Madam Roland

An Appeal to Impartial Posterity

Vol. II.

Madam Roland

An Appeal to Impartial Posterity
Vol. II.

ISBN/EAN: 9783744793483

Printed in Europe, USA, Canada, Australia, Japan

Cover: Foto ©ninafisch / pixelio.de

More available books at **www.hansebooks.com**

AN

APPEAL

TO

IMPARTIAL POSTERITY,

BY

MADAME ROLAND,

WIFE OF THE MINISTER OF THE INTERIOR;

OR,

A COLLECTION OF TRACTS

WRITTEN BY HER DURING HER CONFINEMENT IN THE PRISONS OF THE ABBEY, AND ST. PÉLAGIE, IN PARIS.

IN FOUR PARTS.

TRANSLATED FROM THE FRENCH ORIGINAL,

Published for the Benefit of her only Daughter, deprived of the Fortune of her Parents by Sequestration.

SECOND EDITION, REVISED AND CORRECTED.

VOL. II.

Containing PART III. and IV.

May my laſt letter to my daughter fix her attention to that object which appears likely to become her effential duty; and may the remembrance of her mother attach her for ever to thofe virtues which afford confolation in all circumſtances.

Extracted from the piece entitled *My Laſt Thoughts*, in Part II. p. 120.

LONDON:

PRINTED FOR J. JOHNSON, ST. PAUL'S CHURCH-YARD.

1796.

PART THE THIRD.

PRIVATE MEMOIRS.

SECTION I.

Prifon of St. Pélagie,
Aug. 9, 1793.

THE daughter of an artift, the wife of a man of letters (who afterwards became a minifter, and remained an honeft man), now a prifoner, deftined perhaps to a violent and unexpected death, I have been acquainted with happinefs and with adverfity, I have feen glory at hand, and I have experienced injuftice.

Born in an obfcure ftation, but of honeft parents, I fpent my youth in the bofom of the fine arts, nourifhed by the charms of ftudy, and ignorant of all fuperiority but that of merit, of all greatnefs but that of virtue.

Arrived at years of maturity, I loft all hopes of that fortune, which might have placed me in a condition fuitable to the education I had received.

A mar-

A marriage with a refpectable man appeared to compenfate this lofs; it ferved to lay the foundation of new misfortunes.

A gentle difpofition, a ftrong mind, a folid underftanding, an extremely affectionate heart, and an exterior which announced thefe qualities, rendered me dear to all thofe with whom I was acquainted. The fituation into which I have been thrown has created me enemies; perfonally I have none: to thofe who have fpoken the worft of me I am utterly unknown.

It is fo true that things are feldom what they appear to be, that the periods of my life in which I have felt the moft pleafure, or experienced the greateft vexation, were often the very contrary of thofe that others might have fuppofed: the folution is, that happinefs depends on the affections more than on events.

It is my purpofe to employ the leifure of my captivity in retracing what has happened to me from my tendereft infancy to the prefent moment. Thus to tread over again all the fteps of our career, is to live a fecond time; and what, in the gloom of a prifon, can we do better than to tranfport our exiftence elfewhere by pleafing fictions, or by the recollection of interefting occurrences?

If we gain lefs experience by acting, than by reflecting on what we fee and do, mine will be greatly augmented by my prefent undertaking.

Public

Public affairs, and my own private fentiments, afforded me ample matter for thinking, and fubjects enough for my pen, during two months imprifonment, without obliging me to have recourfe to diftant times. Accordingly, the firft five weeks were devoted to my *Hiftoric Notices*, which formed perhaps no interefting collection. They have juft been deftroyed; and I have felt all the bitternefs of a lofs, which I fhall never repair. But I fhould defpife myfelf, could I fuffer my mind to fink in any circumftances whatever. In all the troubles I have experienced, the moft lively impreffion of forrow has been almoft immediately accompanied by the ambition of oppofing my ftrength to the evil, and of furmounting it, either by doing good to others, or by exerting my own fortitude to the utmoft. Thus misfortune may purfue, but cannot overwhelm me; tyrants may perfecute, but never, no never fhall they debafe me. My *Hiftoric Notices* are gone: I mean to write my *Memoirs*; and, prudently accommodating myfelf to my weaknefs, at a moment when my feelings are acute, I fhall talk of my own perfon, that my thoughts may be the lefs at home. I fhall exhibit my fair and my unfavourable fide with equal freedom. He who dares not fpeak well of himfelf is almoft always a coward, who knows and dreads the ill that may be faid of him; and he who hefitates to confefs his faults, has neither spirit to vindicate, nor virtue to repair them. Thus frank with respect to myself, I shall not be scrupulous in regard to others: father, mother, friends, husband, I shall paint them all in their proper colours, or in the colours at least in which they appeared to me.

While I remained in a quiet and retired station, my natural sensibility so absorbed my other qualities, that it displayed itself alone, or governed all the rest. My first objects were to please and to do good. I was a little like that good man, Mr. de Gourville, of whom Madame de Sévigné said, that the love of his neighbour cut off half his words; nor was I undeserving of the character given me by Sainte-Lette, who said, that though possessed of wit to point an epigram, I never suffered one to escape my lips.

Since the energy of my character has been unfolded by circumstances, by political and other storms, my frankness takes place of every thing, without considering too nicely the little scratches it may give in its way. Still, however, I deal not in epigrams; they indicate a mind pleased at irritating others by satirical observations; and, as to me, I never yet could find amusement in killing flies. But I love to do justice by the utterance of truths, and refrain not from the most severe, in presence of the parties concerned, without suffering myself to be alarmed, or moved, or angry,

angry, whatever may be the effects they produce.

Gatien Phlipon, my father, was by profession an engraver; he also professed painting, and applied himself to that in enamel, less from taste than expectation of profit: but the fire which enamelling requires, agreeing neither with his sight nor his constitution, he was obliged to relinquish that branch of the art. He confined himself therefore to the first, the profits of which were moderate. But, though he was industrious, though the times were favourable to the exercise of his art, though he had much business, and though he employed a considerable number of workmen, the desire of making a fortune induced him to enter into trade. He purchased diamonds, and other jewels, or took them in payment from the tradesmen who employed him, to sell them again when opportunities might occur. I mention this circumstance, because I have observed, that ambition is generally fatal to all classes of men; for the few whose wishes it crowns with success, multitudes become its victims. The example of my father will afford me more than one application of this maxim. His art was sufficient to procure him a comfortable subsistence; he went in pursuit of riches, and met with ruin on his way.

Strong and healthy, active and vain, he loved his wife, and was fond of dress. Without learning, he had that superficial degree of taste and knowledge which the fine arts never fail to give, however inferior the line in which they are pursued. Accordingly, in spite of his regard for wealth, and whatever could procure it, though he trafficked with tradesmen, he formed connexions with artists, painters, and sculptors alone. He led a very regular life while his ambition was kept within bounds, and had suffered no reverse of fortune. He could not be said to be a virtuous man, but he had a great deal of what is called honour. He would have had no objection to selling a thing for more than it was worth, but he would have killed himself rather than not pay the stipulated price of what he had agreed to purchase.

Margaret Bimont, his wife, brought him, as a dower, very little money, but a heavenly mind, and a charming figure. The eldest of six children, to whom she had been a second mother, she married at six-and-twenty, only to resign her place to her sisters. Her affectionate heart and captivating mind ought to have procured her an union with a man of delicate feelings and an enlightened understanding; but her parents proposed to her an honest man, whose talents insured her a subsistence, and her reason accepted him. Instead of that happiness, which she could not expect, she was sensible that she should be able to attain domestic quiet, its most desirable substitute. It is a proof of wisdom to be able to contract our desires: enjoyments

ments are always more rare than is imagined; but virtue is never without its confolation.

I was their fecond child. My father and mother had feven; but all the reft died at nurfe, or from accidents in coming into the world; and my mother fometimes took a pleafure in remarking, that I was the only one from whom fhe had experienced no difafter; for her delivery had been as happy as her pregnancy: it feemed as if I had contributed to eftablifh her health.

An aunt of my father felected for me, in the neighbourhood of Arpajon, whither fhe made frequent excurfions in the fummer, a healthy and well-difpofed nurfe, who was much efteemed in the place, and the more fo, becaufe her hufband's brutality rendered her unhappy, without making her alter her difpofition or her conduct. Madame Befnard (for that was the name of my great aunt) had no children; her hufband was my godfather; and they both looked upon me as their own daughter. Their kindnefs to me has been conftant and invariable; they are ftill alive, and in the decline of life are overwhelmed with forrow, lamenting the fate of their darling niece, in whom they had placed their hopes and their glory. Aged and refpectable friends, be comforted: it is given to few to complete their career in that filence and tranquillity which attend you. I am not unequal to the misfortunes that affail me, nor fhall I ever ceafe to honour your virtues.

The

The vigilance of my nurfe was encouraged or recompenfed by the kindnefs of my good relations; her zeal and fuccefs procured her the friendfhip of my whole family; nor did fhe, as long as fhe lived, ever fuffer two years to elapfe, without taking a journey to Paris, on purpofe to fee me. She haftened to me when fhe heard that a cruel death had deprived me of my mother. I ftill recollect her fudden appearance: I was confined to my bed with affliction; and as her prefence recalled a recent calamity, the firft misfortune of my life, very forcibly to my mind, I fell into convulfions, which terrified her to fuch a degree, that fhe withdrew, and I faw her no more: foon after fhe died. I had been to vifit her at the cottage in which fhe fuckled me, and liftened with emotion to the tales which her good-natured fimplicity took a pleafure in telling, while pointing out the places I had preferred, and relating the tricks I had played her, with the frolicfome gaiety of which fhe was ftill entertained.——At two years of age I was brought home to my father's. I have frequently been told of the furprife I teftified at the lighting of the lamps, which I called " Pretty bottles!" of my repugnance to make ufe of what is called a *pot-de-chambre*, for a purpofe for which the corner of the garden had always ferved me; and of the air of ridicule with which I pointed to the falad-difhes and *terrenes*, afking if they too were made for the fame ufe. Thefe little anecdotes, and

others

others of equal importance, interefting to nurfes, and fit only to be related to uncles and aunts, fhall be paffed over in filence; nor will it be expected that I fhould here depict a little brunette, of two years of age, whofe dark hair fell in graceful ringlets over a face animated with a glowing complexion, and breathing the happinefs of that age of which it wore the ruddy livery. I know a better moment for drawing my portrait, and I am not fo injudicious as to anticipate it here.

The difcretion, and other excellent qualities, of my mother, foon gave her an afcendancy over my mild and affectionate difpofition, which fhe never employed but for my good. So great was this afcendancy, that, in thofe little difputes, unavoidable between authoritative reafon and refifting infancy, fhe never found it neceffary to inflict any other punifhment than that of gravely calling me *Mademoifelle,* and fixing on me an eye of reproof. I ftill feel the impreffion made upon me by her look, at other times fo affectionate; I ftill hear, with a palpitating heart, the word *Mademoifelle* fubftituted, with heart-rending dignity, for the kind name of daughter, or the elegant appellation of *Manon.* Yes, *Manon*; for fo I was called. I am forry for the lovers of romance: there is certainly nothing noble in the name, nor is it at all fuitable to a heroine of the lofty kind; but it was mine; and, as an hiftorian, I cannot difguife the truth :—befides, sides, the ears of the most delicate would have been reconciled to this name, had they heard it pronounced by my mother, and seen the object to which it was addressed. What expression could want elegance, when conveyed in her affectionate tones? And when her touching voice made its way to my heart, did it not teach me to resemble so amiable a parent?

Lively, without being turbulent or troublesome, and naturally of a reflective turn of mind, I desired nothing more than to be employed, and readily laid hold of every idea that was held out to me. This disposition was turned to so good account, that I never remember having been taught to read. I have been told, that at four years old the business was in a manner completed, and that the trouble of teaching me was over at that epoch, since all that was in future necessary, was not to let me want a supply of books. Whatever they were that were put into my hands, or that I could anywhere meet with, they were sure to engross all my attention, which could no longer be called away by any thing but a nosegay. The sight of a flower delights my imagination, and flatters my senses to an inexpressible degree; it awakens me to a luxurious consciousness of my existence. Under the tranquil shelter of my paternal roof, I was happy from my infancy with flowers and books: in the narrow confines of a prison, amidst the

chains

chains impofed by the moſt ſhocking tyranny, I forget the injuſtice of men, their follies, and my misfortunes, with books and flowers.

It was too good an opportunity of making me acquainted with the Old and New Teſtaments, and with the Catechiſm, both great and ſmall, to be neglected. I learned every thing it was thought proper to give me, and ſhould have repeated the Koran had I been taught to read it. I remember a painter of the name of Guibol, who afterwards ſettled at Studgard, and whoſe panegyric on Pouſſin, which obtained the prize from the academy of Rouen, fell into my hands a few years ago. He uſed to come frequently to my father's, and was a merry fellow, who told me many extravagant tales, which I have not forgotten, and by which I was exceedingly amuſed; nor was he leſs diverted with making me diſplay my ſlender ſtock of knowledge in my turn. I think I ſee him now, with a figure bordering on the groteſque, ſitting in an armed chair, taking me between his knees, on which I reſted my elbows, and making me repeat *St. Athanaſius's creed*; then rewarding my compliance with the ſtory of *Tanger*, whoſe noſe was ſo long, than he was obliged, when he walked, to twiſt it round his arm: this is not the moſt abſurd contraſt that might be exhibited.

When ſeven years old, I was ſent every Sunday to the pariſh-church, to attend *catechiſm*, as it is called, in order to prepare me for confirmation.

From

From the prefent courfe of things, it is poffible that they who read this paffage may afk what I mean. I will inform them. In the corner of a church, chapel, or charnel-houfe, a few rows of chairs, or benches, extending to a certain length, were placed oppofite to each other. A fufficient opening was referved in the middle, in which was placed a feat fomewhat higher than the reft. This was the curule chair of the young prieft, whofe office it was to inftruct the children that attended. They were made to repeat by heart the epiftle and gofpel for the day, the collect, and fuch a portion of the catechifm as was appointed for their weekly tafk. When the children were numerous, the catechifing prieft had a little clerk, who heard them repeat their leffons, while the mafter took upon himfelf to explain the queftions effential to the fubject. In fome parifhes the children of both fexes attended together, and were only placed on feparate forms; but in general their hours of inftruction were entirely diftinct. The pious matrons to whom the children belonged, always greedy of the bread of the word, however coarfely prepared, were prefent at thefe lectures, feated according to their ages, as well as at the preparation for being confirmed, and receiving the firft communion. The zealous paftors alfo occafionally made their appearance amidft their young flock, who were taught to rife refpectfully at their approach. They put a few queftions to the beft dreffed, in

order

order to ascertain the progress they had made. The mothers of those who were interrogated, were puffed up with pride at the distinction, and the reverend pastor withdrew in the midst of their obeisances. Mr. *Garat*, the rector of my parish, which was St. Bartholomew's, within the precinct of what was then called *the City*—a good sort of man, said to be very learned, though he could not deliver two words of common sense from the pulpit, in which he had the rage of exhibiting himself, much in the same manner as Mr. *Garat*, minister of state, is reputed a man of ability, though totally ignorant of his trade—Mr. Garat, my rector, came one day to the catechism; and, in order to sound the depth of my theological erudition, and display his own sagacity, asked me how many orders of spirits there were in the celestial hierarchy. From the ironical tone and air of triumph with which he put the question, I was persuaded that he expected to puzzle me. I answered, with a smile, that, though many were enumerated in the preface to the Missal, I had found from other books that there were nine; and so I marshalled before him in their proper order, the whole host of *angels, archangels, thrones, dominions,* &c. Never was priest so satisfied with the knowledge of his neophyte: it was quite enough to establish my reputation among all the devout matrons; and, accordingly, I became a chosen vessel, as hereafter will appear. Some persons perhaps will say, that, with my

mother's

mother's caution and good fenfe, it is aftonifhing that fhe fhould have fent me to thefe *catechifms*: but there is a reafon for every thing. My mother had a younger brother, an ecclefiaftic belonging to her parifh, to whofe care was committed the *catechifm of confirmation*, to ufe the technical term. The prefence of his niece was an admirable example, calculated to induce thofe who were not of what is called the lower order of the people, to fend their children alfo: a circumftance that could not fail to be pleafing to the rector.—Befides, I had a memory which was fure to fecure me the firft rank; and every thing elfe about me fupporting this kind of fuperiority, my parents gratified their vanity, while appearing only to purfue the path of humility. It happened, that, in the diftribution of prizes, which took place, with no fmall parade, at the end of the year, I obtained the firft, without the leaft partiality being fhown me: on this, all the grave churchwardens, and all the reverend clergy of the parifh, congratulated my uncle; who, in confequence of my fuccefs, began to be more noticed, which was all that was neceffary to prepoffefs every one in his favour. A handfome perfon, the greateft good-nature, an eafy temper, the moft gentle manners, and the utmoft gaiety, attended him to thefe latter times, when he died a canon of Vincennes, juft as the revolution was about to abolifh all ecclefiaftical dignities. It feemed to me, as if I had loft the

laft

laſt of my relations on the maternal ſide, nor can I recollect a ſingle circumſtance reſpecting him without emotion. My eagerneſs to learn, and quickneſs of apprehenſion, ſuggeſted to him the idea of teaching me Latin. I was delighted with it; for it was a feaſt to me to find a new ſubject of ſtudy. I had at home maſters for writing, geography, dancing, and muſic; and my father had made me begin drawing: but in all this I was far from finding an exceſs of occupation. Riſing at five in the morning, when every body in the houſe was aſleep, I ſtole ſoftly, in my bed-gown, regardleſs of ſhoes or ſtockings, to a corner of my mother's chamber, where was the table on which my books were laid; and there I copied or repeated my leſſons with ſuch aſſiduity, that my progreſs was aſtoniſhing. My maſters became in conſequence more affectionate; gave me long leſſons; and took ſuch an intereſt in my inſtruction, as called forth on my part additional attention. I had not a ſingle maſter who did not appear as much flattered by teaching me, as I was grateful for being taught; nor one who, after attending me for a year or two, was not the firſt to ſay, that his inſtructions were no longer neceſſary, and that he ought no longer to be paid; but that he ſhould be glad of permiſſion to viſit my parents in order to converſe with me now and then. I ſhall ever honour the memory of the good Mr. *Marchand,* who, when I was five years old, taught me to write,

write, and afterwards inftructed me in geography and hiftory. He was a difcreet, patient, clearheaded, and methodical perfonage, to whom I gave the nickname of Mr. *Demure*. I faw him married to a worthy woman, a dependant of the family of Nefle; and went to vifit him in his laft ficknefs, when a fit of the gout, tranflated to his cheft by an injudicious bleeding, occafioned his death at the age of fifty.—I was then eighteen.

I have not forgotten my mufic-mafter, *Cajon*, a little, lively, talkative being, born at Macon, where he had been a finging-boy. He was afterwards by turns a foldier, a deferter, a capuchin friar, a clerk in a counting-houfe, and laftly a vagrant, arriving at Paris with his wife and children without a penny in his pocket; but he had a very pleafing counter voice, rarely to be met with in men who have not undergone a certain operation, and admirably adapted to the teaching of young perfons to fing. Introduced to my father, I know not by whom, he had me for his firft fcholar. He beftowed on me confiderable pains: frequently borrowed money of my parents, which was foon fpent; never returned me a collection of leffons by Bordier, which he plundered with fo much art, as to compile from it the *Elements of Mufic*, that he publifhed in his own name; lived in great ftyle without being rich, and, at the end of fifteen years, terminated his career by quitting Paris, where he had contracted heavy debts, and by repairing

to

to Ruffia, where I know not what became of him.

Of *Mozon*, the dancing-mafter, an honeft Savoyard, frightfully ugly, whofe wen I think I ftill fee embellifhing his right cheek while he inclined his pock-fretted and flat-nofed vifage to the left on his inftrument, I might relate fome humorous anecdotes; as well as of poor *Mignard*, my mafter for the guitar, a fort of Spanifh Coloffus, whofe hands refembled thofe of Efau, and who, in gravity, over-ftrained politenefs, and rodomontade, was inferior to none of his countrymen.

The timid *Wattin*, of fifty years of age, whofe periwig, fpectacles, and carbuncled face, feemed all in commotion while he was placing the fingers of his little fcholar on the violoncello, and teaching her to hold her bow, did not continue long with me: but, on the other hand, the reverend father *Colomb*, a Barnabite, formerly a miffionary, fuperior of his convent at the age of feventy-five, and my mother's confeffor, fent his bafs-viol to her houfe to confole me for the defertion of my mafter of the violoncello, and, when he came to fee us, accompanied me himfelf while I played on my guitar. He was not a little aftonifhed, when one day, taking up his bafs, I played a few airs that I had ftudied in private with tolerable execution. Had there been a double-bafs in the houfe, I fhould have got up in a chair to try and make fomething of it. To avoid anachronifm, however, it muft be obferved, that

I am

I am here anticipating things, and that I am arrived in my narrative at the period only of seven years, to which I return.

I have advanced thus far without noticing my father's influence over my education. It was indeed trifling, for he interfered in it but little; but it may not be amiss to relate an occurrence that induced him to interfere still less.

I was extremely obstinate; that is to say, I did not readily consent to any thing of which I saw not the reason; and when the exercise of authority alone appeared, or I fancied that I perceived the dictates of caprice, I could not submit. My mother, sagacious and discreet, rightly judged that I must be governed by reason, or drawn by the cords of affection; and, treating me accordingly, experienced no opposition to her will. My father, hasty in his manner, issued his orders imperiously, and my compliance was either reluctant, or wholly withheld. If, despot-like, he attempted to punish me, his gentle little daughter was converted into a lion. On two or three occasions while he was whipping me, I bit the thigh across which I was laid, and protested against his injunctions. One day, when I was a little indisposed, it was thought proper that I should take physic. The nauseous draught was brought me; and I put it to my lips; but the smell alone made me reject it with abhorrence. My mother made use of all her influence to overcome my repugnance; she inspired me with the

desire

defire of obeying her; and I fincerely did my beft; but every time the horrid potion approached my nofe, my fenfes revolted, and made me turn afide my head. My mother fatigued herfelf to no purpofe; I wept both for her fufferings and my own, and became ftill lefs capable of complying with her will. My father came, put himfelf into a paffion, and, afcribing my refiftance to ftubbornnefs, recurred to the remedy of the rod. From that inftant all defire of obedience vanifhed, and I declared that I would not take the medicine at all. A violent uproar, repeated threats, and a fecond whipping, followed. I was only the more indignant, uttering terrible cries, lifting up my eyes to heaven, and preparing to throw away the draught which they were about to prefent to me again. My geftures betrayed me; and my father, in a rage, threatened to whip me a third time. I feel, while I write this, the revolution, and developement of fortitude, which took place in my mind. My tears ceafed at once to flow, my fobbings were at an end, and a fudden calm concentrated my faculties into a fingle refolution. I raifed myfelf, turned to the bed-fide, leaned my head againft the wall, lifted up my chemife, and expofed myfelf to the rod in filence. My father might have killed me on the fpot, without drawing from me a fingle figh.

My mother, who was dreadfully agitated by the fcene, and who ftood in need of all her prudence not to increase my father's rage, at last got him out of the room: she then put me to bed without saying a word; and, when I had rested two hours, returned, and conjured me, with tears in her eyes, to give her no farther vexation, but to take the medicine. I looked stedfastly in her face, took the glass, and swallowed it at a draught. In a quarter of an hour, however, it was thrown up again; and I was seized with a violent paroxysm of fever, which it was found necessary to cure by other means than by nauseous drugs or by the rod. I was at that time little more than six years old.

All the circumstances of this scene are as present to my mind, all the sensations I experienced as distinct to my imagination, as if they had recently occurred. It was the same inflexible firmness that I have since felt on great and trying occasions; nor would it at this moment cost me more to ascend undauntedly the scaffold, than it did then to resign myself to brutal treatment, which might have killed, but could not conquer me.

From that instant my father never laid his hand upon me, nor did he even undertake to reprimand me; but, on the contrary, caressed me frequently, taught me to draw, took me out to walk, and treated me with a kindness that rendered him more respectable in my eyes, and insured him my entire submission. The seventh anniversary of my birth was celebrated as the attainment of the age of reason, when it might be expected of me to

follow

follow its dictates. This was a politic sort of plea for obferving towards me a more refpectful treatment, that fhould give me confidence in myfelf, without exciting my vanity. My days flowed gently on in domeftic quiet and in great activity of mind. My mother was almoft always at home, and received little company. Two days in the week however we went abroad; once to vifit my father's relations, and once, which was on Sunday, to fee my grandmother Bimont, to go to church, and to take a walk. The vifit to my grandmother always took place as foon as vefpers were over. She was a corpulent but handfome woman, who at an early age had fuffered an attack of the palfy, from which her underftanding had fuftained a permanent injury. From that time fhe had gradually declined into a ftate of dotage, fpending her days in her eafy chair, either at the window or the firefide, according to the feafon. An old fervant, who had been forty years in the family, had the care of her. The fervant, whofe name was Mary, regularly upon my entrance, gave me my afternoon's repaft. So far all went well; but when that was over, I grew dreadfully tired of the vifit. I fought for books; could find none but the Pfalter; and, for want of better, have twenty times read over the French, and chanted the Latin. When I was gay, my grandmother would weep; if I fell down, or got a blow, fhe would burft into a fit of laughter. That did not pleafe me. It was in vain to tell me it it was the effect of her difeafe: I did not find it on that account the lefs difagreeable. I could have borne with her laughing at me, but fhe never fhed tears without their being accompanied by cries at once grievous and imbecile, which rent my heart and infpired me with terror. In the mean time old Mary indulged herfelf to her heart's content in the garrulity of age, with my mother, who confidered it as a facred duty to pafs two hours with hers, while complaifantly liftening to the fervant's tales. This was no doubt a painful exercife of my patience; but I was forced to fubmit; for one day, when I cried for vexation, and begged to go away, my mother, as a punifhment, ftaid the whole evening. Nor did fhe fail, at proper times, to reprefent her affiduity as a ftrict and becoming duty, in which it was honourable for me to participate. I know not how fhe managed it, but my heart received the leffon with emotion. When the Abbé Bimont could meet us at his mother's, my joy was inexpreffible. That dear little uncle made me dance, and fing, and play; but unfortunately it was feldom in his power, as he was mafter of the chorifters, and much confined to the houfe. This brings to my mind one of his pupils, a lad of a prepoffeffing countenance, whom he was fond of praifing, becaufe he was the fcholar that gave him the leaft trouble. His promifing difpofition obtained him, a few years after, an exhibition at fome college, and he is now no other than the Abbé *Noel,*

known

known at firſt by ſome little productions, employed afterwards by the miniſter Le Brun in the diplomatic line, envoy laſt year at London, and now in Italy.

My ſtudies completely occupied my days, which ſeemed very ſhort; for I had never time to get through all that I was inclined to undertake. Together with the elementary books, with which care had been taken to ſupply me, I ſoon exhauſted all thoſe that the little family library contained. I devoured every volume, and began the ſame over again, when no new ones were to be got. I remember two folio lives of the ſaints, a bible of the ſame ſize in an old verſion, a tranſlation of Appian's civil wars, and a deſcription of Turkey written in a wretched ſtyle, all of which I read over and over again. I alſo found the Comical Romance of Scarron; ſome collections of pretended bon mots, on which I did not beſtow a ſecond peruſal; the memoirs of the brave De Pontis, which diverted me much; thoſe of Mademoiſelle de Montpenſier, whoſe pride did not diſpleaſe me; and ſeveral other antiquated works; the contents, binding, and ſpots of which I have ſtill before my eyes. The paſſion for learning poſſeſſed me indeed to ſuch a degree, that, having picked up a treatiſe on the art of heraldry, I ſet myſelf inſtantly to ſtudy it. It had coloured plates, with which I was diverted, and I was glad to know the names of all the little figures they contained. My father was aſtoniſhed when, soon after, I gave him a specimen of my science, by making some remarks on a seal that was not engraved agreeably to the rules of art. On this subject I became his oracle, nor did I ever mislead him. A short treatise on contracts fell into my hands; and this also I endeavoured to learn; for I read nothing which I was not desirous of retaining: but it tired me so soon, that I did not get to the fourth chapter.

The Bible had peculiar attraction for me; and I returned frequently to its perusal. In the old translations it speaks as plain a language as that of the sons of Esculapius; and certain crude and simple expressions struck me so forcibly, that they have never since escaped my memory. Hence I derived information not usually given to girls of my age; but I saw it in a light that was far from seducing. I had too much employment for my thoughts to dwell upon things of a mere material nature, that seemed to me to have nothing attractive about them. I could not however help laughing, when my grandmama talked to me of little children dug out of the parsley-bed; and I used to say, that my Ave-Maria informed me they came from another place, without troubling my head how they got there.

In rummaging the house I found a source of reading which I husbanded for a considerable time. What my father called his work-shop was adjoining to the apartment where I usually sat,

which

which was a handsome room, that might not improperly have been styled a drawing-room, but which my mother modestly called a parlour, neatly furnished, and ornamented with looking-glasses and a few pictures. It was here I received my lessons. The recess on one side of the fire-place was converted into a light closet, in which was placed a bed, so confined for want of room that I was obliged to get into it at the foot; a chair, a small table, and a few shelves. That was my sanctuary. On the opposite side was a large room, serving as a work-shop, my father having placed in it his bench, various pieces of sculpture, and the different instruments of his art. Thither I used to steal in an evening, or at hours of the day when all were absent. I had there remarked a recess where one of the young men kept his books; a volume of which I carried off at a time, and hastened to my little closet to devour it, taking great care to put it in its place again, without saying a word of the matter to any one. They were in general very good books. One day I perceived that my mother had made the same discovery as myself. Recognising a volume in her hands which had previously passed through mine, I no longer felt myself under any restraint; and, without telling a falsehood, but at the same time without saying a word concerning what had passed, I seemed to be only following her example. The young man, whose name was Courson, to

which

which he afterwards prefixed the *de**, when he contrived to get into place at Verfailles as teacher to the pages, did not at all refemble his comrades: he was not deftitute of politenefs, was decent in his demeanour, and fond of ftudy. He faid nothing of the occafional difappearance of his books; fo that it feemed as if there were a tacit agreement between all the parties. In this way I read a great many volumes of travels, of which I was paffionately fond; among others, thofe of Renard, which were the firft; fome plays of fecond-rate authors, and Dacier's Plutarch. This laft work was more to my tafte than any thing I had yet feen, not excepting even pathetic ftories, which however affected me much; as for inftance, that of the unfortunate couple, by Labedoyère, which is ftill prefent to my mind, although I have never read it fince that early period. But Plutarch feemed to be exactly the intellectual food that fuited me. I fhall never forget the Lent of 1763, at which time I was nine years of age, when I carried it to church inftead of the Exercifes of the Holy Week. It is from that period that I may date the impreffions and ideas which rendered me a republican, without my dreaming of ever becoming one.

Telemachus, and Jerufalem Delivered, interfered a little with the current of thefe majeftic thoughts. The tender Fenelon moved my heart, and Taffo

* *De* before a name in France was generally the fymbol of a noble family.—*Tranf.*

fired

fired my imagination. Sometimes I read aloud at my mother's requeſt, of which I was by no means fond, as it diverted me from that cloſe attention which conſtituted my delight, and obliged me to proceed with leſs rapidity. But I would have plucked out my tongue rather than have read in that manner the epiſodes of the iſland of Calypſo, and a number of paſſages in Taſſo. My reſpiration quickened, a ſudden glow overſpread my countenance, and an agitation followed, which my faltering voice would have betrayed. With Telemachus I was Eucharis, and Herminia with Tancred. Completely transformed into theſe heroines, I thought not as yet of being ſomething myſelf with ſome other perſonage. None of my reflections came home to me. I look around me for nothing. I was the very characters themſelves, and ſaw only the objects which exiſted on their account. It was a kind of waking dream, that led to nothing more ſubſtantial. I recollect however having ſeen with conſiderable emotion a young painter of the name of *Taboral*, who came occaſionally to my father's houſe. He was about twenty, his voice was ſoft, his features languiſhing, and he bluſhed like a girl. When I heard him in the work-ſhop, I had always a crayon or ſomething elſe to ſeek; but as the ſight of him embarraſſed no leſs than it pleaſed me, I ran out again more ſpeedily than I entered, with a palpitation of my heart and a trembling of my limbs that I haſtened to conceal in my little cloſet. I can readily believe, that, with ſuch

a diſa difpofition, affifted by leifure and a certain kind of company, both my imagination and my perfon might have been greatly affected.

The works of which I have been fpeaking gave place to others, which foftened the powerful impreffions they had produced. Some of the writings of Voltaire ferved to operate this diverfion. One day, when I was reading Candide, my mother having deferted her party of piquet, the lady with whom fhe was playing calling me from the corner in which I was fitting, defired to fee the book I had in my hand; and on my mother's return expreffed her aftonifhment at the nature of my ftudies. My mother, without making any anfwer, contented herfelf with merely ordering me to carry it back to the place whence it came. I caft an evil eye upon this woman, of forbidding countenance, monftrous rotundity of waift, and affected importance; nor from that day forward did I ever beftow a fmile upon Madame Charbonné. My good mother, however, made no alteration in her truly unaccountable conduct, but permitted me to read all the books I could lay my hands on, without feeming to attend to them, though fhe knew very well what they were. I muft obferve at the fame time, that no immoral publication ever came in my way; and even now I am only acquainted with the titles of two or three; the tafte I have acquired having ever prevented my feeling the fmalleft temptation to procure them. As I preferred books to every thing elfe, my father fometimes made me prefents of that kind; but,

piquing

piquing himself, as he did, on feconding my propenfity to ferious ftudies, his choice was whimfical: he gave me, for inftance, Fenelon on female education, and Locke on that of children in general; thus putting into the hands of the pupil what were defigned for the tutor. I am perfuaded, however, that the incongruity was not unproductive of benefit, and that chance perhaps ferved me better than the ufual confiderations of propriety would have done. I was very forward for my age; I loved to reflect; I thought ferioufly of improving myfelf; that is to fay, I ftudied the movements of my mind; I fought to know myfelf; and I felt that I had a deftination which it was requifite I fhould enable myfelf to fill. Religious notions began to ferment in my brain, and foon produced a violent explofion. But before I defcribe them, it may be proper for my reader to know what became of my Latin.

The firft rudiments of grammar were well arranged in my head. I declined nouns and conjugated verbs, though it appeared to me tirefome enough; but the hope of being able on fome future day to read in that language the admirable productions of which I heard fo much, and of which my books afforded me fome idea, gave me refolution to get through the dry and difficult tafk. It was not thus with my little uncle, for fo I called the Abbé Bimont. Young, good-humoured, indolent, and gay, giving not the fmalleft trouble to any body, caring little to give himfelf any for others, and

heartily

heartily tired of his trade of pedagogue with the choristers; he liked better to take a walk with me than to give me a lesson, and to make me laugh and play, than to hear me repeat my rudiments. He was far from being punctual either as to the hour or the day of coming to our house, and a thousand circumstances combined to procrastinate his lessons. I was desirous however of learning, and loath to relinquish what I had once begun. It was therefore resolved upon, that I should go to him three mornings a week; but he was too giddy to keep himself at liberty to devote a few moments to my instruction. I was sure to find him either busied in parish affairs, diverting himself with his boys, or breakfasting with a friend. I lost my time, the winter season came on, and my Latin was abandoned. From that attempt I have preserved only a sort of glimmering or instinct of knowledge, which, during the days of devotion, enabled me to repeat or chant the Psalms without being absolutely ignorant of what I was saying, and a considerable facility for the study of languages in general, particularly the Italian, which I learnt a few years after, without a master, and without difficulty.

My father took but little pains to forward me in drawing: he rather amused himself with my aptitude, than endeavoured to give me extraordinary talents. A few words that dropped in a conversation with my mother, gave me to understand that, from prudential motives, she was not desirous of my

making

making any great proficiency in the art. 'I would not have her become a painter,' said she; ' it would require an intercommunity of ftudies, and connexions that we can very well difpenfe with.' I was alfo fet to engrave; learnt to hold the graver, and got over the firft difficulties in a fhort time; for nothing came amifs to me. On the birth-days of my good old relations, which were always religioufly celebrated, I carried for my prefent, either a pretty head, which I had been at great pains to draw for the occafion, or a neat little copper-plate, on which I had engraved a flower, with a compliment beneath, written with great care, and in verfes hammered out by *Mr. Demure*. In return I received almanacs*, which greatly amufed me, and prefents of fuch little articles as were adapted to my ufe, in general ornaments of drefs, of which I was very fond. My mother took a pleafure in feeing me fine. In her own drefs fhe was plain, and frequently even negligent; but her daughter was her doll, and from my early infancy I was dreffed with a degree of elegance, and even richnefs, that feemed un-fuitable to my condition. Young ladies at that time wore what was called a *corps-de-robe*, a drefs refembling court robes, and fitting very

---

* French almanacs are very different from the Englifh: moft of them are without calendars, fuch as l'Almanach Chantant, confifting entirely of fongs, l'Almanach des Mufes, containing a mixture of fugitive pieces in profe and verfe, &c.—*Tranf.*

clofely

closely at the waist; of which it displayed the form to advantage, but full below, with a long train that swept the ground, adorned with different trimmings, according to the taste of the wearer. Mine were of fine silk, of some simple pattern and modest colour, but in price and quality equal to my mother's best gala suits. My toilet was a grievous business to me, for my hair was frequently frizzed, papered, and tortured with hot irons, and all the other ridiculous and barbarous implements at that time in use. My head was so extremely tender, and the pulling I was obliged to undergo so painful, that, upon occasions of full dress, my sufferings always forced tears from my eyes, although I uttered no complaint.

Methinks I hear it asked, For whose eyes, in the retired life I led, was all this finery intended? They who ask the question ought to recollect, that I went out two days in the week; and if they were acquainted with the manners of what was at that time called the *bourgeoisie* of Paris, they must know there were thousands of them whose expence in dress, by no means small, had no other object, than an exhibition of a few hours on Sunday in the *Tuileries*; to which their wives joined the display of their finery at church, and the pleasure of parading their own quarter of the town, before their admiring neighbours. Add to this, family visits on great festivals, new year's day, weddings and christenings, and there
will

will be found sufficient opportunities for the gratification of vanity. By the way, more than one contrast may be observed in my education. The young lady, exhibited on Sundays at church, and in the public walks, in an elegant drefs, who you would have suppofed to be just alighted from a carriage, and whofe demeanour and language were perfectly confonant to her appearance, would go neverthelefs to market in the week with her mother, in a linen frock, or would ftep into the ftreet alone, to buy a little parfley or falad, which the fervant had forgotten. It muft be confeffed, I was not much pleafed with it; but I fhowed no figns of diflike, and acquitted myfelf of my commiffion in fuch a way as to render it agreeable. I behaved with fo much civility, and at the fame time with fo much dignity, that the fruiterer, or other fhopkeeper, took a pleafure in ferving me firft; and yet thofe who came before me were never offended: I was fure to pick up fome compliment or other in the way, which only ferved to make me more polite. The fame child, who read fyftematic works, who could explain the circles of the celeftial fphere, handle the crayon and the graver, and who, at eight years of age, was the beft dancer in the youthful parties that met occafionally to affift at fome little family feftival, was frequently called into the kitchen to make an omelet, pick herbs, or fkim the pot. That mixture of ferious ftudies, agreeable relaxations, and domeftic cares, properly ordered, and rendered agreeable by my mother's good management, made me fit for every thing, seemed to forebode the viciflitudes of my fortune, and enabled me to support them. In every place I am at home: I can prepare my own dinner with as much addrefs as Philopœmen cut wood; but no one seeing me so engaged, would think it an office in which I ought to be employed.

It may be suppofed, from what I have already related, that my mother did not neglect what is called religion. She was pious without being a bigot; she had faith, or endeavoured to have faith; and conformed her conduct to the rules of the church with the humility and regularity of a person who, finding it neceffary for her peace of mind to adopt great principles, does not hefitate at trifling details. The refpectful air with which the firft notions of religion had been prefented to me, had difpofed me to receive them with attention. They were of a nature calculated to make confiderable impreffion on a lively imagination; and notwithftanding the troublefome doubts frequently excited by my infant reafon, which regarded with furprife the transformation of the devil into a ferpent, and thought it cruel in God to have permitted it, I at laft believed and adored.

I had received confirmation with the deep attention of a mind that calculates the importance of its actions, and meditates on its duties. The preparing

paring me for my firſt communion was talked of, and I felt a ſacred terror take poſſeſſion of my ſoul.

I read books of devotion; I was ſeized with an irreſiſtible deſire to employ my mind about the great objects of eternal miſery and happineſs; and, by inſenſible degrees, all my thoughts centred in thoſe points. Religious ideas gained a complete aſcendance over my heart, and concurred with my natural forwardneſs in bringing on the reign of ſentiment before its time. It began with the love of God, the ſublime raptures of which rendered the firſt years of my adoleſcence ſafe and happy, reſigned the reſt to the care of philoſophy, and ſeemed likely to protect me for ever from the ſtorm of thoſe paſſions, from which, with a conſtitution as vigorous as that of a prize-fighter, it is with difficulty that I preſerve my riper age.

The fit of devotion which agitated me, produced an aſtoniſhing alteration in my mind. I became profoundly humble and inexpreſſibly timid. I looked upon men with a ſort of terror, which increaſed when any of them ſtruck me as amiable. I watched over my thoughts with extreme ſcrupuloſity; the leaſt profane image that offered itſelf to my mind, however confuſedly, ſeemed a crime. I contracted ſuch a habit of reſerve, that, peruſing Buffon's Natural Hiſtory at the age of ſixteen, when no longer a devotee, I ſkipped the article Man, and turned over the plates relating to it, with the ſpeed and terror of a perſon who ſees a

precipice

precipice beneath his feet. In short, I did not marry till I was twenty-five; and with a heart such as may be imagined, senses highly inflammable, and considerable information as to several points, I had so well avoided all knowledge concerning one circumstance, that the consequences of marriage were as surprising to me as they were unpleasant.

My life, which every day grew more and more retired, appeared still too worldly to admit of my preparing for my first communion. That important transaction, which was to have such influence on my eternal salvation, occupied all my thoughts. I acquired a taste for divine service; I was struck with its solemnity; I read with avidity the explanation of the church ceremonies, and treasured up their mystic signification in my mind. Every day I turned over my folio Lives of the Saints, and regretted those happy days when the persecuting fury of paganism conferred the crown of martyrdom upon courageous christians. I began to think seriously of embracing a new kind of life, and, after profound meditations, fixed upon my plan. Until then, the idea of parting from my mother used to draw a flood of tears from my eyes; and whenever any of my friends wished to divert themselves with the sudden clouds that sensibility spread over my expressive brow, they never failed to talk of convents, and of the propriety of sending young women to inhabit them for a short space of time. But what ought we not to sacrifice to the Lord? I had formed,

of

of the folitude and filence of a cloifter, thofe grand or romantic ideas which an active imagination would naturally engender. The more folemn its abode, the better it fuited the enthufiaftic difpofition of my mind. One evening, after fupper, being alone with my parents, I fell at their feet, fhedding at the fame time a torrent of tears, which deprived me of utterance. Aftonifhed and uneafy, they afked the meaning of this ftrange emotion. 'I beg of you,' faid I, fobbing, ' to do a thing, which is moft painful to my heart, but which is called for by my confcience. Send me to a convent.' They raifed me from the ground. My excellent mother was affected, and no doubt would have been alarmed, if my having been conftantly in her prefence for fome time before, had not removed all grounds of fear: fhe afked me what it was that made me defirous of leaving them, obferving at the fame time, I had never been refufed any reafonable requeft. I anfwered, it was my wifh to receive the communion for the firft time in a difpofition of mind fuitable to the folemnity of the occafion. My father commended my zeal, and expreffed his readinefs to comply with my defire. The next difficulty was, the making a choice among the different religious houfes, in none of which my parents had any connexions; but they recollected that my mufic-mafter had fpoken of a convent in which he gave leffons to feveral young ladies, and refolved to make inquiry concerning it. They found it to

be

be a respectable house, and of an order not very strict. The nuns had consequently the reputation of not practising those extravagancies and mummeries for which nuns are generally remarkable: the education of youth was also their profession. They kept a day-school for children of the lower clafs, whom they taught *gratis*, in conformity with their vows, and who came from their own homes to a room set apart for them; the boarding-school for such young women as were confided to their care, being entirely detached.

My mother took the necessary steps; and after carrying me to visit all my relations of the superior degree, and informing them of my resolution, which was highly commended, conducted me to the sisterhood of the Congregation, in the Rue Neuve St. Etienne, Fauxbourg St. Marceau, very near the prison in which I am now confined. While pressing my dear mother in my arms at the moment of parting with her for the first time in my life, I thought my heart would have burst; but I was acting in obedience to the voice of God, and passed the threshold of the cloister, offering up to him, with tears, the greatest sacrifice I was capable of making. That was the seventh of May 1765, when I was *eleven years* and two months old.

In the gloom of a prison, in the midst of those political commotions which ravage my country, and sweep away all that is dear to me, how shall I recall to my mind, and how describe, that period

of

of rapture and tranquillity? What lively colours can exprefs the foft emotions of a young heart endued with tendernefs and fenfibility, greedy of happinefs, beginning to be alive to the feelings of nature, and perceiving the Deity alone? The firft night that I fpent at the convent was a night of agitation. I was no longer under the paternal roof. I was at a diftance from that kind mother, who was doubtlefs thinking of me with affectionate emotion. A dim light diffufed itfelf through the room in which I had been put to bed, with four children of my own age. I ftole foftly from my couch, and drew near the window, the light of the moon enabling me to diftinguifh the garden, which it overlooked. The deepeft filence prevailed around, and I liftened to it, if I may ufe the expreffion, with a fort of refpect. Lofty trees caft their gigantic fhadows along the ground, and promifed a fecure afylum to peaceful meditation. I lifted up my eyes to the heavens; they were unclouded and ferene. I imagined that I felt the prefence of the Deity fmiling on my facrifice, and already offering me a reward in the confolatory peace of a celeftial abode. Tears of delight flowed gently down my cheeks. I repeated my vows with holy ecftacy, and went to bed again to tafte the flumber of the elect.

As it was evening when I came to the convent, I had not yet feen all my fellow-boarders. They were thirty-four in number, and were affembled sembled in one school-room, from the age of six to that of seventeen or eighteen, but were divided into two tables at meals, and as it were into two sections in the course of the day, to perform their exercises. There was so much of the little woman about me, that it was immediately judged proper to include me in the elder set. I accordingly became the twelfth at their table, and found myself the youngest of them all. The tone of politeness which my mother had rendered familiar, the sedate air which was become habitual to me, and my courteous and correct mode of speaking, in no way resembled the noisy and thoughtless mirth of my volatile companions. The children addressed themselves to me with a sort of confidence, because I never gave them a rough answer; and the elder girls treated me with a kind of respect, because my reserve did not render me the less obliging to them, while it procured particular attention from the nuns. Brought up as I had hitherto been, it was not surprising I should be found better informed than most of my class, even than those whose age the most exceeded mine. The nuns perceived they might derive honour from my education, merely from my being under their care, without being obliged to take any pains to continue it. I knew already, or very easily learnt every thing they gave me to study; and became the favourite of the whole sisterhood: it was quite matter of contention who

should

should caress and compliment me. She, whose business it was to teach the boarders to write, was seventy years of age, and had taken the veil at fifty, either out of chagrin at some disappointment, or in consequence of some misfortune. She had been well educated, and joined to that advantage all that could be derived from good breeding and a knowledge of the world. She valued herself on her skill in teaching, still wrote a very fine hand, embroidered with elegance, gave excellent lessons of orthography, and was by no means unacquainted with history. Her diminutive figure, her age itself, and some small tincture of pedantry, occasioned old sister St. Sophia to be treated, by her giddy little pupils, with less respect than she deserved; and if I recollect aright, the jealousy of the good nuns, who were fond of exposing her defects because they did not possess her talents, tended not a little to encourage their impertinence. This excellent woman soon became much attached to me on account of my studious turn. After having given a lesson to the whole class, she would take me aside, make me repeat my grammar, go over my maps, and extract passages from history. She even obtained permission to take me to her cell, where I used to read to her.

Of my former tutors I had retained only one, and that was my music-master, of whom I received lessons in the parlour, with two of my fellow-boarders, under the inspection of a nun: and in

order

order to keep up my drawing, I was attended by a female artift, who was admitted into the interior of the convent.

The regularity of a life filled up with fuch a variety of ftudies, was perfectly fuitable to the activity of my mind, as well as to my natural tafte for method and application. I was one of the firft at every thing; and ftill I had leifure, becaufe I was diligent, and did not lofe a moment of my time. In the hours fet apart for walking and recreation, I felt no defire to run and play with the crowd, but retired to fome folitary fpot to read and meditate. How delighted was I with the beauty of the foliage, the breath of the zephyrs, and the fragrance of the furrounding flowers! Everywhere I perceived the hand of the Deity; I was fenfible of his beneficent care of his creatures; and I admired his wonderful works. Full of gratitude, I went to adore him in the church, where the majeftic founds of the organ, accompanied by the captivating voices of the young nuns chanting their anthems, completed my ecftacy. Independently of mafs, to which all the boarders were regularly conducted in the morning, half an hour in the afternoon of every working day was confecrated to meditation, to which thofe only were admitted who appeared capable of it, or at leaft of filling up that interval of time by the attentive reading of religious works. It was not even neceffary for me to folicit this favour, which they were eager

to

to confer upon me as a recompence for my zeal: but I earneftly requefted to be allowed to receive my firft communion at the next great feftival, which happened to be the Affumption. Though it followed foon after my entrance into the convent, my requeft was granted with the unanimous confent of the fuperiors, and of the director. The latter was a man of good fenfe, and a monk of the monaftery of St. Victor, where he officiated as rector. He had undertaken the tafk of confeffing the boarders of the Congregation, and was well fitted for it by his age, which was upwards of fifty, by the mildnefs of his temper, and by his great good fenfe, which tempered the aufterity of his morals and demeanour. At the time I was confided to his care, Mr. *Garat*, the prieft of my parifh, had the condefcenfion to come himfelf to the convent to depofit his tender lamb in the hands of his fpiritual brother. They had an interview in the parlour in my prefence, and converfed in Latin, which I did not perfectly underftand, but of which I comprehended a few words very much to my advantage. Thefe never efcape the penetration of a female, whatever may be her age, or the language in which they are uttered. I gained confiderably by the change. Garat was a mere pedant, in whom I fhould have found all the fternnefs of a fpiritual judge: the monk of St. Victor was an upright and enlightened man, who directed my pious affections to all that is great and

fublime

fublime in morality; and who took a pleafure in developing the germs of virtue, by the inftrumentality of religion, without any abfurd mixture of its myfticifm. I loved him as much as if he had been my father; and during the three years that he furvived, after my quitting the convent, went regularly from a confiderable diftance to St. Victor's, on the eve of great feftivals, to confefs myfelf to him.

It cannot be denied, that the catholic religion, though little fuited to a found judgment and an enlightened mind, that fubjects its faith to the rules of reafon, is well calculated to captivate the imagination, which it lays hold of by means of the grand and the terrific, while at the fame time it occupies the fenfes by myfterious ceremonies, alternately foothing and melancholy. Eternity, always prefent to the mind of its fectaries, calls them to contemplation. It renders them fcrupulous appreciators of good and evil, while its daily practices and awful rites ferve both to keep up the attention, and offer the eafy means of advancing towards the end propofed. Women are wonderful adepts in giving a grace to thofe practices, and in accompanying rites with whatever can add to their charms and fplendour — an art in which nuns particularly excel. A novice took the veil foon after my arrival at the convent. The church and the altar were decorated with flowers, brilliant luftres, filk curtains, and other

rich

rich ornaments. The assembly was numerous, and came crowding into the outer part of the church, with that festive air, which a family usually affects on such an occasion, as if it were the wedding of one of the children. The young victim appeared at the grate in the most splendid dress, which however she soon pulled off, to appear again covered with a white veil, and crowned with roses. I still feel the agitation which her slightly tremulous voice excited in my bosom, when she melodiously chanted the customary verse, *Elegit*, &c. *Here have I chosen my abode, and will establish it for ever.* I have not forgotten the notes of this little passage; but can repeat them as accurately as if I had heard them only yesterday; and happy should I be if I could chant them in America! Great God! with what emphasis should I utter them now!—But when the novice, after pronouncing her vows, was covered, as she lay prostrate on the ground, with a pall, under which one might have supposed her to be buried, I trembled with horror. To me it represented the image of an absolute dissolution of every earthly tie, and the renunciation of all that was dear to her. I was no longer myself: I was the very victim of the sacrifice. I thought they were tearing me from my mother, and shed a torrent of tears. With sensibility like this, which renders impressions so profound, and occasions so many things to strike us, that pass away like shadows before the eyes of the vulgar,

our

our exiftence never grows languid. Accordingly, I have reflected on mine from an early period, without having ever found it a burden, even in the midft of the fevereft trials; and though not yet forty, I have lived to a prodigious age, if life be meafured by the fentiment which has marked every moment of its duration.

I fhould have too many fcenes of a fimilar nature to recount, were I to go over all which the emotions of a tender piety have engraven on my heart. The charm and habit of thefe fenfations made an impreffion upon me which nothing can efface. Philofophy has difpelled the illufions of an empty faith, but it has not annihilated the effect of certain objects on my fenfes, or their affociation with the ideas and difpofition of mind which they were accuftomed to excite. I can ftill attend divine fervice with pleafure, if performed with folemnity. I forget the quackery of priefts, their ridiculous fables and abfurd myfteries, and fee nothing but weak mortals affembled together to implore the fuccour of the Supreme Being. The miferies of mankind, and the confolatory hope of an omnipotent remunerator, occupy my thoughts. Every extraneous idea is excluded; the paffions fubfide into tranquillity, and the fenfe of my duties is quickened. If mufic form a part of the ceremony, I find myfelf tranfported to another world; and I come out with an amended heart from a place, to which the imbecil and

ignorant

ignorant crowd refort, without reflection, to adore a morfel of bread. It is with religion as with many other human inftitutions : it does not change the difpofition of an individual, but affimilates itfelf to his nature, and they are together exalted or enfeebled The herd of mankind think but little, take every thing on hearfay, and act from inftinct; fo that there prevails a perpetual contradiction between the principles they admit, and the conduct they purfue. Strong minds proceed upon a different plan; they require confiftency, and their actions are a faithful tranfcript of their faith. In my infancy, I neceffarily embraced the creed that was offered me : it was mine, until my mind was fufficiently enlightened to examine it; but even then all my actions were in ftrict conformity with it's precepts. I was aftonifhed at the levity of thofe, who, profeffing a fimilar faith, acted in a contrary way; in like manner as I am now indignant at the cowardice of men, who would wifh to fee their country free, and yet fet a value upon life when an opportunity offers of rifking it for the public weal.

Though wifhing to avoid repetitions upon the fame fubject, I will neverthelefs relate an incident that marks the fituation of my mind at the moment of my firft communion. Prepared by all the means cuftomary in convents, by retirement, long prayers, filence, and meditation, I confidered it as a folemn engagement, and the pledge of eternal felicity.
This

This idea engroffed the whole of my attention. It fo inflamed my imagination, and foftened my heart to fuch a degree, that, bathed in tears, and enraptured with divine love, I was incapable of walking to the altar without the affiftance of a nun, who came and took me under both arms, and helped me to advance to the facred table. Thefe demonftrations, which were by no means affected, but the natural confequence of a fentiment I could not reprefs, obtained me great confideration, and all the good old women I met upon my way were fure to recommend themfelves to my prayers.

Methinks I hear my reader afk, if this heart fo tender, this extreme fenfibility, were not at length exercifed on more fubftantial objects; and whether thefe early dreams of blifs were not afterwards realifed by a paffion, of which fome happy individual fhared the fruits?

To all this my anfwer is, let us not anticipate. Dwell with me awhile upon thofe peaceful days of holy delufion. Think you that, in an age fo corrupt, and in a focial order fo perverfe, it is poffible to tafte the delights of nature and innocence? Vulgar fouls indeed may find pleafure in fuch an age; but as to thofe for whom pleafure alone would be too little, impelled on the one hand by paffions that promife them more, and reftrained on the other by duties which they are bound to refpect, however abfurd and fevere, their enjoyments confift of little elfe but the

dear-

dear-bought glory of facrificing the feelings of nature to the tyrannical inftitutions of mankind. Let us then, for the prefent, feek repofe of fpirit in the pure joys of friendfhip, which came to offer me its comforts, and to which I have been indebted for fo many happy days.

Some months had elapfed fince my arrival at the convent, where I fpent my time in the way defcribed above. Once a week I was vifited by my parents, who took me out on Sundays, after divine fervice, to walk in the *Jardin du Roi*, now called *le Jardin des Plantes*. I never quitted them without fhedding tears, which proceeded from affection to their perfons, and not from diflike to my fituation; for I returned with pleafure to the filent cloifters, and walked through them with meafured fteps, the better to enjoy their folitude. Sometimes I would flop at a tomb, on which the eulogy of a pious maiden was engraved. 'She is happy!' faid I to myfelf, with a figh: and then a melancholy, which was not without its charms, would take poffeffion of my foul, and make me long to be received into the bofom of the Deity, where I hoped to find that perfect felicity of which I felt the want.

The arrival of new boarders was an event which put all our youthful fpirits on the wing, the curiofity of girls in a convent being ftronger upon fuch occafions than can well be imagined. Young ladies from Amiens had been announced. It was on a summer's evening, and we were walking down an avenue of trees, when the exclamation, 'There they are! there they are!' passed suddenly from mouth to mouth. The principal mistress committed the strangers to the care of the nun whose business at that time it happened to be to superintend the boarders. The crowd gathered round them, walked away, returned again, fell at length into regular order, and paraded up and down the same walk in parties to examine the Miss Cannets. They were two sisters. The eldest was about eighteen, of a fine shape, a forward air, and easy carriage, and was rendered remarkable by something about her which indicated at the same time sensibility, pride, and discontent. The youngest was not more than fourteen: a veil of white gauze covered her charming countenance, and ill concealed the tears in which it was bathed. I felt a liking for her at first sight, stopped to get a better view of her person, and then mixed with the talkers to inquire what they knew of her.

She was the favourite, they said, of her mother, whom she tenderly loved, and with whom she was so loth to part, that her sister had been sent with her in order to enable her the better to bear the separation. Both were seated at supper at the same table with me. Sophia ate but little. Her mute grief was no way repulsive, and could not fail to inspire every body with concern. Her sister appeared less occupied in consoling her, than dissatisfied with

sharing

sharing her lot. Nor was she altogether in the wrong. A girl of eighteen, torn from the world, to which she had been restored, in order to return to a convent as her sister's companion, might naturally enough consider herself as sacrificed by her mother; who in fact had nothing in view but to curb an impetuous temper, which she found herself unable to govern. It was not necessary to be long in the company of the lively Henrietta to discover these things. Frank even to rudeness, impatient even to irascibility, and gay even to folly, she had all the spirit of her age without having any of its reason. Capricious, flighty, sometimes charming, and often insupportable, her bursts of passion were succeeded by the most affectionate atonements. She joined to extreme sensibility the utmost extravagance of imagination. You could not avoid loving, even while you scolded her; and yet it was difficult to live with her upon terms of endearment. Poor Sophia had much to suffer from the disposition of her sister, irritated against her from feelings of jealousy, too just at the same time not to esteem her as she deserved, and consequently finding in their intercourse every thing that could tend to provoke that unevenness of temper, which she herself was the first to lament. The sedateness of premature reason was Sophia's principal characteristic. Her feelings were not very acute, because her head was cool and composed: but she loved to reason and reflect. Gentle, without being forward in her demonſtrations of kindneſs, ſhe courted nobody's good-will, but obliged every body when an opportunity occurred, never anticipating nor ever oppoſing the wiſh of other people. She was fond both of working and reading. Her ſorrows had affected me; I was pleaſed with her demeanour; I felt that I had met with a companion; and we became inſeparable. I attached myſelf to her with that unreſerve which is ſo natural when we are in want of an object on which to place our affections, and meet with a perſon who ſeems fit to fill up the vacancy in our heart. Working, reading, walking, all my occupations and amuſements were ſhared with Sophia. She was of a religious turn, ſomewhat leſs tender than I, but equally ſincere; and that reſemblance between us contributed not a little to our intimacy. It was, if I may ſo expreſs myſelf, under the wing of Providence, and in the tranſports of a common zeal, that our friendſhip was cultivated: we wiſhed reciprocally to ſupport and forward each other in the road to perfection. Sophia was an unmerciful reaſoner: ſhe wanted to analyſe, to diſcuſs, to know every thing. I talked much leſs, and laid little ſtreſs upon any thing but reſults. She took a pleaſure in converſing with me, for I was an adept at liſtening: and when I differed from her in opinion, my oppoſition was ſo gentle, for fear of offending her, that not one of all our arguments ever produced the ſmalleſt diſſenſion between us.

Her

Her fociety was extremely dear to me, for I wifhed to confide to a perfon who could underftand me, the ‾fentiments which I felt, and which feemed to be heightened by participation. About three years older than myfelf, and a little lefs bafhful, fhe had a fort of external advantage which I did not envy her. She prattled prettily and fluently, while I knew only how to anfwer. True it is, that people took a particular pleafure in queftioning me; but that was a tafk every one was not equal to. To my dear friend alone was I truly communicative; others had only, as it were, a glimpfe of me, unlefs, indeed, it were a perfon fufficiently fkilful to lift up the veil, which, without intending to hide, I naturally threw over myfelf.

Henrietta was fometimes, but not often, of our party. She had formed a more *congenial* connection with a Mademoifelle de Cornillon, a girl of eighteen years of age, who was as ugly as fin, and as full of wit and mifchief as the devil; a proper hobgoblin, in fhort, to frighten children, but who would not have chofen to enter the lifts either againft Sophia's fober reafon or mine.

I cannot pafs over in filence the tender marks of affection that were fhewn me from my firft arrival by an excellent girl, whofe unalterable attachment has afforded me confolation on more occafions than one. Angelica Boufflers, born to no inheritance, had taken the veil at the age of feventeen. She was ftill ignorant of her own difpofition. Nature had formed her of the moſt combuſtible materials; and the compreſſion ſuffered by her energies had exalted the ſenſibility of her heart, and the vivacity of her mind, to the higheſt poſſible degree. The want of fortune had aſſigned her a place among the lay ſiſters, with whom ſhe had nothing in common but the ſervility of their functions. There are minds which ſtand in no need of cultivation. St. Agatha (for that was the name ſhe had aſſumed upon taking the veil), without having much education to boaſt of, was ſuperior not only to her companions in ſervitude, but to moſt of the ladies * of the choir. Her worth was known; and though, according to the uſage of thoſe ſocieties, where the majority are always ungrateful, exceſſive labour was impoſed upon her active diſpoſition, ſhe enjoyed, nevertheleſs, the reſpect that was her due. She was appointed, at that time, to wait upon the boarders; and though ſhe had nobody to aſſiſt her, and was entruſted with the care of many things beſide, ſhe found means to get through her buſineſs with equal cheerfulneſs and diſpatch. She had ſcarcely attracted my notice, when I had already obtained a diſtinguiſhed ſhare of hers: her kindneſs prevented my wiſhes, and made me remark her. At table ſhe ſtudied my taſte unknown to me, and endeavoured to gratify it; in my chamber, ſhe ſeemed to take a

* In many of the convents, that were not of the mendicant orders, the nuns were all of noble birth.—*Tranſ.*

pleaſure

pleasure in making my bed, and never let an opportunity escape of saying a civil thing. If I met her, she embraced me with tenderness; and sometimes would take me to her cell, where she had a beautiful canary-bird, which she had tamed, and taught to speak. She even gave me secretly a key to her apartment, that I might have access to it in her absence; and there I read the books that composed her little library—the poems of Father du Cerceau, and mystical works in abundance. When her avocations prevented her from spending a few minutes with me, or were likely to prevent her, I was sure to find a tender billet, which I never failed to answer; and these answers she treasured up like so many jewels, and shewed me them afterwards carefully locked up in her de . The attachment of sister Agatha to little Mademoiselle Phlipon soon became the talk of the whole convent; but any one would have supposed that it was natural it should be so; for my fellow-boarders never appeared hurt at the preference. When any of the nuns spoke of her partiality, she would ask, with her natural frankness, whether, in her place, they would not do the same? and when some peevish sister of fourscore, mother Gertrude for instance, told her, that she loved me too well, she replied, that she only thought so because incapable of feeling the like affection; 'and you yourself,' added she, 'do you not stop her whenever she comes in your way?' Mother

ther Gertrude ufed to turn away, muttering fomething between her teeth; but if fhe met me only half an hour afterwards, fhe was fure to put fome fweetmeats in my hand. When the Mifs Cannets arrived, and I attached myfelf to Sophy, Agatha appeared a little jealous, and the nuns took a pleafure in tormenting her; but her generous affection did not diminifh. It feemed as if fhe was fatisfied with my fuffering myfelf to be loved, and that fhe enjoyed the pleafure I derived from an intimacy with a perfon whofe age was nearer to my own, and whofe fociety I could command every hour of the day. Agatha was at that time four-and-twenty. Her fweet difpofition and her affection have infpired me with the fincereft regard for her, which I have ever taken a pride in teftifying. During the laft years that convents exifted, fhe was the only one that I vifited in hers. Now turned out of it, when her age and infirmities rendered fuch an afylum neceffary, and forced to live upon the fcanty penfion allotted her, fhe vegetates at no great diftance from the place of our ancient abode, or from that in which I am confined; and in the midft of the evils attendant on penury, only laments the captivity of her daughter; for thus has fhe always called me. O my kind friends, you will fometimes ceafe to pity me, when you confider the bleffings which heaven has left me ftill. In the midft of their power, my perfecutors have not the advantage

of

of being beloved by an Agatha, to whom misfortune only renders the objects of her attachment more dear.

The winter had paffed away. During that feafon, I had feen my mother lefs frequently; but my father would never let a Sunday pafs without vifiting me, and taking me to walk in the *Jardin du Roi*, if the weather were any way tolerable; and there we ufed to brave the feverity of the cold, and trip it gaily over the fnow. Delightful walks! the remembrance of which was revived, twenty years 'after, upon reading thofe lines of Thomfon, which I never repeat without emotion:

> Pleas'd was I, in my cheerful morn of life,
> When nurs'd by carelefs folitude I liv'd,
> And fung of nature with unceafing joy;
> Pleas'd was I, wand'ring through your rough domain,
> Through the pure virgin fnows, myfelf as pure.

It had been refolved upon at my entrance into the convent, that I fhould remain there only a year. This I had defired myfelf, as I wifhed to fee bounds fet to the facrifice I was about to make by feparating myfelf from my mother. The nuns, on their part, when they confented to my receiving my firft communion in the fourth month of my refidence among them, had taken great care to ftipulate that I fhould not leave them the fooner on that account, and that I fhould complete the period agreed upon. The year having revolved, I had left the convent. My mother informed me that my grandmother Phlipon,

pon, who was extremely fond of me, wished me much to remain with her some time, and that my mother had confented to my going, conceiving it could not be difagreeable to me, as she should be able to fee me there more frequently than at the convent: that arrangement, befide, was perfectly fuitable to circumftances. My father had been chofen into fome office of his parifh, and on that account was forced to be frequently from home. I readily underftood that my mother, being obliged at prefent to direct her attention to the work entrufted to the young men, about whom fhe had hitherto given herfelf no concern, had loft a portion of her liberty, which fhe would have wifhed to preferve entire, in order to beftow her whole time upon me.

The fituation fhe propofed to me was indeed a gentle tranfition from the abfence I had lately experienced to a complete return to her, and I accepted it the more readily, as I had a great liking for my grandmother. She was a graceful, good-humoured little woman, whofe agreeable manners, polifhed language, gracious fmile, and fignificant looks, ftill announced fome pretenfions to pleafe, or at leaft to remind us that fhe had once been a pleafing object. She was fixty-five or fixty-fix years of age, and ftill paid attention to her drefs, taking care, however, to fuit it to her years; for fhe prided herfelf above all things on the ftudy and obfervance of decorum. Confiderable corpulence, a light

ftep,

step, an upright carriage, handsome little hands, of which the fingers were gracefully displayed, and a sentimental style of converfation, intermingled with fallies of dignified mirth, took away from her every appearance of age. She was a delightful companion for young women, whose fociety pleased her, and of whose attentions she was proud. Becoming a widow immediately upon the termination of the first year of her marriage, my father, born after the death of her husband, was her only child. Misfortunes in trade having reduced her to diftrefs, she had been obliged to have recourse to some diftant relations, who were living in opulence, and who employed her, in preference to any body else, in the education of their children. Thus, for inftance, at Madame Boifmorel's she brought up both her fon Roberge, of whom I shall fpeak in the fequel, and her daughter, afterwards Madame de Favieres. A little eftate, which devolved to her by inheritance, having rendered her independent, she retired to the ifland of St. Louis, where she occupied a decent apartment with her fifter, Mademoifelle Rotiffet, whom she called Angelica. This worthy maiden, afthmatic and devout, as virtuous as an angel, and as fimple as a child, was entirely devoted to her elder fifter. The affairs of the little household devolved entirely on her. A charwoman, who attended twice a day, performed the more menial offices; but every thing elfe was done by Angelica, who dreffed her fifter with the moft reverend care. She naturally became my governante,

nante, at the fame time that Madame Phlipon undertook to be my teacher. Behold me, then, in their hands, after having quitted the houfe of God, regretted, beloved, and embraced by the whole fifterhood of nuns, wept over by my Agatha and my Sophia, lamenting my ' feparation from them, and promifing to mitigate its pains by the frequency of my vifits.

This engagement was too dear to my heart not to be fcrupuloufly fulfilled. My walks were frequently directed towards the Congregation, my aunt Angelica and my father taking a pleafure in accompanying me thither. The news of my arrival in the parlour ufed to run like lightning through the convent; and in the courfe of an hour I had interviews with twenty different perfons. But thofe vifits, after all, were poor fubftitutes for the daily and confidential intercourfe of friendfhip. They became lefs frequent, and I filled up the intervals with an epiftolary correfpondence, in which my Sophy bore the greateft part. That was the origin of my fondnefs for compofition, and one of the caufes that, by giving me a greater habit of writing, gave me alfo a greater facility.

PRIVATE MEMOIRS.

SECTION II.

August 28.

I FEEL the refolution of continuing my undertaking grow weaker. The miferies of my country torment me; the lofs of my friends affects my fpirits; an involuntary fadnefs benumbs my fenfes, overclouds my imagination, and weighs heavy on my heart. France is become a vaft amphitheatre of carnage, a bloody arena, on which her own children are tearing one another to pieces.

The enemy, favoured by her inteftine diffenfions, advances in every quarter; the cities of the North fall into their hands; Flanders and Alface are about to become their prey; the Spaniard is ravaging Roufillon; the Savoyards reject an alliance, which anarchy renders hateful; they return to their old mafter, whofe troops invade our frontiers; the rebels of la Vendée continue to lay wafte a large extent of territory; the Lyonnefe, indifcreetly provoked, burft into open refiftance; Marfeilles pre-
pares

pares for their fuccour; the neighbouring departments take arms: and in this univerfal agitation, and in the midft of thefe multiplied diforders, there is nothing uniform but the meafures of the foreign powers, whofe confpiracy againft freedom and mankind our exceffes have fanctified. Our government is a fpecies of monfter, of which the form and the actions are equally odious; it deftroys whatever it touches, and devours its very felf: this laft effort of its rage is the only confolation of its numerous victims.

The armies, ill conducted, and worfe provided, fight and fly alternately with defperate energy. The moft able commanders are accufed of treafon, becaufe certain reprefentatives, utterly ignorant of war, blame what they do not comprehend, and ftigmatize as ariftocrats all thofe who are more enlightened than themfelves. A legiflative body, characterized by debility from the moment of its exiftence, prefented us at firft with animated debates, which lafted as long as there exifted among the members fufficient wifdom to forefee dangers, and courage enough to announce them. The juft and generous fpirits, who had nothing in view but the welfare of their country, and dared attempt to eftablifh it, after being impudently reprefented under the moft odious colours, and in forms the moft contradictory, were at laft facrificed by ignorance and fear to intrigue and peculation; chafed from that body of which they were the foul,

they

they left behind them an extravagant and corrupt minority, who exercife defpotic fway, and who, by their follies and their crimes, are digging their own graves: but it is, alas! in confummating the ruin of the republic! The nation, fpiritlefs and ill-informed—becaufe the love of felfifh enjoyments makes men indolent, and indolence makes them blind—has accepted a conftitution effentially vicious, which, even if unexceptionable, fhould have been rejected with indignation, becaufe nothing can be accepted from the hands of villainy without degradation to the receiver. They ftill talk of fecurity and freedom, though they fee them both violated with impunity in the perfons of their reprefentatives! They can only change their tyrants; they are already under a rod of iron, and every change appears to them a bleffing; but incapable of effecting it themfelves, they expect it from the firft mafter who fhall chufe to affume the fovereign command. O Brutus! thou, whofe daring hand emancipated the depraved Romans, we have erred in vain, like thee! Thofe juft and enlightened men, whofe ardent fpirits longed for liberty, and who had prepared themfelves for it by the tranquil ftudies, and in the filent retreats of philofophy, flattered themfelves, like thee, that the fubverfion of defpotifm would eftablifh the throne of juftice and peace. Alas! it has only ferved as the fignal for the moft hateful paffions, and the moft execrable vice! After the profcriptions of the triumvirs, thou faidst, thou wert more ashamed of that which had caused Cicero's death, than sorry for the melancholy event; thou blamedst thy friends at Rome for *having become slaves rather by their own fault than that of their tyrants*, and for being *dastards* enough to see and suffer things, the bare recital of which was insupportable, and ought to have filled them with horror. In like manner do I feel indignant in the depth of my dungeon. But the hour of indignation is past; it is too evident that we have no longer a right to hope for any thing good, or to be astonished at any species of evil. Will history ever paint these dreadful times, or the abominable monsters who fill them with their barbarities? They surpass the cruelties of Marius, and the sanguinary achievements of Sylla. The latter, when he shut up and slaughtered six thousand men, who had surrendered to him, in the neighbourhood of the senate, which he encouraged to proceed in the debate amid their dreadful cries, acted like a tyrant, abusing the power he had usurped: but to what can we compare the domination of those hypocrites, who, always wearing the mask of justice, and speaking the language of the law, have created a tribunal to serve as the engine of their personal vengeance, and send to the scaffold, with formalities insultingly judicial, every individual, whose virtues offend them, whose talents excite their jealousy, or whose opulence calls forth their lust of wealth? What Babylon

ever

ever prefented a prototype of Paris, polluted with debauchery and blood, and governed by magiftrates whofe profeffion it is to circulate falfehoods, to fell calumny, and to panegyrize affaffination? What people ever depraved their morals and their nature to fuch a degree, as to contract an appetite for blood, to foam with fury when an execution is delayed, and to be ever ready to exercife their ferocity on all who attempt to calm or mitigate their rage? The days of September were the fole work of a fmall number of inebriated tygers; on the 31ft of May and the 2d of June the triumph of guilt was confirmed by the apathy of the Parifians, and their tame acquiefcence in flavery. Since that epoch the progreffion has been fudden and dreadful; the faction of the Convention called the *Mountain,* offers nothing to the eye but a band of robbers, clothed and fwearing like watermen, preaching maffacre, and fetting the example of rapine. Crowds of people furround the courts of juftice, and vociferate their threats againft the judges, who are thought too tardy in the condemnation of innocence. The prifons are gorged with public functionaries, with generals, and private individuals, of characters that graced and ennobled humanity: a zeal to accufe is received as a proof of civifm, and the fearch and detention of perfons of merit and property comprehend all the duties of an ignorant and unprincipled magiftracy.

The victims of Orleans are fallen. *Charlotte Corday* has not produced the smallest movement in a city which did not deserve to be delivered from a monster. *Briſſot**, *Genſonné*, and a multitude of other members, still remain under impeachment; proofs are wanting, but the fury of their enemies knows no bounds; and for want of reasons to condemn them, an appeal is made to the perverted will of the sovereign people, who impatiently expect their heads as a wild beast awaits his prey. *Cuſtine* † is no more; *Robeſpierre* triumphs; *Hebert* marks the victims; *Chabot* counts them; the tribunal is in haste to condemn, while the populace is preparing to accelerate and generalize the work

---

* Some women who belong to a club that meets in the church of St Euſtatius, said one day, setting up a howl, that they muſt have the head of Briſſot, without permitting the judges to proceed upon his trial with the same tedious formalities they had obſerved upon that of Cuſtine. Two thousand persons ſurrounded the court the day that judgment was pronounced on that general, trembled for fear he ſhould eſcape, and declared aloud, that if he were whitewaſhed, he muſt be treated like Montmorin, and with him, all the villains in the priſons.

† His property is confiſcated. His daughter-in-law, a young and charming woman, at that time pregnant, who divided her days between her father in-law, dragged to the tribunal, and her huſband confined at the *Force*, was impriſoned immediately after the execution of the former. She miſcarried;—but what does that signify to theſe monſters? The public accuſer had received of her 200,000 livres to save innocence: he returned them; but he had her arreſted for fear ſhe ſhould denounce his infamous behaviour.

of

of death. In the mean time famine invades the land; pernicious laws put an end to all induftry, ftop the circulation of commodities, and annihilate commerce; the public money is fquandered; diforganization becomes general; and in this total overthrow of the public fortune, men, devoid of fhame, wallow in ill-acquired wealth, fet a price upon all their actions, and draw up a bill of rates for the life and death of their fellow-citizens.

Dillon and *Caftellane* obtain their releafe: the one from the Magdellonettes, the other from St. Pélagie, by the payment of thirty thoufand livres to Chabot. *Sillery* gets his friends to cheapen his liberty, which he is rich enough to purchafe, and two hundred bottles of his excellent champaign are the overplus of the bargain, driven with the *ftrumpets* of the committee*. Roland's wife, recalled from time to time by the kind care of the Père Duchêne to the recollection of the populace, awaits the laft effort of their rage in the fame prifon, from which a kept girl departs in peace, after paying for her deliverance, and for the impunity

* The money and wine were given and received; Sillery obtained only the liberty of feeing and difcourfing with whom he pleafed. With this mitigation of his imprifonment he is ftill confined in the Luxembourg. Three or four abandoned women, belonging to the infamous wretches of the committees of public and general fafety, form a trading company, in which the pecuniary means of falvation of every remarkable individual are affeffed.

of her accomplice, a fabricator of forged affignats. Henriot, the commandant of the national guards, firſt a lackey, then a cuſtom-houſe officer, and afterwards a ringleader at the maſſacre at St. Firmin, breaks ſeals, empties cellars, and removes furniture, without feeling the ſmalleſt compunction: charged with the care of the deputies confined in the Luxembourg, he preſumes to intrude into their preſence purpoſely to inſult them, deprives them by open force of pens, books, and papers, and adds menaces to outrage. The ſubordination of authorities is a chimera, to which no one is permitted to appeal without incurring the accuſation of *incivifm*, and being ſuppoſed to entertain counter-revolutionary deſigns. Have the fugitive members at length eſcaped from this inhoſpitable land, which devours the virtuous, and drenches itſelf with their blood? O my friends! may propitious fate debark you ſafe in the United States, the only aſylum of liberty! My beſt wiſhes attend you! nor am I without hopes that the winds are now wafting you to that happy land. But *my doom*, alas! is irrevocable! I ſhall never behold you more; and in your departure, ſo much defired for your own ſakes, I ſee with ſorrow our eternal ſeparation. And you, my much revered huſband, grown weak and weary of the world, and ſunk into a premature old age, which you preſerve by painful efforts from the purſuit of the aſſaſſin—ſhall I ever be permitted to ſee you again,

and.

and to pour the balm of confolation into your heart, forely bruifed by the hard hand of misfortune?—— How many days longer am I deftined to remain a witnefs of the defolation of my native land, and of the degradation of my countrymen? Affailed by thefe afflicting images, I find it impracticable to fteel my heart againft affliction; a few fcalding tears ftart from my heavy eyes; and I fuffer the rapid pen to lie idle, that paffed fo lightly over my youthful days.

I will again attempt to recal them to my mind, and to purfue their courfe. In future times perhaps my ingenuous recitals will cheer the gloomy moments of fome unfortunate captive, and make him forget his own calamities while pitying mine: or perhaps fome poet or philofopher, defirous of weaving the paffions of the human heart into the progrefs of a romance, or the action of a drama, will find in my ftory the materials of his work.

Probably not many days will elapfe before the want of provifions, exafperating the impatient populace, will urge them to tumults, which their ringleaders will take care to render deftructive. The 10th of Auguft was intended to be a commemoration of the ides of September. The day before yefterday their renewal was threatened without referve in cafe Cuftine fhould be acquitted. The *Cordeliers* already proclaim the neceffity of getting rid of all fufpected perfons, and punifh-ments are ordained for such as have spoken ill of those glorious days. Is not this providing beforehand the justification of their return? The persons consigned to the revolutionary tribunal are not criminals sent thither to be judged, but victims which it is ordered to immolate. Those who are imprisoned for any thing else than crimes, are not under the protection of the law; but, left at the mercy of suspicion and calumny, it is impossible for them to conceive themselves safe from the fury of a deluded populace. Let us turn from this lamentable era, to which the reign of Tiberius can alone be compared, and call back again the peaceful and delightful days of youth.

I had completed my twelfth year, and the thirteenth was passing away under the care of my grandmother. The quiet of her house, and the piety of my aunt Angelica, accorded admirably with the tender and contemplative disposition I had brought with me from the convent. Every morning Angelica accompanied me to church to hear mass, where I was soon remarked by those monopolizers of consciences, who make a merit with God of peopling the cloisters. The reverend Abbé Géry, with his wry neck and downcast eye, accosted the person whom he took for my governante, to congratulate her on the edification produced by the example of her pupil, and to testify the strong desire he felt to be her guide in the ways of the Lord. He learned with regret, that the grand ceremonies

were

were already over, and that I had put my confcience into other hands. He then defired to know from my own mouth, whether I had not begun to think of my future deftination, and of bidding farewell to the vanities of the world. I anfwered, that I was too young yet to know my vocation. Monfieur Géry fighed, faid feveral fine things to me, and did not fail to place himfelf in my way out, in order to bow to me devoutly. The piety of my young heart did not go fo far as to be gratified with jefuitical affectations; it was too fincere to join hands with the abfurdities of bigotry, and the wry neck of Monfieur Géry was not at all to my tafte. I had neverthelefs a fecret defign of devoting myfelf to the monaftic life. St. Francis de Sales, one of the moft amiable faints in Paradife, had made a conqueft of my heart, and the ladies of the Vifitation, of which he was the founder, were already my adoptive fifters. But I was well fatisfied, that, being an only child, I fhould not obtain my parents' confent to take the veil during my minority, and was unwilling to give them unneceffary concern by any premature difclofure of my fentiments. Befides, fhould my refolution fail during the days of probation, it would only be furnifhing the ungodly with arms. I refolved, therefore, to conceal the intention, and to purfue my plan in filence. I laid my grandmother's little library under contribution; and the *Philotée* of St. Francis de Sales, and

and the Manual of St. Auguftin, became my favourite fources of meditation. What doctrines of fpiritual love! what delicious aliment for the innocence of a fervent foul, abandoned to celeftial illufions! Some controverfial writings of Boffuet furnifhed me with frefh food for my mind: favourable as they were to the caufe which they defended, they fometimes let me into the fecret of objections that might be made to it, and fet me on fcrutinizing my articles of faith. That was my firft ftep; but it was infinitely remote from the fcepticifm, at which in a courfe of years I was deftined to arrive, after having been fucceffively Janfenift, Cartefian, Stoic, and Deift. What a route, to terminate at laft in patriotifm, which has conducted me to a dungeon! In the midft of all this, fome old books of travels, and mythology in abundance, amufed my imagination, while the letters of Madam de Sevigné fixed my tafte. Her delightful eafe, her elegance, her vivacity, her tendernefs, made me enter into her intimacy. I became acquainted with her fociety; I was as much familiarized with her manners and the circumftances of her fituation, as if I had paffed my life with her. My grandmother faw little company, and feldom went out; but her agreeable pleafantry animated the converfation, while I was fitting by her fide, bufied about the different kinds of needle-work which fhe took a pleafure in teaching me. Madam Befnard, the fame great aunt who had paid fo much

atten-

attention to me while I was at nurfe, came every afternoon to pafs an hour or two with her fifter. Her auftere difpofition was always accompanied by a folemn fort of formality, and an air of ceremony, upon which Madam Phlipon would fometimes rally her, but fo tenderly as not to give offence to her fifter, who, after all, generally contributed her fhare to the converfation, by producing fome wholefome truth, delivered in a manner fomewhat harfh and abrupt, but which was readily forgiven, on account of the well-known goodnefs of her heart. My grandmother, who fet the higheft value on the graces, and every thing elfe that embellifhes focial life, was extremely fenfible of the complaifance which my gentle temper, the defire of pleafing every body about me, and her own amiable manners infpired me with towards her. She would fometimes pay me a compliment; and when, as was generally the cafe, I replied with readinefs and propriety, fhe could not conceal her exultation, but would caft a triumphant look upon Madam Befnard, who, elevating her fhoulders, feized the firft moment of my removal to another part of the room, to fay, in a low voice, which I heard very diftinctly, ' You are really infupportable: fhe will be fpoiled; what a pity!' My grandmother on this affumed a more ftately pofture than before, affuring her fifter, with an air of fuperiority, that fhe knew very well what fhe was about; while the worthy Angelica, with her pale face,

face, her prominent chin, her spectacles on her nose, and her knitting-needle in her hand, would tell them both, there was no danger to be apprehended, nothing that would be said could do me any harm, and that I had quite sense enough to be left to my own guidance. This aunt Besnard, so rigid in her manners, and so fearful of the bad effects of flattery, was very uneasy at my lying on a hard bed ; and if my finger chanced to ache, never failed to call twice a day to inquire concerning it. What sincere inquietude, what anxious cares did she not display on these occasions? And how delightful was their contrast with her usual severity and reserve! I verily believe that heaven placed me in the midst of people of kind hearts, on purpose to make mine the most affectionate possible.

My grandmother one day took it into her head to pay a visit to Madam de Boismorel, either for the pleasure of seeing her, or for that of exhibiting her grand-daughter. Great were the preparations in consequence, and tedious my dressing, which began at break of day : at length off we set with my aunt Angelica, for the *Rue St. Louis au Marais*, and reached it about noon. On entering the hotel, all the servants, beginning with the porter, saluted Madam Phlipon with an air of respect and affection, emulous who should treat her with the greatest civility. She answered every body in the kindest but at the same time in the most dignified manner; and so far all went well. But her grand-

daughter

daughter was perceived; for she could not deny herself the pleasure of pointing her out to observation, and the *servants* must needs pay fine compliments to the young lady. I had a sort of uncomfortable feeling, for which I could not account, but which I perceived nevertheless to proceed in part from the idea that servants might look at and admire me, but that it was not their business to pay me compliments. We passed on; were announced by a tall footman, and walked into the parlour, where we found Madam de Boismorel seated upon what was then called not an *ottomane*, but a *canapé*, and embroidering with great gravity. Madam de Boismorel was of the same age, stature, and corpulence as my grandmother; but her dress bespoke less taste than desire to display her opulence and indicate her rank; while her countenance, far from expressing a wish to please, announced her claims to respect, and the consciousness of her merit. A rich lace, puckered into the shape of a little cap, with wings pointed at the ends like the ears of a hare, was placed upon the top of her head, and allowed her hair to be seen, which was probably not of her own growth, and was dressed with that affected discretion which it is very necessary to assume at sixty years of age; while rouge, an inch thick, gave her unmeaning eyes a much more unfeeling look than was necessary, to make me fix mine upon the ground.—
' Ah! Mademoiselle Rotisset, good morning to you!

you!' cried Madam de Boifmorel in a loud and frigid tone, while rifing to receive us. (Mademoifelle?—So my grandmother is mademoifelle in this houfe.) 'I am very glad to fee you indeed. And who is this fine girl?—Your granddaughter I fuppofe?—She promifes to make a pretty woman! Come here, my dear, and fit down by my fide. She is a little bafhful. How old is your grand-daughter, Mademoifelle Rotiffet? She is a little brown to be fure, but her fkin is clear, and will grow fairer a year or two hence—fhe is quite the woman already! I will lay my life that hand muft be a lucky one. ' Did you never venture in the lottery?'— ' Never, Madam; I am not fond of gaming.'— I dare fay not: at your age children are apt to think their game a fure one. What an admirable voice!—fo fweet, and yet fo full-toned.—But how grave fhe is! Pray, my dear, are you not a little of the devotee?'—' I know my duty to God, and I endeavour to fulfil it.'—' That is a good girl! You wifh to take the veil, don't you?'—' I know not what may be my deftination, nor do I feek as yet to divine it.'— ' Very fententious, indeed! Your grand-daughter reads a great deal, does not fhe, Mademoifelle Rotiffet?'—' Reading, Madam, is her greateft delight; fhe always devotes to it fome part of the day.'—' Ay, ay, I fee how it is: but have a care fhe do not turn author; that would be

a pity

a pity indeed.' The converfation between the two ladies next turned upon the family and friends of the miftrefs of the houfe, my grandmother inquiring very refpectfully after the uncle, and the coufin, and the daughter-in-law, and the fon-in-law, and the Abbé Langlois, and the Marchionefs of Levi, and the Counfellor Brion, and Mr. Parent, the rector: they talked of their health, of their family connexions, and of their follies; as for inftance of thofe of Madam Rondé, who, notwithftanding her great age, ftill pretended to have a fine bofom, and made a great difplay of it, except when getting in or out of a carriage, for then fhe hid it with an ample handkerchief which fhe always carried in her pocket for that purpofe, becaufe, as fhe faid, fuch a fight ought not to be thrown away upon footmen. During this dialogue, Madam de Boifmorel made a few ftitches in her work, or elfe patted her little dog, keeping her eyes almoft conftantly fixed upon me. I was careful not to encounter looks I did not like; but took a furvey of the apartment, the decorations of which appeared far more agreeable to me than the lady to whom they belonged. In the mean time my blood circulated with more than ufual rapidity, my cheeks glowed, and my little heart was all in a flutter. I did not as yet afk myfelf, why my grandmother was not fitting upon the *canapé*, and why Madam de Boifmorel was not playing the humble part of *Mademoifelle Rotiffet*; but I had the

feel-

feeling which naturally leads to that reflection, and saw an end put to the visit with as much joy as if relieved from some grievous suffering. 'Mind, now, don't you forget to buy me a ticket in the lottery, and let your grand-daughter chuse the number, do you hear, Mademoiselle Rotisset? I am determined to try her hand. Come, give me a kiss: and you, my little dear, don't look so much upon the ground. You have very good eyes; and even your confessor will not blame you for opening them. — Yes, yes, Mademoiselle Rotisset, many a fine bow will come to your share, take my word for it; and that before you are much older. Good morning to you, ladies.' Thereupon Madam de Boismorel rang her bell, ordered Lafleur to call in a day or two at Mademoiselle Rotisset's for a lottery ticket, chid her dog for barking, and had already resumed her seat upon the *canapé* before we were well out of the room.

Our walk home was a silent one, and I hastened to return to books that might make me forget Madam de Boismorel, whose compliments were no more to my taste than those of her servants. My grandmother, not very well satisfied herself, mentioned her sometimes, and talked of her peculiarities; of her consummate selfishness, which made her say that children were but secondary considerations, when Madam Phlipon took the liberty of reminding her of the interest of her family, in order to check her prodigal expence: she spoke

also

alſo of that freedom of manners, ſo common among women of faſhion, in conſequence of which ſhe received her confeſſor, and other perſons, at her toilet, and changed her linen in their preſence. This ſort of behaviour ſtruck me as very ſtrange: and my curioſity induced me to ſet my grandmother talking about all theſe matters; but I kept the impreſſions they made on my mind to myſelf; not thinking them exactly ſuch as I could make known to her with propriety.

A fortnight after our viſit, we received one from Madam de Boiſmorel's ſon, who was not at home when we called upon his mother. He was a man verging upon forty; his aſpect was grave but gentle; and his behavour equally decent and dignified. His eyes, which were large, and even a little too full, ſent forth frequent flaſhes of lightning; and his bold and manly voice, ſoftened by reſpect, ſpoke the language of the ſoul in tones expreſſive of a gracious kind of politeneſs that ſeemed to flow directly from the heart. He addreſſed himſelf reſpectfully to my grandmother, calling her his good old friend, and bowed to me with that ſort of reverence which men of ſuſceptible minds take a pride in ſhewing to young women. Our converſation was at once guarded and familiar: M. de Boiſmorel took care not to let ſlip the opportunity of making handſome mention of the obligations he owed to my grandmother's care; and I eaſily underſtood that he was hinting to her

in

in an obfcure but delicate manner, that providence had rewarded her generous attention to other people's children, by giving her fo promifing a grandchild of her own.

I thought M. de Boifmorel infinitely more amiable than his mother, and was delighted whenever he called upon us, which was generally once in two or three months. He had married, at an early age, a very charming woman, and had a fon by her, whofe education occupied a confiderable portion of his thoughts. He had undertaken it himfelf, and was defirous of directing it by philofophical views, in which he was not a little thwarted by the prejudices of his mother, and the enthufiaftic devotion of his wife. He was accufed of fingularity; and as his nerves had been affected in confequence of a dreadful inflammatory diforder, the old counteffes, the folemn lawyers, and the fpruce abbés of his family, or of his mother's acquaintance, afcribed to a derangement of the brain, refulting from difeafe, the conduct he purfued in bringing up his boy. Thefe circumftances, when they came to my knowledge, excited much of my attention: it appeared to me that every thing which this fingular man faid was very much to the purpofe, and I began to fufpect there were two forts of reafon, if I may fay fo, one for the clofet and another for the world; a morality of principle, and a morality of practice, from the contradiction of which refulted fo many abfurdities, fome of which

which did not altogether escape my observation; in short, that persons of the gay world called every body insane, who was not affected with the common insanity: and thus did materials for reflection insensibly accumulate in my active brain.

My grandmother sometimes compared the sentiments and behaviour of Mr. de Boismorel with those of his sister, Madam de Favières, of whom she had some reason to complain; whose brother had found it necessary to remind her that Mademoiselle Rotisset was their own relation (a circumstance, said I to myself, that their mother appears either not to know, or not inclined to acknowledge), and to whom she had no desire to introduce me, any more than I to be introduced—which indeed she was so well aware of, that she never even proposed a second visit to Madam de Boismorel.

My father had vacated his office; the year to be spent with my grandmother had elapsed; and I returned to the arms of my indulgent mother. But it was not without regret that I left the handsome streets of the *Isle St. Louis*, the pleasant quays, and the tranquil banks of the Seine, where I was accustomed to take the air with my aunt Angelica, in the serene summer evenings, contemplating the winding course of the river, and the extensive landscape beyond it—quays, along which I used to pass, without meeting in my solitary way with any object to interrupt my meditations, when in the fervency of my zeal I was repairing to the temple in order to pour out my whole foul at the foot of the altar. My grandmother's gaiety gave charms to her habitation, in which I had fpent many pleafant and peaceful days. I took leave of her with a flood of tears; notwithftanding my attachment to my mother, whofe merit, of a more folid kind, was accompanied by a referve, with which I had not till then made any comparifon that could make it appear lefs attractive, as at that moment it ftruck me in a confufed manner. Child of the Seine, it was ftill upon its banks that I was going to refide; but the fituation of my father's houfe was not quiet and folitary like that of my grandmother. The moving picture of the *Pont-Neuf* varied the fcene every moment, and I entered literally as well as figuratively into the world, when I returned under my paternal roof. A free air, however, and an unconfined fpace, ftill gave fcope to my romantic and wandering imagination. How many times from my window, which fronted the north, have I contemplated, with emotion, the vaft expanfe of heaven, and its azure dome, defigned with fo much grandeur, and ftretching from the grey caft beyond the *Pont-au-Change* to the trees of the mall, and the houfes of Chaillot, refplendent with the ruddy beams of the fetting fun ! Never did I fail to employ a few moments in this way at the clofe of every fine day, and often have tears of delight ftolen down my cheeks in filence, while my heart, dilated by a fentiment not to be defcribed,

and

and happy in the idea and confcioufnefs of exiftence, was offering to the Supreme Being a pure homage of gratitude worthy of his acceptance. I know not if fenfibility give a more vivid hue to every object, or if certain fituations, which do not appear very remarkable, contribute powerfully to develope it, or if both be not reciprocally caufe and effect: but when I review the events of my life, I find it difficult to affign to circumftances, or to my difpofition, that variety and that plenitude of affection which have marked fo ftrongly every point of its duration, and left me fo clear a remembrance of every place at which I have been.

Cajou had ftill continued to teach me mufic. He was fond of making me talk over the theory, or rather the mechanifm of his art; for, though fomething of a compofer, he underftood little of mathematics, and of metaphyfics lefs: but he was ambitious of communicating to me all he knew. He was almoft as much afflicted at my want of expreffion in finging, as aftonifhed at the eafe with which I purfued a chain of reafoning. 'Put foul into it!' he would continually exclaim: 'You fing an air as nuns chant an anthem.' The poor man did not perceive that I had too much foul to be able to put it in a fong: and indeed I was as much embarraffed to give the proper expreffion to a tender paffage of mufic, as I fhould formerly have been in reading aloud the epifode of Eucharis or Erminia. Being fuddenly transformed into the perfonage fuppofed to be

speak-

speaking, I was no longer capable of imitation; I experienced the fentiment to be defcribed; my breathing grew fhort; my voice faltered; and difficulties refulted thence, which I could not overcome in a flat and ferious ftyle of finging; for I could not prevail upon myfelf to act the impaffioned lover.

Mignard, whofe Spanifh politenefs gained him the efteem of my grandmother, had begun, while I was with her, to teach me the guitar, and continued to give me leffons when I returned to my father's. The common accompaniments did not coft me many months to execute; and *Mignard* afterwards took a pleafure in forwarding my improvement, till in the end I furpaffed my mafter. *Mozon* was recalled to perfect my dancing, as was *Mr. Demure*, to keep up my arithmetic, geography, writing, and hiftory. My father made me refume the graver, confining me to the moft trifling branch of the art, to which he thought to attach me by the tie of intereft; for having taught me enough to make me of fome ufe, he gave me little jobs to do, of which he fhared the profit with me at the end of the week, according to a book which he defired me to keep. But I foon became weary of this; nothing was fo infipid to me, as to engrave the edge of a watch-cafe, or to ornament a bauble: I liked much better to read a good author, than to buy a riband. I did not conceal my difguft; and as no conftraint was laid upon me, I threw afide the graver, and have never touched it fince. I went out every

morn-

morning with my mother to hear mafs: after which we fometimes made our little purchafes. When the time required for thefe purpofes, and the hours devoted to the leffons of my different mafters, were over, I retired to my clofet to read, to write, and to meditate. The long evenings made me return to my needle-works, during which my mother had the complaifance to read to me for hours together. Thefe readings gave me great pleafure; but as they did not permit me to digeft things to my entire fatisfaction, I conceived the idea of making extracts. Accordingly, my firft employment in the morning was to confign to paper what had ftruck me moft forcibly the preceding evening; and this done, I returned to the book to recover the connexion, or to copy a paffage, that I was defirous of having entire. This grew into a habit, a paffion, a perfect rage. My father having only the little library, which I had formerly exhaufted, I borrowed and hired books, and could not bear the idea of returning them till I had made what I conceived the beft part of their contents my own. In this manner I demolifhed *Pluche, Rollin, Crevier*, the *Père d'Orleans, St. Real*, the *Abbé de Vertot*, and *Mezeray*, who fo little refembles the latter; Mezeray, the drieft of all poffible writers, but the hiftorian of my country, with the annals of which I wifhed to be acquainted.

My grandmother Bimont was dead. My little uncle fettled at St. Bartholomew's, in a better place

than

than that of mafter of the choir, boarded with the firft vicar, the Abbé le Jay, who kept a very tolerable houfe, where we ufed to go and pafs the evening on Sundays and holidays, after divine fervice.

The Abbé le Jay was a good old man, clumfy both in body and mind, a wretched preacher, an unmerciful confeffor, a cafuift, and the Lord knows what befide. But he was by no means blind to his own intereft: he had found means to help on his two brothers, and to get them eftablifhed as notaries at Paris, where they made a figure in their profeffion, at that time both reputable and lucrative. His own houfe was kept by one of his relations, a Mademoifelle d'Hannaches, tall, dry, and fallow, with a fhrill voice, proud of her defcent, and tiring every body with her economical arrangements, and her pedigree. She was a woman however, and that always enlivens the houfe of a prieft: befides, fhe contrived to keep a neat and plentiful table for her coufin, who was a great *amateur* of good eating. The Abbé found it extremely agreeable to have a boarder in his houfe of the amiable difpofition of my uncle Bimont: his table was more cheerful, Mademoifelle d'Hannaches better tempered, and his party of tric-trac* never failed: my mother and the coufin were partners; and as to me, who feemed thus to be deferted, I was not at all difpleaf-

---

* A game refembling backgammon, but fometimes played by four perfons.—*Tranf.*

ed at my four friends amusing themselves in that way; for the Abbé le Jay received company in a large library, which I laid under contribution without mercy. That was a source which I recurred to as long as he lived; something less than three years. One of his brothers having ruined himself, the Abbé lost his senses, languished for six weeks, threw himself out of a window, and died of his fall. Mademoiselle d'Hannaches, then at law for the inheritance of her uncle, *the captain,* was accommodated in my mother's house, and resided with us a year and a half. During that period I was her secretary: I wrote her letters, copied her dear genealogy, drew up petitions which she presented to the president and attorney-general of the parliament of Paris, who were left trustees of the annuities bequeathed by a Mr. de St. Vallier to poor gentlewomen; and sometimes accompanied her when she went to make interest with various persons of consequence. I easily perceived that, notwithstanding her ignorance, her stiff demeanour, her bad way of expressing herself, her old-fashioned dress, and her other absurdities, respect was paid to her origin. The names of her ancestors, which she never failed to repeat, were attended to, and great pains were taken to obtain for her what she desired. I compared the honourable reception she met with, with that given me by Madam de Boismorel, which had left a deep impression on my mind; I could not help feeling my superiority over

Made-

Mademoifelle d'Hannaches, who with her genealogy, and at the age of forty, was unable to write a line of common fenfe, or a legible hand; and it appeared to me that the world was extremely unjuft, and the inftitutions of fociety highly abfurd.

But let us fee for a moment what was become of my friends at the convent. My Agatha now and then wrote me letters in the ftyle of tendernefs peculiar to thofe plaintive doves, who dared not indulge in any thing farther than friendfhip; a ftyle rendered ftill more affectionate by her ardent foul. Little boxes, pincufhions, and fweetmeats, accompanied them, whenever fuch prefents were within her reach. I went occafionally to fee her; and was even admitted into the interior of the convent at a feftival given in honour of the fuperior; a privilege they had taken care to infure me, by obtaining unknown to me a licence from the archbifhop, which was afterwards prefented to me as a fpecial favour, and received by me as fuch. Every thing was in motion, the young ladies were well dreffed, the hall was adorned with flowers, and the refectory ftuffed full of dainty cates. It muft be confeffed, that in thefe entertainments of poor fecluded virgins, in which no doubt fomething childifh may be found, there is alfo fomething amiable, ingenuous, and graceful, which belongs only to the gentlenefs of women, to their lively imagination, and innocent playfulnefs, when they make merry among themfelves at a diftance from a fex, that always

ways renders them more ferious, when it does not completely turn their brain. A fhort drama, rather dull, but enlivened by the voices of little girls finging a few ftanzas in chorus, was the firft rallying point: fportive dances fucceeded; at one time fome excellent joke, and at another an arch laugh, the more humorous, becaufe making a greater contraft with their habitual gravity, gave a true Saturnalian character to the fports of the good fifters and their pupils.

The phyfician coming by chance to the infirmary to vifit his patients, it was impoffible to do otherwife than invite him to a fight of the entertainment. He was accordingly conducted under a cloifter hung with feftoons of flowers, where a fort of fair was eftablifhed. There young novices were felling ballads, others were diftributing cakes, one was drawing a lottery, and another telling fortunes, while the little girls were loaded with bafkets of fruit, and a concert was performing on the oppofite fide. At the fight of the doctor's wig, the novices pulled their veils over their faces; the elder boarders looked at their drefs, to fee whether it was in diforder; the younger girls affumed a graver air; and I held my guitar in a lefs negligent manner. It was fufpended before me by a riband paffed over my fhoulder. The nuns had infifted upon hearing me fing, and the occafion had infpired me with two ftanzas indifferent in themfelves, but fo well timed as to be received with unbounded

bounded applaufe. Even Cajou would have been fatisfied with the manner in which I fung them; for having no fentiments to exprefs but fuch as I could indulge, my accents were perfectly unreftrained. I was defired to repeat them before the phyfician: but that was a very different affair; my voice faltered, and my expreffion became obfcure. An old nun remarked it, and faid with an arch look, that it only made my countenance fo much the more interefting. At length the doctor withdrew, every body being glad he was gone, though nobody would have wifhed him not to have been there.

Sophia had returned to her family at Amiens; but previoufly to her departure we had prevailed upon our mothers to fee one another. They had in a manner confecrated our connexion, had reciprocally applauded their daughters' choice, and fmiled at our promifes, of never forgetting each other, which we called upon them to witnefs. Thofe promifes, however, were better kept than they imagined, notwithftanding certain modifications of which my readers hereafter will be able to judge. My correfpondence with my friend was regularly carried on. I wrote to her always once a week, and generally twice.—' And what,' methinks I hear it afked, ' could you have to relate?'—Every thing I faw, thought, felt, or perceived: furely then I could not be in want of fomething to fay! Our correfpondence gave facility to itfelf, and furnifhed its

own

own materials. By communicating my reflections, I learned the better to reflect; I studied with more ardour, because I took a pleasure in sharing what I acquired; and I made my observations with the greater care, because I found entertainment in committing them to paper. Sophia's letters were less frequent: a numerous family, a crowded house, the forms of society, and the very nature of a provincial life, occupied by trifles, by unmeaning visits, and of which a part is necessarily devoted to cards, left her neither the leisure to write, nor the means of collecting such abundant materials. For that reason perhaps she set the greater value on the letters she received from me, and pressed me more earnestly to write.

The death of the Abbé le Jay having deprived me of the use of his library, in which I had found historians, mythologists, fathers of the church, and literati:—*Cotrou* and *Rouillé*, for instance, who call Horatius Cocles a *one-eyed worthy*; *Maimbourg*, of a taste equally elevated; *Berruyere*, who wrote the history of the people of God in the style wherein *Bitaubé* has composed his poem called Joseph; the chevalier *de Folard*, of a very different cast, whose military details appeared to me much more rational than the reflections of the Jesuits; the Abbé *Banier*, who amused me a great deal more than the Abbé *Fleury*; *Condillac*, and father *André*, whose metaphysics, applied to eloquence, and to the *beautiful* of every kind, gave me singular delight;

light; some poems by *Voltaire*; the moral essays of *Nicole*; the Lives of the *Fathers in the Wilderness*, and that of *Descartes* by *André Baillet*; *Bossuet*'s Universal History; the letters of *St. Jerôme*, and the romance of *Don Quixote*, with a thousand others equally congruous:—this library failing me, I was forced to have recourse to the bookfellers. My father being ill qualified to select, asked for whatever I pointed out, my choice generally falling on the works of which I had been enabled to form some idea by the quotations and extracts I had found in those I had already read. In that way translations of Diodorus Siculus, and other ancient historians, attracted my notice. I was also desirous of reading the history of my own country in some other writer besides Mezeray, and accordingly pitched upon the Abbé *Velly*, and his continuators far less interesting than himself, in periods, where, with his talents, they might have been more so. *Pascal*, *Montesquieu*, *Locke*, *Burlamaqui*, and the principal French dramatists, next engaged my attention. I had no plan, nor any end in view, but to improve myself and acquire knowledge. I felt a sort of necessity of exercising the activity of my mind, and of gratifying my serious propensities. I panted after happiness, and could find it only in a powerful exertion of my faculties. I know not what I might have become, if placed in the hands of a skilful preceptor: it is probable that by applying solely or principally to a particular study, I

might

might have extended some branch of science, or have acquired talents of a superior kind. But should I have been better or more useful? That is a question which I leave others to resolve: certain it is, that I could not have been more happy. I know of nothing comparable to that plenitude of life, of peace, of satisfaction, to those days of innocence and study. They were not, however, unmixed with trouble, from which the life of man upon earth is never exempt.

I had generally several books on hand at a time, some serving for study, others standing me in the stead of recreation. Historical works of length, as I have already observed, were read aloud in the evening, which was almost the only time I spent with my mother. The whole of the day I passed in the solitude of the closet, in making extracts, or in meditation. As long as the fine weather lasted, we went on holidays to the public walks; and my father regularly carried me besides to all the exhibitions either of pictures or other works of art, so frequent at Paris in those days of luxury, and of prosperity, as it was then called. He enjoyed himself much on these occasions, when he had it in his power to make an agreeable display of his superiority by pointing out to my observation what he understood better than I; and was proud of the taste I discovered as of his own work. That was our point of contact: in those cases we were truly in unison. My father never lost an opportunity of shewing himself felf to advantage; and it was evident that he was fond of being feen in public, giving his arm to a well-dreffed young woman, whofe blooming appearance frequently produced a murmur of admiration grateful to his ears. If any one accofted him, doubtful of the relation in which we ftood to each other, he would fay, ' My daughter,' with an air of modeft triumph, which I was not the laft to perceive, and which affected me without making me vain, for I afcribed it entirely to parental affection. If I chanced to fpeak, he might be feen examining, in thofe around, the effect of my voice, or of the good fenfe I might have uttered, and afking them by his looks, if he had not reafon to be proud. I was fenfible of thefe things; and they fometimes made me more timid, without producing any awkward feeling: it feemed incumbent upon me to make amends by my modefty for my father's pride. In the mean time, how did thefe worldly amufements, thefe arts, the images they call up, and the defire to pleafe, fo natural and fo ftrong in womankind, agree with my devotion, my ftudies, my fober reafon, and my faith? That was precifely the origin of the trouble of which I have been fpeaking, and of which the progrefs and effects are well worthy of an explanation rather difficult to give.

With the bulk of mankind, formed rather to feel than to think, the paffions give the firft fhock to their creed, when that creed has been imbibed
from

from education. What but paffion produces fuch contradictions between the principles that have been adopted, the defires that thofe principles cannot extinguifh, and the inftitutions of a government ill calculated to reconcile them? But in a young mind accuftomed to reflect, and placed out of the reach of the feductions of the world, it is reafon which firft gives the alarm, and urges us to examine, before we have any intereft to doubt. If my inquietude, however, had no felfifh confiderations in view, it was not, on that account, independent of my fenfibility: I thought through the medium of my heart; while my reafon, though obferving a ftrict impartiality, was by no means unconcerned in the operations of the mind.

The firft thing that fhocked me in that religion, which I profeffed with the ferioufnefs of a folid and confiftent mind, was the univerfal damnation of all thofe by whom it is denied, or to whom it has remained unknown. When, inftructed by hiftory, I had well confidered the extent of the earth, the fucceffion of ages, the progrefs of empires, the virtues and the errors of fo many nations, I perceived weaknefs, abfurdity, and impiety, in the idea of a creator, who devotes to eternal torments thofe innumerable beings, the frail works of his hands, caft on the earth in the midft of fo many perils, and loft in a night of ignorance, from which they have already had fo much to fuffer. ' I am deceived in
this

this article of my creed, it is evident; am I not equally wrong in some other? Let me examine.'—From the moment a Catholic has arrived at this stage of reasoning, he is lost for ever to the church. I easily conceive why priests require a blind submission, and preach up so strenuously that religious faith, which adopts without examination, and adores without murmuring; this is the basis of their empire, which is destroyed as soon as we begin to investigate. Next to the cruelty of damnation, the absurdity of infallibility struck me the most; and very soon it was rejected likewise. 'What truth is there then remaining?'—That became the object of a research continued, during a number of years, with an activity, and sometimes an anxiety, of mind, difficult to describe. Critical, moral, philosophical, and metaphysical writers became my favourite study. I was on the hunt after whatever could point them out to me; and their analysis and comparison became my principal employ. I had lost my confessor, the monk of St. Victor's: the good M. Lallement was dead, to whose worth and discretion I am happy to have an opportunity of bearing witness. Being under the necessity of making choice of some person to succeed him, I cast my eyes upon the Abbé Morel, who belonged to our parish, and whom I had seen at my uncle's: he was a little man, by no means wanting in understanding, and professing the greatest austerity of principles, which was the motive

that

that determined me in my choice. When my faith wavered, he was fure to be the firft informed of it; for I never could tell any thing but the truth. He was eager to put into my hands the apologifts and champions of Chriftianity. Behold me then clofetted with the Abbé *Gauchat*, the Abbé *Bergier*, *Abbadie*, *Holland*, *Clarke*, and the reft of the reverend phalanx.—I perufed them with critical feverity, and fometimes made notes, which I left in the book when I returned it to the Abbé Morel, who afked with aftonifhment if I had written and conceived them. The moft whimfical part of the ftory is, that it was from thefe works that I firft got an idea of thofe which they pretended to refute, and noted down their titles in order to procure them. In this way did the treatife on *Toleration*, the *Dictionnaire Philofophique*, *Queftions concerning the Encyclopedie*, the *Bon Sens* of the Marquis d'Argens, the *Jewifh Letters*, the *Turkifh Spy*, *les Mœurs*, *l'Efprit*, *Diderot*, *d'Alembert*, *Raynal*, and the *Syfteme de la Nature*, pafs fucceffively through my hands.

The progrefs of my mind was not going on alone. Nature was making hers in every way. Although my mother had never precifely told me what I had to expect, fhe had occafionally faid enough on the fubject in my prefence, and my grandmother in particular had amufed herfelf too much by certain predictions, to leave any room for aftonifhment at the event.

I re-

I remarked it with a fort of joy, as an initiation into the clafs of grown perfons, and I announced it to my mother, who embraced me tenderly, delighted at idea the of my having paffed fo happily through a period, during which fhe had been alarmed for my health. Previoufly to this occurrence I had been fometimes roufed in a furprifing manner from the moft profound fleep. My imagination had no concern in the bufinefs: it was too much occupied with ferious fubjects, and my timorous confcience guarded it too fcrupuloufly againft amufing itfelf with others, for it to be poffible that it fhould prefent to me what I had never allowed myfelf to try to comprehend. But an extraordinary ebullition irritated my fenfes during the hours of repofe, and operated of itfelf, by the mere force of an excellent conftitution, an effect which was as perfectly unknown to me as the caufe. The firft fentiment that refulted from it was an unaccountable fort of terror. I had read in my *Philotée*, that we are not permitted to derive any pleafure from our bodies unlefs in lawful marriage. This precept recurred to my mind. What I had experienced might be called a pleafure: I was therefore culpable, and in a way too that might occafion me the greateft fhame and forrow, fince it was precifely the offence moft difpleafing to the Lamb without fpot. Great was the agitation in my poor heart, fervent were my prayers, and my mortifications

tions fevere! How was a fimilar event to be avoided in future? for after all I had not forefeen it. True; but I had not taken pains to prevent it, at the inftant it was coming on. My vigilance accordingly became extreme. I perceived that one pofition expofed me more to it than another; and carefully avoided it. My uneafinefs was fo great, that it ufed afterwards to wake me before the cataftrophe. When I had been unable to prevent it, I leaped out of bed, and ftanding in the midft of winter, with my naked feet on the bare pavement*, I fupplicated the Lord, with folded arms, to preferve me from the temptations of the devil. I loft no time in putting myfelf upon low diet; and it has happened to me to practife literally what the royal prophet has perhaps only given us, as an oriental figure of fpeech; I mixed afhes with my bread, and moiftened it with my tears. I have made more than one breakfaft on toaft fprinkled with afhes inftead of falt, by way of penance. Thefe repafts did me no more harm than the nocturnal accidents, for the reparation of which, I put myfelf upon fo ftrange a regimen. At laft I conceived that they might be trials which heaven permitted in order to keep us in humble diftruft of ourfelves; and I called to mind the complaints of St. Paul, and his prayers to be delivered from '*the thorn in the flefh, the meffenger of Satan*

* In France the bed-rooms are generally paved with hexagonal tiles.—*Tranf.*

that was given to buffet him.' I fancied that it was on this account, that St. Bernard ufed to throw himfelf in the fnow; that St. Jerome covered his body with fackcloth; and that abftinence was fo ftrenuoufly recommended to thofe who afpire to perfection. How humble and fervent was my devotion whenever fuch an accident had happened to me! How much muft my earneft voice, my humble attitude, the extraordinary glow of my complexion, and my bright and humid eyes, have added to the expreffion of a countenance full of candour and fenfibility! What a mixture of innocence, of premature fentiment, of good fenfe, and of fimplicity! In truth, I almoft confider myfelf as fortunate in being fent to prifon, in order to call to mind thefe interefting peculiarities, which never before came into my head, and by which I am highly affected.

I already fee the curious at a lofs to know what I could fay on this fubject to my confeffor: but moft affuredly the difficulty they may find in conceiving it, is not greater than the embarraffment I underwent. It was in vain that the moft fcrupulous examination quieted my confcience as to my will: I always returned to the principle of the *Philotée*, and the argument thence to be inferred; and, in fhort, if it were only a trial, it ought ftill to be laid before my confeffor. How fhall I attempt it? What name fhall I give it? What fhall I defcribe? or how exprefs myfelf?——' Father, I accufe cuſe myſelf.'—' Well, child!' What could I ſay next? My heart began to beat, the blood ruſhed into my face, and a dewy moiſture diffuſed itſelf over my whole frame. ' I accuſe myſelf—of having had emotions contrary to the chaſtity of a chriſtian.' Oh! what an excellent phraſe! Santeuil was not more delighted at finding his rhime, nor Archimedes with the ſolution of his problem, than I was pleaſed with the expreſſion. But if he ſhould queſtion me further? Nay, but I have told all I can; it is his buſineſs to know the reſt. I trembled that day much more than uſual in kneeling before the holy tribunal; and my veil was pulled down to my chin. I was anxious, however, to eaſe my heart of the heavieſt of my accuſations. ' Have you at all contributed thereto?'— ' I do not know, but my will was not concerned.' —' Have you read no bad books?'—' Never.'— ' Entertained no improper thoughts?'—' Oh no! I abhor them.'—' Hem! go on.' I know not whether the Abbé Morel had any bad thoughts to combat at that moment, but his prudent reſerve not ſuffering him to add any thing more, I looked upon his *Hem! Go on*, as tantamount to the order of the day, and concluded, that I was not ſo criminal as I had ſuppoſed. He took care, however, in his final exhortation, to recommend to me to be watchful, and to remind me, that angelic purity was the virtue moſt agreeable in the eyes of the Lord, with other common-place maxims which I

read

read every day. I was confirmed in my idea that it was a trial, and that I was right in my applications of St. Paul and other holy writers. My confcience was delivered from a very painful fcruple, and I became in future free from agitation. It is inconceivable what good effects this habit of reftraint has produced on the whole courfe of my life, notwithftanding the way in which it was contracted. It has gained fuch an afcendance over me, that I have maintained, from delicacy and a fenfe of rectitude, the feverity that firft fprung from devotion. I became miftrefs of my imagination by dint of curbing it; I took a fort of diflike to every brutal and folitary gratification; and in dangerous fituations have found a pleafure in remaining prudent, when feduction would have led me to forget my reafon and my principles. Pleafure, like happinefs, I can fee only in the union of what charms the heart as well as the fenfes, and leaves behind it no regret. With fuch fentiments, it is difficult to forget, and impoffible to degrade, one's felf, at the fame time that they do not exempt us from what is properly called a tender paffion; on the contrary, they perhaps increafe the quantity of fuel by which it is fed. I might add here, as in geometry, Q. E. D. But have a little patience! we have plenty of time to come at the proof.

To the newly acquired fenfations of a well organized frame, were infenfibly joined all the modifications of the defire to pleafe. I was fond of *look-*

ing well, I was pleafed at hearing it faid, and willingly employed myfelf in whatever feemed likely to procure me that fatisfaction. This, perhaps, is the place to draw my portrait, and it will be quite as well to infert it here as elfewhere. At fourteen years old, having already attained my full height, my ftature was, as now, about five feet*; my leg was well made; my foot well fet on; my hips high and prominent; my cheft broad, and nobly decorated; my fhoulders flat; my carriage firm and graceful; and my walk light and quick:—fuch was the firft *coup d'œil*. My face had nothing ftriking in it, except a great deal of colour, and much foftnefs and expreffion. On examining each feature, 'Where,' it might be faid, 'is the beauty?' Not a fingle one is regular, and yet all pleafe. My mouth is a little wide; you may fee prettier every day; but you will fee none with a fmile more tender or engaging. My eyes, on the contrary, are not very large, and the colour of the iris is hazel; but they are fufficiently prominent, and are crowned with well-arched eye-brows, which, like my hair, are of a dark brown. My look is open, frank, lively, and tender, varying in its expreffion like the affectionate heart of which it indicates the movements: ferious and lofty, it fometimes aftonifhes; but it charms much more, and never fails to keep attention awake. My nofe gave me fome uneafinefs; I thought it a little too full at the end;

---

* Near five feet four inches Englifh meafure.—*Tranf.*

but

but taken with the reſt, eſpecially in profile, its effect is not amiſs. My forehead, broad, high, with the hair retiring, at that early age, ſupported by a very elevated orbit of the eye, and marked by veins in the form of a Y, that dilated on the ſlighteſt emotion, was far from making ſuch an inſignificant figure as it does in many faces. As to my chin, which turns up a little at the end, it has preciſely the marks attributed by phyſiognomiſts to the voluptuary. Indeed, when I combine all the peculiarities of my character, I doubt if ever an individual ſo well formed for pleaſure, taſted it ſo little. A complexion clear rather than fair, a freſh colour, frequently heightened by the ſudden fluſh of a rapid circulation excited by the moſt irritable nerves; a ſmooth ſkin, a well-turned arm, a hand, which, without being ſmall, is elegant, becauſe its long and taper fingers give it grace, and indicate addreſs; teeth white and regular; and the plumpneſs of perfect health:—ſuch are the gifts with which nature had endowed me. I have loſt many of them, particularly the fulneſs of my form, and the bloom and ruddineſs of my complexion; but thoſe which remain ſtill hide five or ſix years of my age, without any aſſiſtance of art, ſo that the perſons who are in the daily habit of ſeeing me, will hardly believe me to be more than two or three and thirty. It is only ſince my beauty has begun to fade, that I know what was its extent: while in its bloom I was unconſcious of its value, which was probably augmented by my ignorance.

I do

I do not regret its lofs, becaufe I have never abufed it; but I certainly fhould not be forry, provided my duty could be reconciled with my inclination, to turn the portion that remains to better account. My portrait has frequently been drawn, painted, and engraved, but none of thefe imitations gives an idea of my perfon*: my likenefs is very hard to hit, becaufe the expreffion of my foul is more ftrongly marked than the lines of my countenance. This an artift of common abilities cannot reprefent; poffibly he does not even fee it. My face takes animation in proportion to the intereft with which I am infpired, in the fame manner as my mind is developed in proportion to the mind with which I communicate. I feel myfelf fo ftupid with many people, that upon perceiving my readinefs with perfons of wit, I have thought in the fimplicity of my heart that I was indebted for it to their clevernefs. I generally pleafe, becaufe I am fearful of offending; but it is not given to all to find me handfome, or to difcover what I am worth. I can fuppofe that an old coxcomb, enamoured of himfelf, and vain of difplaying the flender ftock of fcience he has been fo long in acquiring, might be in the habit of feeing me for ten years together without fufpecting I could do more than caft up a bill, or cut out a fhirt. It was not without reafon that Camille Defmoulins was

* The cameo of Langlois is the leaft defective.

aftonifhed

astonished that '*at my age, and with so little beauty,*' I had still what he calls adorers. I never spoke to him in my life, but it is probable that with a personage of his stamp I should be cold and silent, if not absolutely repulsive. He was not right in supposing me to hold a court. I hate gallants as much as I despise slaves, and know perfectly well how to get rid of a flatterer. What I want is esteem and goodwill; admire me afterwards if you please; but esteem and affection I must have at any rate: this seldom fails with those who see me often, and who possess, at the same time, a sound understanding and a heart.

That desire to please, which animates a youthful breast, and excites so delicious an emotion when we perceive the flattering looks of which we are the object, was curiously combined with my virgin bashfulness, and the austerity of my principles, and diffused a peculiar charm over my person and my dress. Nothing could be more decent than my garb, nor any thing more modest than my deportment: though wishing them to bespeak reserve, and aspiring only to neatness, the greatest commendations were bestowed upon my taste. Meanwhile, that renunciation of the world, that contempt of its pomps and vanities, so strongly recommended by christian morality, accorded ill with the suggestions of nature. Their contradictions at first tormented me, but my reasoning necessarily extended to rules of conduct, as well as to articles of faith. I applied

plied myfelf with equal attention to the inveftigation of what I ought to do, and the examination of what it was poffible for me to believe: the ftudy of philofophy, confidered as the moral fcience, and the bafis of happinefs, became my only one, and I referred to it all my reading and obfervation.

The fame thing happened to me in metaphyfics and morality, that I had experienced in reading poetry: I fancied myfelf transformed into the perfonage of the drama that had moft analogy with myfelf, or that I moft efteemed; and adopted the propofitions, with the novelty or brilliancy of which I had been ftruck: they remained my own, till fome newer or more profound difcuffion came in my way. Thus, in the controverfial clafs, I fided with the authors of Port Royal; their logic and their aufterity agreed with my temper of mind, while I felt an inftinctive averfion to the fophiftical, evafive, and flexible faith of the Jefuits. When I became acquainted with the ancient fects of philofophers, I gave the palm to the ftoics; and endeavoured, like them, to maintain that pain was no evil. That folly could not laft, but I perfifted in determining at leaft not to be overcome by it; and my little experiments convinced me that I could endure the greateft torments without uttering a cry. The night of my marriage deftroyed the confidence I had till then preferved: it is true, furprife had fome fhare in the bufinefs, and a novice of that rigid order may be expected to

bear

bear an evil foreseen, better than one that came unawares, when the very contrary was looked for.

During two months that I studied Descartes and Malebranche, I considered my kitten, when she mewed, merely as a piece of mechanism performing its movements; but in thus separating sentiment from its signs, it seemed to me that I was dissecting nature, and robbing it of all its charms. I thought it infinitely more agreeable to give every thing a soul; and should have adopted that of Spinosa, rather than go without one. Helvetius hurt me: he annihilated the most ravishing illusions; and shewed me everywhere a mean and revolting self-interest: yet what sagacity! what happy ideas! I persuaded myself that Helvetius delineated mankind in the state to which they had been reduced by the corruption of society: I thought it right to study him, in order to frequent what is called the world, without being its dupe; but I took good care not to adopt his principles for the purpose of estimating man in his unadulterated state, or appreciating my own actions. I felt myself possessed of a generosity of soul, of which he denied the existence. With what delight did I oppose to his system the sublime traits of history, and the virtues of the heroes it has celebrated! I never read the recital of a glorious deed without saying to myself, ' It is thus that I should have acted.' I became a passionate admirer of republics,

lics, because it was there that I found the moſt virtues to awaken my admiration, and the men beſt deſerving of my eſteem. I was perſuaded, that their form of polity was the only one calculated to produce both: I felt myſelf not unequal to the former; I rejected with diſdain the idea of uniting myſelf with a man inferior to the latter; and I aſked, with a ſigh, why I was not born a republican.

My mother, my amiable little uncle, Mademoiſelle d'Hannaches, and myſelf, made a journey to Verſailles, which was ſolely intended to ſhew me the court, and the place it inhabited, and to amuſe me with its pageantry. We lodged in the palace. Madam le Grand, the Dauphineſs's woman, well known to the Abbé Bimont, by means of her ſon, who was his ſchool-fellow, and of whom I ſhall have occaſion to ſpeak hereafter, not being in waiting, lent us her apartment. It was a garret, in the ſame corridor with that of the Archbiſhop of Paris, and ſo cloſely adjoining, that it was neceſſary for the prelate to ſpeak in a low tone of voice, to avoid being overheard: the ſame precaution was neceſſary on our part. Two rooms indifferently furniſhed, over one of which it was contrived to lodge a valet, and to which the avenue was dark, and rendered inſupportable by the ſtench of the privies—ſuch was the habitation which a duke and peer of France did not diſdain to occupy, that he might be more at hand to go creeping every morning to their majeſties levee: this prelate, however, was no other

than

than the rigid Beaumont. For one entire week we were conſtant ſpectators of the public and private dinners *(les petits et grand couverts)* of all the royal family, whether aſſembled in one party, or divided into ſeveral, and attended them at maſs, in their walks, at their card parties, and in the drawing-room.

The different acquaintances of Madam le Grand facilitated our admiſſion; while Mademoiſelle d'Hannaches thruſt herſelf forward with the greateſt aſſurance upon every occaſion, ready to throw her name in any one's face who ſhould dare to oppoſe her paſſage, and taking it for granted, that they muſt needs read in her groteſque countenance ſix hundred years of well-aſcertained nobility. She recollected two or three of the king's guards, whoſe pedigrees ſhe recited with the greateſt accuracy, taking care to prove herſelf preciſely the relation of him whoſe name was the moſt ancient, and who appeared to me nevertheleſs to be a very inſignificant perſonage at court. The handſome face of a ſpruce young clergyman, like my uncle Bimont, and the imbecil hauteur of the ugly d'Hannaches, were not wholly out of place at Verſailles; but the cheeks of my reſpectable mother, unplaſtered with rouge, and the plainneſs of my apparel, beſpoke us citizens; and if my youth or my eyes drew forth a word or two, they were modulated with a tone of condeſcenſion that gave me little leſs offence than the compliments of Madam Boiſmorel. Philoſo-

phy,

phy, imagination, fentiment, and calculation, were all bufy upon this occafion. I was not infenfible to the effect of a great difplay of magnificence, but I felt indignant at its being intended to fet off a few certain individuals, already too powerful, though in themfelves deferving little regard. I liked better to look at the ftatues in the gardens than at the great perfonages in the palace; and when my mother afked me if I were pleafed with my excurfion, ' Yes,' faid I, ' if it terminate fpeedily: if we ftay but a few days longer, I fhall fo perfectly deteft the people I fee, that I fhall not know what to do with my hatred.'—' Why, what harm do they do you?'—' They give me the feeling of injuftice, and oblige me every moment to contemplate abfurdity.' I fighed at the recollection of Athens, where I could have equally admired the fine arts, without being annoyed with the fpectacle of defpotifm. Fancy tranfported me all over Greece; I affifted at the Olympic games, and was out of all patience at being a Frenchwoman. Enchanted with what I had feen in the golden period of the republic, I paffed over the ftorms by which it had been agitated: I forgot the exile of Ariftides, the death of Socrates, and the condemnation of Phocion. I little thought that heaven referved me to be witnefs of errors, fimilar to thofe of which *they* were the victims, and to participate in the glory of the fame perfecution, after having profeffed the fame principles. Heaven knows that

the

the misfortunes which affect only myself have extorted from me neither sighs nor complaints: I only feel thofe which afflict my country. At the time of the diffenfion between the court and the parliament in 1771, my difpofition and opinions attached me to the party of the latter; I procured all their remonftrances, and was moft pleafed with thofe which contained the ftrongeft things expreffed in the boldeft ftyle. The fphere of my ideas continually enlarged. My own happinefs, and the duties to the performance of which it might be attached, occupied my mind at a very early period; the love of knowledge made me afterwards ftudy hiftory, and turn my thoughts to every thing about me; the relation of our fpecies to the divinity fo varioufly reprefented, caricatured, and disfigured, attracted my attention; and at length the welfare of man in fociety fixed it to a determinate point.

In the midft of doubts, uncertainty, and inveftigation, relative to thefe important matters, I readily concluded, that the unity of the individual, if I may fo exprefs myself, that is to fay, the moft entire harmony between his opinions and actions, was neceffary to his perfonal happinefs. Accordingly, we ought to examine well what is right, and when we have found it, we fhould practife it rigoroufly. There is a kind of juftice due to a man's felf, even were he living in the world alone: it is incumbent on him fo to regulate all his affections and habits, that he may be the flave of none. A

being

being is *good* in itfelf, when all its parts concur to its prefervation, its maintenance, or its perfection: this is not lefs true in the moral, than in the phyfical world. Juftnefs of organization, and an equipoife of humours, conftitute health: wholefome aliments, and moderate exercife, preferve it. The due proportion of our defires, and the harmony of the paffions, form the moral conftitution, of which wifdom alone can fecure the excellence and duration. Its firft principles originate in the intereft of the individual; and in this refpect it may be truly faid, that virtue is nothing more than good fenfe applied to moral purpofes. But virtue, properly fo called, can only fpring from the relations of a being with his fellow-creatures: a man is prudent as far as felf is concerned, virtuous in regard to other people. In fociety every thing is relative: there is no independent happinefs: we are obliged to facrifice a part of what we might enjoy, in order to run no rifk of lofing the whole, and to keep a portion out of the reach of accident. Even here the balance is in favour of reafon. However laborious may be the life of the honeft, that of the vicious muft be ftill more fo. That man can feldom be tranquil, who ftands in oppofition to the intereft of the majority; it is impoffible for him not to feel that he is furrounded by enemies, or by individuals about to become fo; and this fituation is always painful, however flattering may be its appearances. Let us add to thefe confiderations the fublime inftinct, instinct, which corruption may mislead, but which no false philosophy can ever annihilate; which impels us to admire and love wisdom and generosity of conduct, as we do grandeur and symmetry in nature and the arts—and we shall have the source of human virtue independent of every religious system, of the idle fancies of metaphysics, and of the imposture of priests. As soon as I had combined and demonstrated these truths, my heart expanded with joy; they offered me a port in the storm, and I could now examine with less anxiety the errors of national creeds and social institutions. Can the sublime idea of a divine Creator, whose providence watches over the world, the immateriality of the soul, and its immortality, that consolatory hope of persecuted virtue, be nothing more than amiable and splendid chimeras? But in how much obscurity are these difficult problems involved? What accumulated objections arise when we wish to examine them with mathematical rigour! No; it is not given to the human mind to behold these truths in the full day of perfect evidence: but why should the man of sensibility repine at not being able to demonstrate what he feels to be true?

In the silence of the closet, and the dryness of discussion, I can agree with the atheist or the materialist, as to the insolubility of certain questions; but when in the country, and contemplating nature, my soul, full of emotion, soars aleft to the vivifying

principle

principle that animates them, to the almighty intellect that pervades them, and to the goodnefs that makes the fcene fo delightful to my fenfes. Now, when immenfe walls feparate me from all I love, and when all the evils of fociety fall upon us together, as if to punifh us for having defired its greateft bleffings, I fee beyond the limits of life the reward of our facrifices.

How? In what manner?—I cannot fay; I only feel that fo it ought to be *.

The atheift is not, in my eyes, an evil-minded man : I can live with him as well, nay better than with the devotee; for he reafons more; but he wants a certain fenfe that I poffefs, and my mind does not perfectly harmonize with his: he is unmoved at the moft enchanting fpectacle, and is feeking for a fyllogifm, while I am offering up my thankfgivings.

It was not all at once that I fixed myfelf in this firm and peaceful feat, in which, enjoying the truths that are demonftrated to me, and giving

* I write this on the 4th of September at eleven at night, the apartment next to me refounding with peals of laughter. The actreffes of the *Theatre Français* were arrefted yefterday, and conducted to St. Pélagie. To-day they were taken to their own apartments, to witnefs the ceremony of the taking off the feals, and are now returned to the prifon, where the peace-officer is fupping and amufing himfelf in their company. The repaft is noify and frolicfome; I catch the found of coarfe jefts, while foreign wines fparkle in the goblet. The place, the object, the perfons, and my occupation, form a contraft not a little curious.

way without scruple to feelings so full of delight, I am content to remain ignorant of what cannot be known, and give myself no disturbance about the opinions of others. I have here set down in a few words the result of several years of meditation and study, in the course of which I have sometimes shared in the sentiments of the deist, in the atheist's incredulity, and in the sceptic's indifference. But always sincere, because I had no inducement to change my faith in order to relax my morals, which were fixed upon principles that no prejudices could affect, I sometimes felt the agitation of doubt, but never the torment of fear. I conformed to the established worship, because my age, my sex, and my situation, made it my duty so to do; but, incapable of deceiving any one, I used to say to the Abbé Morel, ' I come to confession for the edification of my neighbour, and to preserve my mother's peace of mind; but I scarcely know of what to accuse myself: I lead so quiet a life, and my desires are so moderate, that my conscience has nothing to reproach me with, at the same time that I have no great merit in behaving with propriety. I am sometimes, however, too much taken up with the desire of pleasing, and give way to too great violence of temper, when any thing goes wrong. I am also too severe perhaps in my judgment of others; and, without suffering it to manifest itself, I conceive too hasty an aversion to those who appear to be stupid or dull; but in this I will be careful to

correct,

correct myself. In the laſt place, I am too abſent and too careleſs while attending divine ſervice; for I acknowledge that we ought to be attentive to whatever we think it requiſite to perform, be the motive what it may.' The worthy prieſt, who had exhauſted his library and his rhetoric to keep me in the path of belief, had the good ſenſe to be pleaſed at finding me ſo reaſonable: he exhorted me, however, to diſtruſt the ſpirit of pride; repreſented to me the advantages of religion in the beſt way he was able; thought proper to give me abſolution; and was tolerably well ſatisfied with my attending at the holy table three or four times a year, out of philoſophical toleration, ſince it was no longer the work of faith. When I went to receive the divine aliment, I could not help thinking on the words of Cicero, who ſaid, that, to complete the follies of men, with reſpect to the Deity, it only remained for them to transform him into food, and then to eat him. My mother's devotion growing greater every day, I became leſs able to deviate from the ordinary practices of religion; for there was nothing that I dreaded ſo much as to afflict her.

The Abbé le Grand, my uncle Bimont's friend, ſometimes viſited us. He was a man of great good ſenſe, who had nothing of his proſeſſion about him but his gown, in which he felt himſelf not a little awkward. His family had made him a prieſt, becauſe one out of three ſons muſt neceſſarily enter into holy orders. Appointed chaplain to the prince of Lamballe, and penfioned after the death of his patron by Penthièvre, he had fettled himfelf in a parifh merely that he might have a fixed refidence, and had chofen it near his friend, in order to enjoy his fociety. Affected with great weaknefs of fight, he became blind at a very early age; and this accident, by foftering his tafte for reflection, had given him a very meditative turn. He was fond of chatting with me, and often brought me books, generally works of philofophy, on the principles of which he fpoke with great freedom. My mother hardly ever bearing a part in the difcuffion, I was afraid of carrying things to any great length: fhe did not, however, hinder me from reading, nor did fhe blame the choice of my fubjects. A Genevefe watchmaker, connected in bufinefs with my father, a worthy man, who always kept a book among his tools, and had a tolerable library, with which he was better acquainted than many great lords are with theirs; offered me the ufe of a treafure fo fuited to my tafte, and I availed myfelf of his kindnefs. That kind M. Moré was a man of good fenfe, and could reafon, not only concerning his art, but concerning morals and politics alfo; and though he expreffed himfelf with a difficulty and tardinefs, that my patience found it hard to fupport, he fhared with moft of his countrymen that folidity of intellect which makes amends for a want of the graces. From him I procured *Buffon*, and many other works. I mention this author by way of referring

to

to what I have faid, in a former part of my memoirs, of the difcretion with which I read him. Philofophy, in calling forth the energies of my foul, and giving firmnefs to my mind, did not diminifh the fcruples of fentiment, or the fufceptibility of my imagination, againft which I had reafon to be fo much upon my guard. Natural philofophy firft, and then mathematics, exercifed my activity for a time. *Nollet, Réaumur,* and *Bonnet,* who indulges his fancy upon what others defcribe, amufed me in their turns; as did *Maupertuis,* who enters into woful lamentations while particularizing the pleafures of fnails. At length *Rivard* infpired me with the defire of becoming a geometrician. Guéring, a ftone-mafon and furveyor, who with all his fimplicity was a man of great good fenfe and good nature, coming one day to talk with my father, found me fo clofely rivetted to Rivard's quarto, that I did not perceive his arrival. He entered into converfation with me, obferved that *Clairaut*'s Elements would much better anfwer the purpofe I had in view; and the next day brought me the copy he had in his poffeffion. I found it to contain a fimple reduction of the firft principles of the fcience, and recollecting at once that the work might be ufeful to me, and that I could not with decency detain it from the proprietor fo long as I fhould like to keep it, I came to a refolution to copy it from the beginning to the end, including fix plates of diagrams. I cannot help laughing at this operation whenever it recurs to my mind; any body but myfelf would have determined to buy the book, but the thought never came into my head, while the idea of copying it occurred as naturally as that of pricking a pattern for a ruffle, and was almoſt as foon effected; for the work was but a fmall octavo. This curious manufcript is ſtill, I believe, among my papers. I was amufed with geometry as long as there was no need of algebra, with the drynefs of which I was difgufted as foon as I had got through fimple equations. I accordingly gave to the winds the multiplicity of fractions, and thought it better to feaſt upon a good poem than to ſtarve myſelf with *roots*. In vain, fome years after, did M. Roland, while paying his addreſſes, endeavour to recal my former taſte; we made, indeed, a great many figures; but the fcience of reafoning by X and Y was never fufficiently attractive to obtain much of my attention.

September 5. I cut the ſheet to inclofe what I have written in the little box; for when I fee a revolutionary army decreed, new tribunals formed for ſhedding innocent blood, famine impending, and the tyrants at bay, I augur that they muſt have new victims, and conclude that no one is fure of living another day.

My

My correspondence with Sophia was still one of my greatest pleasures, the bonds of our friendship having been drawn closer by several journies which she had made to Paris. My susceptible heart stood in need, I will not say of a chimera, but of a principal object for its affections, especially for confidence and communication. Friendship offered them, and I cultivated it with delight. The footing I lived upon with my mother, agreeable as it was, would not have supplied the place of this affection; it had too much of the gravity resulting from respect on the one part, and of authority on the other. My mother might know every thing; I had nothing to conceal from her; but I could not tell her every thing: to a parent we may address confessions; but it is to an equal alone, that we entrust the secrets of the heart.

Accordingly, without asking to read the letters I wrote to Sophia, my mother was desirous that I should let her see them; and our arrangement in this respect had something whimsical in it. We had understood one another without a word on the subject. When I heard from my friend, which I did regularly every week, I read to her a few sentences of the letter, but did not communicate the whole. When I had written an answer, I left it for a day, made up and directed, upon my table, but unsealed; my mother scarcely ever failed to run it over, though seldom in my presence, or if it so happened, I always found some

pretence

pretence for retiring. Whether she saw it or not, the period supposed necessary for her doing so being elapsed, I sealed my letter, but not always without adding a postscript. It never happened to her to make any mention of what she had read; but I did not fail to inform her by this means of all that I wished her to know of my disposition, my taste, and my opinions; and I set them forth with a freedom which I should not have dared to take with her in person. My frankness had its full scope, for I felt that I had a right to exercise it without any one's having a right to take it amiss. I have often thought since, that, had I been in my mother's place, I should have wished to become my daughter's friend in the fullest sense of the word; and if I have any regret at present, it is that mine is not what I was at that time: we should then be companions, and I should be happy. But my mother, though her heart was excellent, had something cold in her manner: she had more prudence than sensibility, and was rather reserved than affectionate. Perhaps too, perceiving an ardour in me that would have hurried me to greater lengths than herself, she so conducted herself, as to let me go on without restraint, but without familiarity. She was sparing of caresses, although her eyes beamed with tenderness and love, and were generally fixed upon me. I was sensible of the kindness of her heart, and my own returned the vibrations of affection; but the reserve that hung

hung about her, called forth a circumfpection on my part, from which I fhould otherwife have been free. Any one would have fuppofed that the diftance between us had increafed when I was no longer a child. There was a dignity about my mother, of a gentle kind it is true, but it was dignity ftill. The tranfports of my ardent foul were repreffed by it, and I only knew the full extent of my attachment to her, by the defpair and delirium that I fell into at her death. My days paffed away in delightful tranquillity. I fpent the greater part in folitary ftudies, tranfported by my imagination to the remote ages of antiquity, of which I reviewed the hiftory and the arts, and examined the precepts and opinions. Mafs in the morning, a few hours that we fpent in reading together, our repafts and our vifits, made up the only portion of time that I paffed in my mother's company. We went abroad but feldom, and when vifitors came who were not to my liking, I contrived to remain in my clofet, which my mother was too kind to oblige me to quit. Sundays and holidays were devoted to our walks: fometimes we extended them to a confiderable diftance, and at laft got into the habit of doing fo, in confequence of the preference I gave to the country over the formal gardens of the metropolis. I was, however, by no means infenfible to the pleafure of appearing occafionally in the public walks. They afforded, at that period, a very brilliant fpectacle, in which the youth of both fexes
always

always had an agreeable part to play. Perſonal graces conſtantly obtained there the homage of admiration, which modeſty cannot but perceive, and of which the heart of a young girl is always covetous. But it did not ſatisfy mine: I experienced after theſe walks, during which my vanity, powerfully excited, was upon the watch for whatever could ſhew me off to advantage, and prove to me that I had not loſt my time, an inſupportable vacuity, an uneaſineſs and difguſt, which made the pleaſures of vanity too dear a purchaſe. Accuſtomed to reflect, and to render an account of my ſenſations to myſelf, I made a ſtrict inquiry into the cauſe of this inquietude, and found ſufficient room to exerciſe my philoſophy.

'Is it then,' ſaid I to myſelf, ' to pleaſe the eye, like the flowers of a parterre, and to receive a few evaneſcent praiſes, that perſons of my ſex are brought up in the practice of virtue, and enriched with talents ? What means this intenſe deſire of pleaſure which preys upon me, and which does not make me happy, even when it ſhould ſeem that it ought to be moſt gratified ? What are to me the admiring eyes, and ſoftly murmured compliments, of a crowd, of which I have no knowledge, and which is compoſed of perſons, whom, did I know them, I ſhould probably deſpiſe ? Did I come into the world to waſte my exiſtence in frivolous cares and tumultuous ſenſations ?—No: I have doubtleſs a nobler deſtination! The admiration which I

ſo

so ardently feel for whatever is virtuous, wise, exalted, and generous, tells me that I am called to practise these things. The sublime and rapturous duties of a wife and a mother will on some future day be mine; it is in rendering myself capable of fulfilling them, that my early years ought to be employed; I ought to study their importance, and to learn, by keeping my own inclinations within bounds, how to direct hereafter those of my children; by the habit of governing my passions, and by the care of cultivating my mind, I ought to secure to myself the means of giving happiness to the most delightful of societies, of providing a never-failing source of felicity for the man who shall deserve my heart, and of communicating to all about us, a portion of the bliss with which I shall crown his wishes, and which ought to be the entire work of my own hands.'

Such were the thoughts that agitated my bosom. Overcome with emotion, I shed a flood of tears, while my heart exalted itself to that supreme intelligence, that first cause, that gracious providence, that principle of thought and of sentiment, which it felt the necessity of believing and acknowledging. 'O thou who hast placed me on the earth, enable me to fulfil my destination in the manner most conformable to thy divine will, and most beneficial to the welfare of my fellow-creatures.'

This unaffected prayer, as simple as the heart that dictated it, is become my only one; never have
the

the doubts of philosophy, nor any species of dissipation, been able to dry up its source. In the midst of the tumult of the world, and in the depth of a dungeon, I have pronounced it with equal fervour. I pronounced it with transport in the most brilliant circumstances of my life; I repeat it in fetters with resignation; anxious in the former to guard against every affection unworthy of my situation; careful in the latter to preserve the necessary fortitude for supporting me in the trials to which I am exposed; persuaded that, in the course of things, there are events which human wisdom cannot prevent; and convinced that the most calamitous ones cannot overpower a firm mind; and that peace at home, and submission to necessity, are the elements of happiness, and constitute the true independence of the sage and of the hero.

The country presented objects more analogous to my habits of meditation, to my serious, tender, and pensive disposition, fortified by reflection and the developement of a feeling heart. We often went to Meudon: it was my favourite walk. I preferred its wild woods, its solitary ponds, its avenues of pines, and its towering trees, to the frequented paths and uniform coppices of the *Bois de Boulogne*, to the ornamented gardens of Belle-vue, or the clipt and right-lined vistas of St. Cloud.—
' Where shall we go to-morrow, if the weather be fine?' said my father on the Saturday evenings during summer—He then looked at me with a smile—
' shall

' fhall we go to St. Cloud? The water-works are to play: there will be a world of company.'—'Ah, papa! if you would go to Meudon I fhould be much better pleafed.' By five o'clock on Sunday morning every body was ftirring; a light, neat, and fimple drefs, a few flowers, and a gauze veil, announced the project of the day. The odes of Rouffeau, a volume of Corneille, or of fome other author, were the only baggage I took with me. We fet off all three, and embarked at the Pont-royal, which I could fee from my window, on board of a little boat, that, in the filence of a fmooth and rapid navigation, conducted us to the fhores of Belle-vue, not far from the glafs-houfe, of which the black column of fmoke is vifible at a confiderable diftance. Thence by a fteep afcent we proceeded to the avenue of Meudon, about the middle of which ftood a little cottage on the right, that became one of our refting-places. It was the abode of a milk-woman, a widow, who lived there, having two cows and fome poultry. As it was advifeable to make the moft of day-light for our excurfion, it was agreed it fhould ferve us as a halting-place on our return, and that the good woman fhould furnifh us with a bowl of milk from the cow. That was fo regular a thing, that in walking up the avenue we never failed to call at the milk-woman's to tell her we fhould be with her in the evening or the next morning, and not to forget the bowl of milk. The good woman received

ceived us with much kindnefs; and our repaft, feafoned with a little brown bread and a great deal of good humour, had the appearance of a little feaft, of which fome memorial was fure to remain in the milk-woman's pocket. We took our dinner at the lodge of one of the porters belonging to the park: but the defire I had of ftriking into a folitary path led us to the difcovery of a retreat very much to my tafte. One day, after having wandered a long time in an unfrequented part of the wood, we came to an open and folitary fpot, at the end of an avenue of lofty trees, under which a paffenger was feldom feen. A few other trees fcattered over a charming lawn ferved to mafk a neat little cottage two ftories high. 'Ah! what have we here?'—Two fine children were playing before the door, which was ftanding wide open. They had neither the appearance of children of the town, nor thofe enfigns of wretchednefs fo common in the country. We drew near; and perceived upon the left a kitchen garden, where an old man was at work. To walk in, and enter into converfation with him, was the bufinefs of a moment. We learned that the name of the place was *Ville-bonne*; that its inhabitant was the water-bailiff of the *Moulin Rouge*, whofe office it was to fee that the canals conveying water to different parts of the park were kept in repair; that the flender falary of that place helped to fupport a young couple, the parents of the children whom we had feen, and of

whom

whom the old man was the grandfather; and that the wife employed herfelf in the cares of the houfehold, while he cultivated the garden, the produce of which, the fon carried to town to fell at his leifure. The garden was a long fquare, divided into four parts, round each of which was a walk of fufficient width; in the centre a bafon of water, which facilitated the bufinefs of watering; and at the farther end an arbour of yews inclofing a ftone bench, affording at once both fhelter and repofe. Flowers interfperfed among the culinary herbs gave the garden a gay and agreeable appearance; while the robuft and contented gardener, who converfed with equal good humour and good fenfe, reminded me of the old man of the banks of the Galefus, whom Virgil has fung. A tafte for fimplicity would alone have made fuch an encounter agreeable; but my fancy did not fail to inveft it with a thoufand imaginary charms. We afked whether they were in the habit of affording entertainment to ftrangers?—' Very few come here,' faid the old man; ' the place is little known; but when they do, we willingly ferve up to them the produce of our farm-yard and our garden. We begged to have fomething for dinner, and were furnifhed with new-laid eggs, vegetables, and a falad, in a delightful arbour of honeyfuckle behind the houfe. I never made fo agreeable a repaft: my heart dilated in contemplating the

tran-

tranquillity and innocence of so charming a situation. I fondled the little children, and expressed great veneration for the old man. The young woman seemed delighted at having us in the house. We were told that they had two rooms which they should have no objection to let to any body that would take them for three months, and we had some idea of taking them. But that agreeable project was never realized; nor have I ever been at Ville-bonne since; for Meudon had been our place of resort long before we made that discovery, and we had fixed upon a little inn in the village for our lodging whenever two holydays coming together permitted us to prolong our absence. It was at that inn, the sign of which I think was the Queen of France, we met with a laughable adventure. We were put into a room with two beds, in the largest of which I slept with my mother; the other in a corner served for my father alone. One night, just after he had got into bed, the fancy took him of drawing his curtains perfectly close, and he pulled them so strongly that the tester fell upon him and covered him up completely. After a moment of alarm, we all began to laugh very heartily at the accident; the tester having fallen exactly in such a way as to inclose my father without hurting him. We called for assistance to set him at liberty; the good woman of the house came; was astonished to see her bed decapitated; and exclaimed, with the utmost

most simplicity, 'My God! how could this happen? it is seventeen years since the bed was put up; and in all that time it has never budged an inch.' The logic of the hostess made me laugh more than the fall of the tester. I often found an occasion to apply it, or rather to compare it with the arguments I heard in company; and used to say to my mother in a whisper, This is quite as good as the seventeen years to prove that the bed ought not to have given way.

Delightful Meudon! how often beneath thy refreshing shade have I blessed the great Author of my existence, desiring what might at some future time render it complete; but it was that charming sentiment of desire without impatience, which only serves to gild the clouds of futurity with the rays of hope. How often in thy cool retreats have I gathered the variegated fern, and the brilliant flowers of the orchis! How did I love to rest myself under the lofty trees bordering the glades, through which I used to see the swift and timorous doe go bounding along! I recollect the more *sombre* spots, whither we retired during the heat of the day. There, while my father, stretched upon the greensward, and my mother, softly reclined on a heap of leaves which I had collected for the purpose, enjoyed their afternoon's nap, did I contemplate the majesty of thy silent groves, admire the beauty of nature, and adore the Providence whose benefits I felt! The glow of sentiment heightened the colour of my humid

humid cheeks, and my heart enjoyed all the delight of the terreftrial paradife. An account of my ex-curfions, and of the pleafure they afforded me, found its way into my correfpondence with Sophia: fometimes my profe was intermingled with verfe, the irregular, but eafy, and fometimes happy effu-fions of a mind to which all was picture, life, and felicity.

Sophia, as I have already obferved, found her-felf thrown into a fociety, where fhe had none of the comforts which fhe knew me to enjoy in my folitude. I was acquainted with feveral of her fa-mily, and learned from their company to rate my retirement at a higher price.

In her journies to Paris with her mother fhe ufed to alight at the houfe of two coufins, whofe names were *De Lamotte.* They were old maidens, one of whom, a four devotee, never ftirred from her chamber, where fhe faid her prayers, fcolded the fervants, knitted ftockings, and reafon-ed with tolerable acutenefs about her perfonal in-terefts: the other, a good fort of woman, fat in the parlour, did the honours of the houfe, read the pfalms, and took a hand of cards. Both of them were very proud of their noble birth, and could fcarcely conceive it poffible to keep company with perfons whofe father at leaft had not been ennobled; and, without daring to wear it, carefully preferved the *fack* of which their mother had had the train borne after her to church, as a mark of family

con-

consequence. They had taken under their care a young woman, their relation, whose slender fortune they purposed augmenting, provided she could find a gentleman to marry her. The young woman, Mademoiselle d'Hangard, was a tall, lusty brunette, of a ruddy complexion, and enjoying a state of health so vigorous as almost to alarm, whose rusticity of appearance ill concealed a petulant temper and a narrow mind. But the most curious piece of household goods was counsellor *Perdu*, a widower, who had consumed his estate in doing nothing, and who had been put to board with his cousins by his sister (my Sophia's mother), that he might pass the last years of his worthless existence in a decent way. Mr. Perdu, who was wonderfully plump and sleek, devoted the greater part of the morning to the care of his person, dined with an excellent appetite while cursing the dishes, and passed in dissertations at the Luxemburg *, several hours of every day, which was sure to close with a game of piquet. He was still prouder of his gentility than his old cousins, and piqued himself upon having all the airs and principles of a man of noble birth. When speaking to Sophia of her uncle, I always called him *the commandant*, so strongly did he resemble *the commandant* in Crebillon's *Père de Famille*. The *commandant* then always assumed a great air of superiority with his nieces, affecting to temper it with the condescen-

* A public garden at Paris.—*Transl.*

sions of politeness; but there was something whimsical in his behaviour to Mademoiselle d'Hangard, whose fresh complexion and continual presence, inflaming his imagination, inspired him with sensations which he dared not betray, and which sometimes put him out of humour with his nephew.

The nephew, who took the name of *Selincour* *, was a tall young man, with a gentle look and a soft voice, not unlike his sister Sophia, sensible in his conversation, and agreeable in his manners, to which a sort of bashfulness was no disadvantage; such at least was my opinion, even when it became more than usually perceptible in his intercourse with me. Probabilities, and the wishes of the family, appeared to point him out as a proper suitor for Mademoiselle d'Hangard.

As to Mesdemoiselles Lamotte's society, it was composed of a *Count d'Essales*, created a Chevalier of St. Louis in Canada, where he had married the governor's daughter; taking care to keep at a respectful distance from great guns, ignorant, overbearing, and garrulous, he came to play a party of piquet with the Marchioness de *Cailiavelle*, an antiquated dowager, with whom he had more than one game going on, which the good old damsels did not perceive. Madam *Bernier*, a rigid Jansenist, but otherwise a sensible woman, whose hus-

---

* In France it is customary for the sons to assume the names of the different estates, and sometimes such as are merely dictated by fancy.—*Transf.*

band

band had quitted the parliament of Brittany after the affair of la Chalotais, ufed to come alfo, but lefs frequently, with her two daughters, the one a fcholar, the other a devotee. The tender heart of the latter would have gained my affection; but her wry neck fupported with difficulty a head fo crammed with religion, that there was no room for any thing like reafon. The fcholar, with rather too much loquacity, was poffeffed of judgment and tafte enough juft to render a repulfive figure fupportable. But *M. de Vouglans* foared above them all. A delineation of his character would be fuperfluous to thofe who have read the book entitled *Reafons for my Faith in Jefus Chrift, by a Magiftrate*, and his *Collection of Penal Laws*, an elaborate compilation, in which equal induftry, fanaticifm, and atrocity were difplayed. I never met with a man by whofe fanguinary intolerance I was fo much fhocked. He took particular pleafure in converfing with father Romain Joly, a little old monk, Mefdemoifelles Lamotte's confeffor, who made verfes againft Voltaire, in which he compared him to the devil, and who was for ever quoting in the pulpit the *Capitularies* of Charlemagne, and the edicts of our monarchs. I have had the good fortune to dine with him at the table of the Lamottes, to hear him preach at my own parifh church, and to read his *Phaeton*; and he would afford me an excellent caricature, if I had courage enough to fhake folly, hypocrify, and the moft puerile learning, out of his gown. Sophia's friend made

made a curious figure in this fociety, of which the members lamented when her back was turned, that fo well difpofed a young woman was not of noble birth. I do not even doubt but that the commandant had, in his great wifdom, deliberated whether fuch a connexion were proper for his niece. But *the young woman* was well bred, and behaved with a decorum which the old maids highly approved; and unlefs when expreffions efcaped her, which *favoured of wit*, and which he was fure to animadvert upon to his nieces, the *commandant* himfelf could not altogether withhold his praife. He would even take charge of Sophia's letters, and bring them to my mother's; a thing that Selincour would have done more readily, if his fifter had confented to entruft them to his care.

The infignificance and oddities of thefe perfonages, to whom, no doubt, many people of the great world bore a refemblance, made me reflect on the inanity of fafhionable circles, and the advantage of not being obliged to frequent them. Sophia enumerated all the perfons with whom fhe affociated at Amiens, and gave me a fketch of their characters, which enabled me to judge of the infignificance of moft of them; fo that when the balance was ftruck, it appeared that, at the end of the year, I had feen in my folitude more people of merit, than fhe had perceived in her round of routs and affemblies. This may eafily be conceived, when it is remembered that my father's bufinefs connected him with none but artifts, many of whom came occafionally to the houfe, house, though none were regular visitors. Those who inhabit the capital, even if not of the first rank, acquire a fund of information, and a kind of urbanity, which most assuredly is neither to be found among the little provincial gentry, nor among mercantile people in haste to make a fortune that may serve as the means of ennobling their family. The conversation of the worthy *Jollain*, a painter of the academy, of the honest *l'Epine*, a pupil of Pigal, of *Desmarteau*, who professed the same art as my father, of *Falconet*'s son, of *d'Hauterne*, whom his talents would have borne on rapid wings to the academy, if his quality of Protestant had not been an exclusion, and of the Genevese watch-makers *Ballaxferd* and *Moré*, the former of whom has written upon Physical Education, was certainly far preferable to that of the opulent *Cannet*, who upon seeing the success of a tragedy written by his kinsman Belloy, and calculating the profits, exclaimed in sober sadness, ' Why did not my father teach me to compose tragedies ? I could have worked upon them on Sundays and holydays.'—And yet these wealthy blockheads, these pitiful possessors of purchased nobility, these impertinent soldiers like d'Essales, and these wretched magistrates like Vouglans, considered themselves as the props of civil society, and actually enjoyed privileges which merit could not obtain. I compared these absurdities of human arrogance with the pictures of Pope, tracing its effects in the satisfaction of the artisan, who is as proud of his

his leather apron as the king of his crown. I endeavoured to think with him, that every thing was right; but my pride told me that things were ordered better in a republic.

There is no doubt that our fituation in life has a confiderable influence on our charaƈters and opinions: but, in the education I received, in the ideas I acquired, whether by ftudy or by obfervation of the world, every thing may be faid to have concurred in infpiring me with republican enthufiafm, by making me perceive the folly, or feel the injuftice, of a multitude of privileges and diftinƈtions. Accordingly, in all my readings, I took the fide of the champions of equality; I was Agis and Cleomenes at Sparta; the Gracchi at Rome; and, like Cornelia, I fhould have reproached my fons with being called nothing but the mother-in-law of Scipio. I retired with the plebeians to the Aventine hill; and gave my vote to the tribunes. Now that experience has taught me to appreciate every thing with impartiality, I fee in the enterprife of the Gracchi, and in the conduƈt of the tribunes, crimes and mifchiefs, of which I was not at that time fufficiently aware.

When I happened to be prefent at any of that fort of fights which the capital fo frequently afforded, fuch as the *entry* of the queen or princeffes, *thankfgiving* after a lying-in, &c. I compared with grief, this Afiatic luxury and infolent pomp, with the abjeƈt mifery of the *brutified* populace,
who

who proftrated themfelves before idols of their own making, and foolifhly applauded the oftentatious magnificence which they paid for by depriving themfelves of the neceffaries of life. The diffolute conduct of the court during the laft years of Lewis XV. that contempt of morality, which pervaded all ranks of the nation, and thofe exceffes, which were the fubject of all private converfation, filled me with aftonifhment and indignation. Not perceiving as yet the germs of a revolution, I inquired with furprife, how things could fubfift in fuch a ftate? Obferving in hiftory, the invariable decline and fubverfion of empires when arrived at this pitch of corruption, and hearing the French nation finging and laughing at its own misfortunes, I felt that our neighbours, the Englifh, were right in regarding us as children. I attached myfelf to thofe neighbours; the work of De Lolme had familiarifed me with their conftitution; I fought an acquaintance with their writers, and ftudied their literature, but as yet only through the medium of tranflations.

The arguments of Ballexferd not having been able to overcome my parents' repugnance to having me inoculated, I caught the fmall-pox when eighteen years of age. The era has left deep impreffions on my mind; not from any apprehenfions on account of the diforder, for I had already too much philofophy not to fupport fuch a trial with fortitude; but from my mother's incredible and

affecting

affecting folicitude. What forrow, and yet what activity! In what agitation was fhe kept by her uneafinefs! and what tendernefs was difplayed in all her attentions! Even during the night, when I thought I was taking fomething from the nurfe, I felt my mother's hand, and heard her voice while getting out of her bed every moment to come to the fide of mine; her anxious eyes devoured the looks, and, if I may fo exprefs myfelf, the words of my phyfician; and in fpite of her refolution to fupprefs them, the tears ftole from her eyes, when looking at me, while I endeavoured, in vain, by a cheerful afpect, to pacify her feelings. Neither fhe nor my father had ever had the fmall-pox, and yet neither of them would fuffer a day to pafs without kiffing the disfigured cheek, which I ftrove in vain to keep out of their way, for fear the contact fhould be followed by fatal effects. My Agatha, grieved at being confined to her cloifter, fent me one of her relations, the amiable mother of four children, whom fhe had infpired with a portion of her attachment to me, and who obftinately perfifted in feeing and embracing me without confideration for herfelf. It was thought proper to conceal from Sophia, who was then at Paris, the condition of her friend. I was fuppofed to have fet off fuddenly for the country, that the period of contagion might elapfe without our meeting; but Selincour called every day on the part of his mother to inquire after my health; and I heard from my chamber his mournful

ful exclamation when he was told, that a complication of the putrid fever and small pox was feared. I had the miliary fever; the eruption peculiar to which, checking the other, the pustules of small-pox were few, and though large, subsided without suppuration, and left only a dry skin, that fell off of itself. It is the kind of small-pox, said Dr. Missa, that the Italians call *ravaglioni*, pustules of false suppuration, which leave no vestiges behind; and in reality not even the polish of the skin was impaired: but the ravages made by the variolous humour threw me into a state of languor and debility, from which it was four or five months before I was completely recovered. Sedate in health, too tender to be gay, but patient under affliction, my sole object in sickness is to divert my attention from my sufferings, and to render agreeable the troublesome attentions I require from those about me. Indulging my imagination in the most fanciful flights, I say extravagant things: it is the sick person that furnishes those in health with amusement.

Doctor Missa was a sensible man, whom I was very much pleased with. As he was sufficiently advanced in years to relieve me from the constraint that I was kept in by younger men, we conversed freely in his visits, which he willingly prolonged; and conceived a friendship for each other. One or other of us, said he, one day, has been much in the wrong. Either I am come too soon, or you too late. Though Missa's good sense had disposed me

favour-

favourably towards him, his age had prevented me from perceiving that I had been in the wrong to come later than he: I made him no other anfwer than a fmile. He was bringing up nieces, with whom he wifhed me to be acquainted, and we fometimes vifited; but as they never went out without their governefs, any more than I without my mother, and as the uncle's profeffion did not leave him leifure to keep up the connexion between us, it came to nothing in confequence of our diftant abodes and fedentary habits. Miffa fcolded me very much one day upon finding Malebranche's *Recherche de la Verité* lying on my bed. ' Why, my God!' faid I, ' if all your patients were to amufe themfelves in the fame way, inftead of getting angry with their difeafes and their doctor, you would have a great deal lefs to do.'—The perfons who chanced to be then in my room, were talking of fome loan or other, of which the edict of creation had juft made its appearance, and to which all Paris was running in crowds. ' The French,' faid Miffa, ' take all upon *truft*.'—' Say rather,' anfwered I, ' upon *appearances*.'—' True,' replied he ; 'the expreffion is juft and profound.'—' Don't fcold me then for reading Malebranche,' faid I eagerly ; ' you fee that my time is not thrown away.'

Miffa was at that time accompanied in his vifits by a young phyfician, who had recently taken his degree, and whom he fometimes difpatched before him to wait his arrival. This youthful graduate, to

borrow

borrow Miſſa's expreſſion, could not be reproached with coming too ſoon into the world; but though he had a tolerably handſome face, there was a ſelf-ſufficiency about him that I did not like. I have naturally ſo decided an averſion to affectation and airs of conſequence, that I always conſider them as a ſign of an indifferent underſtanding, if not of abſolute imbecility; though it is certain that, under the old government, they were ſometimes no more than the follies of youth. In ſhort, ſo far from pleaſing me, they put me out of humour, and always make me conceive an ill opinion of the perſon by whom they are diſplayed. Theſe are the only traces left in my memory by the young doctor, whom I have never ſeen ſince, and whom I ſhall probably never ſee again.

An excurſion to the country being neceſſary for the perfect re-eſtabliſhment of my health, we went to breathe its ſalutary air at the houſe of M. and Madam Beſnard, with whom two years before my mother and I had ſpent almoſt the whole month of September. Their ſituation was admirably calculated to feed my philoſophy, and to fix my meditations upon the vices of ſocial life.

Madam Beſnard, upon the reverſe of fortune which ſhe had experienced in common with her ſiſters, had entered into the family of a *fermier-general*, whoſe houſe ſhe ſuperintended: it was that of old Haudry. There ſhe had married the ſteward, M. Beſnard, with whom ſhe had long ſince retired

from

from the world, and was living in peace and happinefs, though in an humble way.

The ill-placed pride of Madam Phlipon had led her fometimes to exprefs, in my prefence, and in the privacy of the family, how much this marriage had difpleafed her; but, as far as I can judge, fhe was certainly offended without caufe. M. Befnard was a man of integrity and good moral character, each of which was the more praifeworthy in preportion as it was difficult to meet with among men in the fame line of life. The whole of his conduct to his wife exhibited the greateft delicacy of fentiment. It is impoffible to carry veneration, tendernefs, and attachment, to a greater length. Enjoying the fweets of a perfect union, they ftill prolong a career, in which, like Baucis and Philemon, they attract the refpect of all who witnefs their fimplicity of life, and their virtues. I efteem it an honour to be related to them; and fhould do fo ftill, if, with the fame character and conduct, M. Befnard had been a footman.

Old Haudry, who owed his fortune to his own exertions, was dead; and had left a large fortune to a fon, who, being born in opulence, was likely to fquander it away. That fon, who had already loft a charming wife, lived at a great expence; and, according to the cuftom of the rich, fpent a fmall part of the year at the chateau of Soucy, whither he was much more apt to carry the manners of the town, than to adopt thofe that were fuitable

to

to the country. He had several contiguous estates, of which that nearest to Soucy (Fontenay) had an old mansion belonging to it that he was fond of filling with inhabitants. He had given a lodging there to a notary and an overseer, and requested M. Besnard to take an apartment, which might serve him as a residence during part of the summer. This was no bad way of 'keeping his estate in good order, at the same time that it gave him an air of magnificence. M. and Madam Besnard were well accommodated, and enjoyed the pleasure of walking in a park, the wildness of which made an agreeable contrast with the gardens of Soucy, and pleased me more than the luxury that distinguished the *farmer-general*'s abode. As soon as we arrived at Madam Besnard's, she requested us to go and pay a visit to Soucy, where Haudry's sister-in-law and step-mother resided with him, and did the honours of his house. The visit was modestly paid before dinner. I walked without the smallest pleasurable sensation into the drawing-room, where Madam Penault and her daughter received us with great politeness, it is true, but it was a politeness that favoured a little of superiority. My mother's manner however, and something which appeared in me also in spite of that timidity which proceeds from a consciousness of our worth, and a doubt of its being perceived by others, scarcely allowed them to assume any consequence. I received compliments which gave me little pleasure, and which

I was anfwering with fome degree of ingenuity, when certain parafites, of the order of St. Lewis, who always haunt the manfions of opulence, as ghofts refort to the banks of the Acheron, thought proper to interrupt me with exaggerated praife.

The ladies did not fail, a few days after, to return our vifit. They were attended by the company that happened to be at the chateau, the vifit to Fontenay ferving them for a walk. Upon that occafion, I was more engaging than before, and contrived to put into my fhare of the reception, fuch a portion of modeft and dignified politenefs, as re-eftablifhed the equilibrium between us. It once happened to us to be invited to dinner by Madam Penault; but never was aftonifhment equal to mine, when I learned that we were not to dine at her table, but with the upper fervants in the hall. I was fenfible however, that, as M. Befnard had formerly played a part there, I ought not, out of refpect to him, to appear diffatisfied at appearing in fuch a character; but I was of opinion that Madam Penault might have ordered things otherwife, and have fpared us the contemptuous civility. My great aunt faw it in the fame light; but, to avoid giving offence, we accepted the invitation. It was fomething new to me to mix with thofe deities of the fecond order; nor had I the leaft idea of what chambermaids were when giving themfelves airs of confequence. They were prepared to receive us; and, indeed, played the

doubles

doubles of their superiors admirably well. Dress, gesture, affectation, graces, nothing was forgotten. Their mistresses cast-off clothes, which were hardly soiled, gave a richness to their appearance, that decent persons in trade would have thought out of character. The caricature of fashionable manners superadded a sort of elegance, not less foreign to mercantile simplicity than to the taste of an artist, though there is no doubt but their flippancy of speech, and finery, might have imposed on country ladies. It was still worse with the men. The sword of Mr. steward, the attentions of Mr. cook, and the politeness and gaudy clothes of the valet-de-chambre, could not atone for the awkwardness of their manners and the blunders in their language, when they wished it to be elegant, nor the vulgarity of their expressions when they forgot their parts. The conversation was full of marquises, counts, and financiers, whose titles, fortunes, and alliances, seemed to confer grandeur, riches, and importance upon those who were talking of them. The superfluities of the first table were spread upon the second with a neatness and order which gave them the air of a first appearance, and in such abundance as afterwards to suffice for the third table, that of the *domestics*, properly so called; for the persons who sat at the second were called *officers*. Play followed the repast: the stake was high; it was what the *ladies* were accustomed to play for, and they played every day. I was introduced to a new world, in which were exhibited the prejudices, the vices, and the follies of a world, very little better, in fpite of its greater fhow. I had heard a thoufand times of the origin of old Haudry, who came to Paris from his village; found means to rake thoufands together at the expence of the public; married his daughter to Montulé, and his grand-daughters to the Marquis Duchillau and Count Turpin, and left his fon heir to an immenfe eftate. I recollected Montefquieu's expreffion, who fays, that financiers fupport the ftate as the cord fupports the criminal; nor could I help thinking that tax-gatherers who contrive to amafs fuch enormous fums, and then to make their opulence ferve as the means of an alliance with families, which the policy of courts affects to confider as neceffary to a kingdom's fplendour and defence, muft needs belong to a deteftable government, and to a nation highly corrupt. I little thought there was a government ftill more horrible, and a degree of corruption ftill more to be deplored. Who, indeed, could have imagined it? All the philofophers of the age have been deceived as well as I.—I allude to the government and corruption of the prefent time.

Every Sunday there was a dance at Soucy in the open air, under no other fhelter than the trees. Gaiety, on thefe occafions, obliterated diftinctions in a great degree; and as foon as per-

fonal

sonal merit was attended to, I had little fear of missing the place that might chance to suit me best. The new comers used to ask, in a whisper, who I was, but I took care to give nobody a surfeit of my company; and, after an hour's recreation, withdrew with my relations for a walk, of which I would not have exchanged the tranquil enjoyments for all the empty and noisy pleasures that attend any kind of parade.

I sometimes saw Haudry, who was then young, acting the great man, gratifying all his fancies, and wishing to appear generous and noble. His family began to be uneasy at his extravagance with the courtezan La Guerre, by which he was already laying the foundation of his future ruin. He was pitied as imprudent, rather than blamed as vicious; he was a spoiled child of fortune, who, had he been born in moderate circumstances, would certainly have turned out a better man. With a dark complexion, an erect carriage, the airs of a great man, and courteous manners, he was perhaps amiable among those whom he esteemed his equals: but I hated to come in his way, and never failed, when in his presence, to assume an air of dignified reserve.

Last year, coming out of that magnificent dining-room which the elegant Calonne had fitted up in the controller-general's hotel, since occupied by the minister of the interior, I found in my way through the second antichamber, a tall grey-headed old man, of decent appearance, who accosted me respectfully: 'I should be very glad, Madam, to speak with the minister, when his dinner is over; I have something to communicate to him.'—'Sir, you will see him in an instant: he has been detained in the next room; but will be here immediately.' I made my curtesy, and proceeded to my own apartment, where Roland soon after joined me. I inquired if he had seen a person, whom I described, and who appeared apprehensive of not meeting him?—'Yes, it was M. Haudry.'—'What, the quondam *farmer-general*, who squandered an immense fortune?'—'The same.'—'And what has he to do with the minister of the interior?'—'Our business relates to the manufactory at Sèvres, at the head of which he has been placed.' What a theme for meditation do these sports of fortune furnish! I had already found one when I entered for the first time into the apartments occupied by Madam Necker in the days of her glory. I occupy them a second time, and they do but the more strongly attest the instability of the things of this world; but I will at least take care, that no reverse of fortune shall find me unprepared. Such were my reflections in October 1792, when Danton was conferring some celebrity upon me, by detracting from my husband's merit, and was silently preparing the calumnies, by which he meant to assail both. I was ignorant of his proceedings, but I had observed the course of things in revolutions. I was

only

only ambitious of preferving my mind uncontaminated, and of feeing my hufband's reputation free from ftain. I well knew this kind of ambition feldom leads to any other fpecies of fuccefs. My wifh is accomplifhed: Roland, perfecuted and profcribed, will not be forgotten by pofterity. I am a captive, and fhall probably be facrificed; but my confcience ftands in the ftead of every thing. It will happen to me as it did to Solomon, who afked only for wifdom, and obtained other advantages: I wifhed only for the peace of the righteous, and *I alfo* fhall have fome exiftence in future times.—But in the mean while let us return to Fontenay.

The little library of my relations afforded fome employment to my mind. I found there the whole of *Puffendorf*, tedious perhaps in his univerfal hiftory, and more interefting to me in his *Duties of the Man and the Citizen*; the *Maifon Ruftique*, and a variety of works on agriculture and economy, which I ftudied for want of others, becaufe it was neceffary that I fhould always be learning fomething; the agreeable trifles which *Bernis* wrote in verfe, when he was unfettered by the *Roman purple*; a life of *Cromwell*; and a curious medley of other productions.

Here I cannot help remarking, that, in the multitude of books which chance or other circumftances had thrown in my way, and of which I mention loofely fuch as places and perfons recal to my memory, nothing by Rouffeau has yet been noticed: the truth is, I read him very late; and it was well for me I did: he would have turned my brain, and I should have read nothing elfe. Perhaps as it is, he has but too much ftrengthened my weak fide, if I may be allowed to make ufe of fuch an expreffion.

I have reafon to believe that my mother had taken fome care to keep him out of my way; but his name not being unknown to me, I had fought after his works, and was already acquainted with his Letters from the Mountain, and his Letter to Chriftopher de Beaumont, when I loft her, having then read the whole of Voltaire and Boulanger, the Marquis d'Argens and Helvetius, and many other philofophers and critics. Probably my mother, who faw plainly that my mind muft needs be employed, was not much averfe to my making a ferious ftudy of philofophy at the rifk even of a little incredulity; but fhe was of opinion, no doubt, that no ftimulants were wanting for my fufceptible heart, already too obedient to the impulfe of the paffions.— Good heavens! how vain are all our endeavours to efcape from our deftiny ! The fame idea influenced her, when fhe prevented me from ftudying painting, and made her alfo oppofe my learning to play upon the harpfichord, though I had a moft excellent opportunity. Our living in the fame neighbourhood had made us acquainted with an Abbé Jeauket, a great mufician, and a good-natured man,

but

but as ugly as sin, and addicted to the pleasures of the table. He was born in the environs of Prague, had passed many years at Vienna, attached to the nobles of the court, and had given lessons to Marie Antoinette. After having been induced to visit Lisbon by particular circumstances, he had at last chosen Paris, in order to spend in a state of independence, the pensions of which his little fortune was composed. He wished exceedingly that my mother would permit him to teach me the harpsichord. He insisted upon it that my fingers and my head would soon go a great length, and that I could not fail to become a composer. ' What a shame,' he would cry, ' to be humming over a guitar, when possessed of powers to invent and execute the finest pieces upon the first of instruments !' This enthusiasm, and his reiterated entreaties, carried even to supplication, could not overcome my mother's reluctance : as to me, though always ready to avail myself of any instruction that came in my way, I was so much accustomed to respect her decisions, as well as to love her person, that I never importuned her for any thing. Besides, study in general afforded me so vast a field of occupation, that I never felt the pains of idleness. I often said to myself, When I become a mother in my turn, it will be my business to make use of what I shall have acquired: I shall then have no leisure for further studies; and I was the more earnest to turn my time to account, and afraid of losing a single moment. The Abbé Jeauket

was

was now and then vifited by perfons of merit, and whenever he invited them to his houfe, was anxious to include us in his party. Thus, among other individuals not worth remembering, I became acquainted with the learned Rouffier, and the worthy d'Odiment; but I have not forgotten the impertinent Paradelle and Madam de Puifieux. Paradelle was a huge monfter, in the garb of an abbé, the greateft coxcomb and romancer of all the fools I ever met with, who pretended to have kept a carriage at Lyons for twenty years, and who, to keep himfelf from ftarving at Paris, was obliged to give lectures on the Italian language, in which he was very little verfed. Madam Puifieux, who paffed for author of the *Characters*, to which her name is prefixed, retained at the age of fixty, with a hump back and toothlefs gums, the little airs and pretenfions, of which the affectation is fcarcely pardonable even in youth. I had fancied that a female author muft needs be a very refpectable perfonage, efpecially one who had written upon morals. But Madam de Puifieux's abfurdities made me change my mind. Her converfation befpoke very little wit, and her whims indicated very little judgment. I began to perceive it was poffible to collect a great deal of reafon, in order to make a difplay of it, without confuming much for our own purpofes, and that the men who made a jeft of female authors were perhaps no otherwife to blame than in applying to them exclufively, what is equally appli-
cable

cable to themselves. Thus it was, that in a sphere of life exceedingly confined, I found means to add to my stock of observations. I was in a solitary spot; but it was on the confines of the world, and so situated as to allow me to distinguish a great variety of objects without any of them standing in my way. The concerts of Madam l'Epine enlarged my prospect. I have already said that l'Epine was a pupil of Pigal: he was, indeed, his right hand. At Rome he had married a woman, who, I presume, had been an opera singer, and whom his family had at first looked upon with an evil eye, but who proved, by the propriety of her conduct, that she did not deserve their disdain.

She had a concert of amateurs, composed of excellent musicians, to which nobody was admitted but what she called good company. They met every Thursday at her house, whither I was often taken by my mother; and there I heard *Jarnewick, St. George, Duport, Guerin,* and many others. There too I met wits of both sexes: Mademoiselle *de Morville*, Madam *Benoit, Silvain-Marechal*, &c. with haughty baronesses, handsome abbés, old chevaliers, and young fops. What a curious magic lantern! The apartments of Madam l'Epine, in the *Rue Neuve St. Eustache*, were not remarkably superb, nor was the concert-room spacious, but adjoining to another, of which the folding-doors were set open: there, ranged in a circle, the company
had

had the several advantages of hearing the music, seeing the actors, and being able to converse between the acts. Seated by my mother, and keeping the silence that custom prescribes to young women, I was all eyes and ears; but when we chanced to be for a moment in private with Madam l'Epine, I asked her a few questions, the answers to which elucidated my observations.

One day that lady proposed to my mother to accompany her to a *charming* assembly, held at the house of a man of wit, whom we had sometimes seen at her concerts: the company consisted of enlightened men, and women of taste; very agreeable productions were recited: it was indeed *delightful!* The proposal was made several times before it was accepted: 'Let us go,' said I to my mother; 'I begin to know enough of the world to presume that it must either be very agreeable or very absurd; and even in the latter case, it will serve to amuse us once. The party was agreed upon; and on the Wednesday, the day on which M. Vâse's literary assembly was regularly held, we repaired with Madam l'Epine to his residence at the *Barrier du Temple.* After toiling up three pair of stairs we came to a moderately spacious apartment, furnished like a barrack: rush-bottomed chairs, marshalled in close order, and in several ranks, were ready to receive the spectators, and began to be filled; while tallow candles in dirty brass candlesticks illumined this retreat of the

muses,

muses, the grotesque simplicity of which accorded well with philosophical rigour and the poverty of an author. Well-dressed women, young girls, antiquated dowagers, poetasters in abundance, loungers, and adventurers, composed the society.

The master of the house, seated at a table, which served as a desk, opened the sitting by reading a piece of poetry of his own composition: the subject was a little marmoset which the old Marchioness de Préville always carried in her muff, and which she exhibited to the company; for she was there, and thought she could do no less than gratify the eager eyes of the persons present with a sight of the hero of the piece. Loud *bravos* and applauses did justice to M. Vàse's poetic flights. M. Vàse, highly satisfied with himself, wished to give up his seat to M. Delpêches, a poet who wrote little comic dramas for the theatre of Audinot, concerning which he was accustomed to take the opinion of the society, or, in other words, the encouragement of its applause; but that day he was prevented either by a sore throat, or the want of a few verses in some of his scenes. Imbert, the author of the *Judgment of Paris*, was therefore obliged to take the chair, and read an agreeable trifle, which was extolled to the skies. His reward awaited him Mademoiselle de la Coffonnière came next with a *Farewel to Colin*, which if not very ingenious, was at least very tender. It was known directly that it was addressed to Imbert,

about

about to undertake a journey, and a shower of compliments was poured upon him. Imbert discharged his own debt, and that of his muse, by saluting all the females in the assembly. The free and gay ceremony, though conducted with decency, was not at all pleasing to my mother, and appeared in so strange a light to me as to give me an air of embarrassment. After some epigram or distich by no means remarkable, a man of pompous declamation recited a poem in praise of Madam Benoit. She was sitting by, and must be briefly mentioned, for the sake of those who have not read her romances, which were dead long before the revolution, and will be buried beneath heaps of dust before my memoirs see the light.

Albine was born at Lyons, as I have read in the *History of the illustrious Women of France, by a Society of Men of Letters*; a history, in which I was quite astonished to find women whom I met with everywhere, as the lady in question, Madam de Puisieux, Madam Champion, and many more, some of whom perhaps are still alive at the moment I am writing, or have only quitted this terrestrial abode within a few years.

Having united herself in the holy bands of wedlock with Benoit, a draughtsman, she had accompanied him to Rome, and had there been admitted a member of the academy of the *Arcades*. Lately become a widow, and still in mourning for her husband, she had settled at Paris, where she made

verses

verses and novels, sometimes without writing them, kept a gaming-house, and visited women of quality, who paid in presents of money or clothes for the pleasure of having a female wit at their tables.

Madam Benoit had been handsome: the cares of the toilet, and the desire of pleasing, prolonged beyond the age which insures their success, still procured her a few conquests. Her eyes canvassed for them with such ardour; her bosom, always bare, palpitated so anxiously to obtain them; that it was impossible not to grant to the franknefs of desire, and the facility of satisfying it, what men bestow at all times so readily, when constancy is not required. Madam Benoit's air of undisguised voluptuousness, was something new to me. I had seen in the public walks those priestesses of pleasure, whose indecency announced their profession in the most disgusting manner; but her's was quite a different style. I was no less struck by the poetical incense lavished on her, and by the epithets of the *chaste* and *virtuous* Benoit, which occurred repeatedly in the poem, and obliged her now and then to cover her eyes modestly with her fan, while some of the men rapturously applauded those encomiums, which they doubtless conceived to be admirably applied. I recollected all that my reading had enabled me to conceive on the subject of gallantry, and calculated what corruption of heart and perversion of mind must be superadded by the manners

ners of the age, and the diforders of the court. I faw effeminate men giving all their admiration to flimfy verfes, to frivolous talents, and to the defire of feducing every woman that came in their way, and certainly without loving them; for he who devotes himfelf to the happinefs of a beloved object, does not court the looks of the crowd. I experienced a fenfation of difguft and mifanthropy in the midft of objects that fpoke to my imagination, and returned to my folitude in a melancholy mood. We never repeated our vifit to M. Vàfe: I had had quite enough of it; and Imbert's kifs, and the panegyric of Madam Benoit, would at any rate have cured my mother of all defire to take me there again. Neither did the concert of the Baron de Back, very curious, but frequently rendered very tedious alfo by the pretenfions of that mufical maniac, fee much of us, notwithftanding the cards of invitation which Madam l'Epine's politenefs often procured us. The fame referve was extended to that known as the *concert of amateurs*, which was numeroufly attended. We went there but once, attended by a M. Boyard de Creufy, who had amufed himfelf in compofing new inftructions for the guitar, of which he begged my mother's permiffion to offer me a copy. He was a man of polite manners, and I mention him here becaufe he had the good fenfe to believe, that, in a fituation ftill regarded by the vulgar as elevated, I fhould

be

be pleafed to fee the perfons with whom I had been acquainted in my youth. He called on me in the *hôtel de l'interieur*, while Roland was in the miniftry; and the reception he met with was fuch as muft have convinced him, that I derived fatisfaction from the remembrance of a time, on which I have reafon to value myfelf, and indeed on every other period of my life.

As to public places, it was ftill worfe; my mother never went there; and I was taken but once during her life to the Opera, and once to the *Theatre Français*. I was then about fixteen or feventeen. *The Union of Love and the Arts*, by Floquet, contained nothing either in the mufic, or the drama, capable of creating illufion, or of fupporting the idea I had formed of theatrical enchantment. The coldnefs of the fubject, the incoherence of the fcenes, and awkward intrufions of the ballets, difpleafed me. I was ftill more difgufted with the drefs of the dancers, who had not then laid afide their hoops: I had never feen any thing fo abfurd. Accordingly I thought the critique of Piron on the wonders of the Opera much fuperior to the Opera itfelf. At the *Theatre Français* the play was the *Ecoffoife*, which was not very well calculated to infpire me with enthufiafm for the drama; the performance of Mademoifelle Dumefnil alone delighted me. My father fometimes carried me to the theatres of the Foire St. Germain.

Germain *. Their mediocrity infpired me with difguft. Thus was I armed againft every temptation to play the *bel efprit*, precifely as the Spartan children were againft drinking, by feeing the confequences of excefs. My imagination received none of the great fhocks which the fafcination of the theatre might have produced, had I been prefent at the reprefentation of the fineft pieces. What I had feen made me content with reading in my clofet the works of the great mafters of the drama, and with enjoying their beauties at my leifure.

A young man, a conftant attendant at Madam l'Epine's concerts, had thought proper to call in her name at my mother's, to inquire for us, when an abfence unufually prolonged could juftify the fuppofition of our being indifpofed. A genteel deportment, an agreeable vivacity, a great deal of good fenfe, and above all, the unfrequency of his vifits, procured him his pardon for the little contrivance to get admiffion into the houfe. At laft La Blancherie hazarded his declaration.— But fince I am come to the hiftory of my fuitors, I muft march them off *en maſſe*; a delicate expreffion, that may ferve as a date to my writings,

---

* The inferior play-houfes at Paris are called *Theatres forains*; becaufe they remove for the few weeks it lafts to the Foire St. Germain, a fair at Paris not very unlike St. Bartholomew's at London. The reft of the year they perform in neat little theatres upon the *Boulevards*.—*Tranf.*

and

and recal to mind thefe glorious days, when every thing is ordered *en maſſe*, in fpite of the greateſt poſſible fubdiviſion of will and inclination.

The reader cannot have forgotten the Spaniſh coloſſus, with hands like Efau's, the polite M. Mignard, whofe name made fuch a curious contraſt with his face*. After confeſſing, of his own accord, that he was capable of teaching me nothing further on the guitar, he had begged permiſſion to call now and then to hear me, and came at diſtant periods, without being always fure of finding us at home. Flattered with the ſkill of his young fcholar, looking upon it as his own work, imagining that he thence derived fome fort of right, or of excufe, and giving himfelf out for a nobleman of Malaga, whom misfortunes had obliged to recur to his muſical knowledge for fubſiſtence, he began by loſing his fenfes, and ended by talking nonfenfe in order to juſtify his pretenſions. When that was done, he came to the refolution of demanding me in marriage, but had not courage enough to make his declaration in perfon. The friend whom he empowered to do fo, not being able by his remonſtrances to divert him from his intention, executed his commiſſion. The confequence was, a requeſt not to fet his foot within the houfe again, accompanied with thofe civilities which are due to the unfortunate. My father's jokes made me ac-

* The word *Mignard* means in French a delicate little gentleman. — *Tranſ.*

quainted with what had paſſed: he was fond of entertaining me with a relation of the applications made to him on my account; and as he was a little proud of his advantages, he did not ſpare the perſons who laid themſelves open to ridicule.

Poor Mozon was become a widower; he had the wen that embelliſhed his left cheek extirpated; and had ſome thoughts of ſetting up a one-horſe chaiſe: I was then fifteen, and he had been ſent for to perfect me in my dancing. His imagination took fire; he entertained a high opinion of his art; he ſhould have thought it no preſumption in Marcel *; one dancing-maſter was as good as another, why then ſhould he not enter the liſts? He made known his wiſhes, and was difmiſſed like Mignard.

From the moment a young female attains the age that announces maturity, ſwarms of ſuitors come humming round her, like bees about the newly-expanded flower.

Brought up in the ſtricteſt manner, and leading ſo retired a life, I could inſpire but one project; but the reſpectable character of my mother, the appearance of ſome fortune, and my being an only child, might make that project a tempting one to a great number of perſons.

Accordingly they came in crowds; and finding it difficult to obtain a perſonal introduction, the greater part adopted the expedient of writing to my

* A very celebrated French dancing-maſter.

parents.

parents. All letters of this kind were brought to me by my father; and my firſt opinion was always grounded upon the terms in which they were conceived, without the leaſt regard to the ſtatement they contained of the writer's rank and fortune. I undertook to make a rough draught of the anſwers, which my father faithfully tranſcribed. I made him diſmiſs my ſuitors with dignity, without giving room for reſentment or for hope. The youth of our quarter paſſed thus in review; and in the greater number of inſtances I met with no difficulty in getting my refuſal approved. My father looked to little elſe than riches; and, as he thought himſelf authorized to expect great things, whoever was too recently eſtabliſhed, or whoſe actual poſſeſſions or ſpeedy hopes of property did not inſure conſiderable eaſe of circumſtances, was ſure not to obtain his vote; but when once thoſe requiſites were found, he was concerned at ſeeing me refuſe to cloſe with the propoſal. Here began to break out thoſe diſſenſions between my father and me, which continued ever after. He loved and eſteemed commerce, becauſe he regarded it as the ſource of riches; I deteſted and deſpiſed it, becauſe I conſidered it as the foundation for avarice and fraud.

My father was ſenſible that I could not accept of an artiſan, properly ſo called; his vanity would not have ſuffered him to entertain ſuch an idea: but he could not conceive that the elegant jeweller, who touches nothing but fine things, from which he derives a great profit, was not a suitable match, especially when already in good business, and in a fair way to make a fortune. But the spirit of the jeweller, as well as of the little mercer, whom he looks upon as beneath him, and of the rich woollen-draper, who holds himself superior to both, appeared to me entirely engrossed by the lust of gold, and by mercenary calculations and contrivances: the mind of such a man must needs be a stranger to the elevated ideas and refined sentiments by which I appreciated existence.

Occupied from my infancy in considering the relations of man in society, brought up in the strictest morality, and familiarized with the noblest examples, had I then lived with Plutarch, and all the other philosophers, to no better purpose than to connect myself for life with a shop-keeper incapable of seeing any thing in the same light as myself?

I have already said that my provident mother wished me to be as much at home in the kitchen as in the drawing-room, and at market as in a public walk: after my return from the convent, I used still to accompany her, when she went to purchase articles of household consumption, as was often the case; and at last she would sometimes send me on such errands with a maid. The butcher with whom she dealt lost a second wife, and found himself, while still in the prime of life, possessed of a fortune of fifty thousand crowns, which he proposed

to

to augment. I was perfectly ignorant of thefe particulars : I only perceived that I was well ferved, and with abundant civility ; and was much furprifed at feeing this perfonage frequently appear on a funday in a handfome fuit of black and lace ruffles in the fame walk as ourfelves, and put himfelf in my mother's way, to whom he made a low bow, without accofting her. This practice continued a whole fummer. I fell fick; and every morning the butcher fent to inquire what we wanted, and to offer any accommodation in his power. This very pointed attention began to provoke my father's fmiles, who, wifhing to divert himfelf, introduced to me a certain Mademoifelle Michon, a grave church-going woman, one day when fhe came very ceremonioufly to demand my hand in the butcher's name. ' You know, daughter,' faid he, with great gravity, ' that it is a rule with me to lay no conftraint upon your inclinations.—I fhall therefore only ftate to you a propofal in which you are principally concerned. He then repeated what Mademoifelle Michon had intimated. I fcrewed up my mouth, a little vexed that my father's good-humour fhould turn over to me the tafk of giving an anfwer, which he ought to have taken upon himfelf. ' You know, papa,' faid I, parodying his mode of expreffion, ' that I confider myfelf as very happy in my prefent fituation; and that I am firmly refolved not to quit it for fome years to come. You may take any fteps in conformity with this refolution that you think proper:' and on faying this I withdrew.—' Why truly,' faid my father, when we were afterwards alone, ' this reafon you have invented is a very fine one for keeping every body away.'—' I revenged myfelf, papa, for the little trick you played me, by a general anfwer very becoming a girl; and I left it to you to give a formal refufal: a tafk which I ought not to take upon myfelf.'—' It's an excellent evafion; but tell me then who it is that will fuit you?'—' Tell me, papa, why, in bringing me up, you taught me to think, and fuffered me to contract habits of ftudy: I know not what kind of man I fhall marry; but it muft be one who can fhare my fentiments, and to whom I can communicate my thoughts.'—' There are men in bufinefs poffeffed both of politenefs and information.'—' Yes, but not of the kind I want: their politenefs confifts in a few phrafes and bows, and their knowledge always relates to the ftrong box, and would affift me but little in the education of my children.'— ' But you might educate them yourfelf.'—' The tafk would appear laborious, if not fhared by the man to whom they would owe their exiftence.'—' Do you fuppofe that *l'Empereur*'s wife is not happy? They have juft retired from bufinefs, are buying capital places, keep an excellent houfe, and receive the beft company.'—' I am no judge of other people's happinefs; but my own affections are not fixed upon riches: I conceive that the ftricteft

union

union of hearts is requisite to conjugal felicity; nor can I connect myself with a man who does not resemble me: my husband must even be my superior, for since both nature and the laws give him pre-eminence, I should be ashamed of him, if he did not really deserve it.'—' You want a counsellor, I suppose? But women are not very happy with those learned gentlemen: they have a great deal of pride, and very little money.'— ' My God! papa, I do not judge of a man's merit by his cloth; nor have I ever told you that I affect such or such a profession: I want a man I can love.'—' But according to you, such a man is not to be found in trade?'—' I confess that I do not think it likely. I have never seen a tradesman to my liking; and the profession itself is my aversion.'—' It is, however, a very pleasant thing for a woman to sit at her ease in her own apartment, while her husband is carrying on a lucrative trade. Now, there's Madam d'Argens: she understands diamonds as well as her husband: she deals with the brokers in his absence; concludes bargains with private persons, and would be able to carry on the business, even if left a widow: their fortune is already considerable, and they belong to the company which has just bought Bagnolet. You are intelligent; and, indeed, understand that branch of business since you perused the treatise on precious' stones. You would inspire people with confidence; you might do whatever

you

you pleafe; and a happy life would you have had if you could but have fancied Delorme, Dabreuil, or l'Obligeois.'—' Hark ye, papa; I have too well perceived that the only way to make a fortune in trade, is by felling dear what has been bought cheap, by overcharging the cuftomer, and beating down the poor workman. I fhould never be able to defcend to fuch practices, nor to refpect a man who makes them his occupation from morning to night. It is my wifh to be a virtuous wife; but how fhould I be faithful to a man who would hold no place in my efteem, even admitting the poffibility of my marrying fuch a man? Selling diamonds and felling paftry feem nearly the fame thing to me; except that the latter has a fixed price, requires lefs deceit perhaps, but foils the fingers more. I like the one not in any degree better than the other.'—' Do you fuppofe then there are no honeft tradefmen?'—' I will not abfolutely affirm it; but I am perfuaded the number is fmall; and the few honeft folks have not all that I require in a hufband.'—' You are extremely faftidious, methinks; but if you do not find the idol of your imagination?'—' I will die a maid.' —' That would be a harder tafk perhaps, than you imagine. You have time enough, to be fure, to think of it: but *ennui* will come at laft; the crowd will be gone by; and you know the fable!'—' Oh! I would take my revenge by deferving happinefs from the very injuftice that

would

would deprive me of it.'—' Now you are in the clouds again! It is very pleafant to foar to fuch a height; but it is not eafy to keep the elevation: do not forget, however, that I fhould like to have grandchildren before I am too far advanced in years.'

I fhould like to prefent you with fome, faid I to myfelf, when my father put an end to the dialogue, by withdrawing; but moft certainly I never fhall have any, unlefs by a hufband to my mind. I experienced a flight fenfation of melancholy, when on cafting my eyes about me, I could perceive nothing that was fuitable to my tafte; but the fenfation foon fubfided. I was fenfible of my prefent comforts, and hope threw its enlivening beams on the time to come. It was the plenitude of happinefs overflowing its banks, and clearing away every thing unpleafant from my future profpect.

' Shall I fuit you this time, Mademoifelle?' faid my father one day, with affected gravity, and the look of fatisfaction which was vifible upon every new demand. ' Read that letter.' It was very well written as to imagery and ftyle, and brought the blood into my cheeks. Mr. Morizot de Rozain expreffed himfelf handfomely enough, but did not forget to remark that his name was to be found among the nobles of his province. It appeared to me coxcomical and injudicious, to make a parade of an advantage which he knew me not to poffefs, and of which he had no right to fuppofe me ambitious. ' We have here,' faid I, fhaking

my

my head, 'no great cause for confideration: it may be worth while, however, to hear what the gentleman has to fay for himfelf: a letter or two more, and I fhall be able to found the depth of his pretenfions. I will go and draw up an anfwer.' When writing was the queftion, my father was as tractable as a child, and fat down to copy without reluctance. I was much diverted at the idea of acting the papa; and difcuffed my own interefts with all the gravity fuitable to the occafion, and in a ftyle of prudence truly parental. No lefs than three explanatory letters came from Mr. de Rozain, which I preferved for a long time, becaufe they were extremely well written. They proved to me that powers of mind did not fuffice, unlefs accompanied by fuperior judgment, and a foul, which nothing can fupply the want of, or defcribe, but which is recognized at the firft glance. Befides, Rozain had nothing but the title of advocate; my prefent fortune was not enough for two; nor were his qualities fuch as to create a defire of furmounting that obftacle.

In announcing the *rifing en maffe* of my fuitors, I did not promife to name them all, and I fhall be readily excufed. I only wifh to fhow the fingularity of a fituation, which procured me offers from a great many perfons, whofe very faces I was not always acquainted with, and in which the examination of reafons and appearances was left to myfelf. I often, indeed, perceived new faces obferving

ſerving or following me at church, or in the public walks, and uſed to ſay to myſelf, ' I ſhall ſoon have an anſwer to write for my father.' But I never ſaw a figure that ſurpriſed or faſcinated me.

I have already ſaid that La Blancherie had wit enough to make his way into our houſe, and to underſtand, that, before he declared himſelf, it was neceſſary to gain my good opinion. Though ſtill very young, he had already travelled, had read a great deal, and had even tried his fortune as an author. His work was not good for much; but it contained morality in abundance, and ſome ideas that were not amiſs. He had intitled it, *Abſtract of my Travels, intended to ſerve as a School for Fathers and Mothers:* this, as my readers will perceive, was not very modeſt; but one could hardly help forgiving him; for he ſupported himſelf by very reſpectable philoſophical authorities, quoted them happily, and inveighed with all the indignation of an honeſt heart, againſt the coldneſs and negligence of parents, too frequently the cauſe of the deſtructive irregularities of youth. La Blancherie, diminutive, brown, and ordinary, had no hold on my imagination; but I did not diſlike his mind, and thought I could perceive that he had a great liking for my perſon. One evening, returning with my mother from a viſit to our old relations, we found my father in a thoughtful mood. ' I have news for you,' ſaid he, ſmiling. ' La Blancherie is juſt gone away, after paſſing more than

than two hours with me; he has told me a secret; and as it concerns you, Mademoiselle, you muſt be let into it.' (The confequence was not ſtrictly neceſſary, but it was cuſtomary with my father to infer it.) 'He is in love with her, and has propoſed himſelf for my ſon-in-law; but he has no fortune, and it would be a folly, as I have given him to underſtand. He is preparing for the bar, and means to purchaſe a place in the magiſtracy; but what he has to expect from his family, being too little for the purpoſe, he has been thinking, that if we like the match, his wife's fortune would ſupply the deficiency, and that as our girl is an only child, they might live with us for the firſt two or three years. He has been ſaying a great number of fine things upon the ſubject, which may be very ſatisfactory to a youthful fancy; but prudent parents require ſomething more ſolid. Let him ſet up an office, or buy a place; let him, in ſhort, follow his profeſſion: it will be time enough to talk of marriage afterwards; but to begin by marrying, would be abſurd in the extreme. Beſides, it would be neceſſary to inquire into his character; though that indeed might be eaſily done. I had rather he were not noble, and that he had forty thouſand good crowns in his purſe. He is a good young man; we had a great deal of talk together; and though he was a little hurt by my arguments, he liſtened to me with patience. At laſt he requeſted me not to ſhut my

door

door againſt him, and urged his prayer with ſo good a grace, that I conſented, upon condition of his not coming more frequently than before. I told him that I would not ſay a word to you; but as I know your diſcretion, I never like to keep you in the dark.'—A few queſtions from my mother, and ſome prudent reflections concerning the many things to be conſidered before we form an affection, ſaved me the trouble of anſwering; but my thoughts were buſily employed.

Though my father's calculations were well founded, there was nothing unreaſonable in the young man's propoſal; and I felt diſpoſed to ſee him, and to ſtudy his diſpoſition with additional intereſt and curioſity. My opportunities were few: at the end of ſome months La Blancherie ſet off for Orleans, and I ſaw no more of him till two years after. In the mean time I was very near marrying Gardanne, the phyſician; a match recommended by one of our relations. Madam Deſportes, a native of Provence, had married a tradeſman at Paris; and having been left a widow with an only daughter, at a very early age, had continued to deal in jewels, the buſineſs which my father thought ſo very agreeable. Sound ſenſe, civility, good breeding, and a great deal of addreſs, procured her general eſteem: any one, indeed, would have ſuppoſed that ſhe carried on her trade merely to oblige her cuſtomers. Without going out of her apartment, which was neatly furniſhed, nifhed, and in which fhe received a very refpectable fociety, compofed in part of the very perfons who fatisfied their wants or their luxury by purchafing her goods, fhe maintained herfelf in eafy circumftances, without increafing or diminifhing the little fortune fhe poffeffed. Being far advanced in years, fhe needed the affiftance of her daughter, who, out of filial affection, rejected all offers of marriage, that her intimate union with her mother might not be difturbed.

Gardanne was a countryman of Madam Defportes. Natural good fenfe, that lively difpofition fo common among the natives of the fouth, an excellent education, and an extreme defire to get on, promifed the young doctor fuccefs in a career, already aufpicioufly begun. Madam Defportes, who received him with that patronizing kindnefs which became her age and character, and which fhe had the art of rendering agreeable, conceived the idea of giving him her young coufin for a wife; but death overtook her while intent upon this project, which her daughter refolved to execute.

Gardanne both defired and feared the connection. In confidering the advantages and inconveniences of becoming a *Benedict*, he did not, like my romantic brain, attend to perfonal qualities alone: he calculated every thing. My fortune was only twenty thoufand livres*; but the fmallnefs of

* 883l.

this

this fum was compenfated by confiderable expectations. The pecuniary arrangements were made before I knew any thing of the matter, and the *bargain* abfolutely concluded, when I firſt heard that a phyſician had entered the lifts. The profeffion did not difpleafe me; it promifed an enlightened mind: but it was neceffary to become acquainted with his perfon. A walk in the Luxemburg gardens was propofed; we were to be overtaken by the rain; and the rain came, or at leaſt was apprehended. We ran for ſhelter to the houfe of a Mademoifelle de la Barre, a rigid Janfeniſt, and a friend of Madam Defportes, who was overjoyed at the circumſtance, and offered us refrefhments, which we were taking, when her phyſician came with his countrywoman in the very moment to pay her a vifit.

A minute furvey took place on both fides, without any appearance, on my part, of being fo employed, but at the fame time without my fuffering any thing to efcape me. My coufin affumed an air of triumph, as if fhe would have faid, ' I did not tell you fhe was handfome: but what do you think of her?' My good mother looked kind and penfive; Mademoifelle de la Barre was equally profufe of her wit and her confectionary; the phyſician chattered away, and made great havoc among the fugar-plums, faying, with a fort of gallantry, that favoured a little of the fchool-boy, that he was very fond of every thing fweet; upon which the young lady obferved with a foft voice, a blufh, and a half fmile, that the men were accufed of loving fweet things, becaufe it was neceffary to make ufe of great fweetnefs in dealing with them. The cunning doctor was quite tickled with the epigram. My father would willingly have given us his benediction, and was fo polite, that I was out of all patience with him. The doctor retired firft to pay his evening vifits; we returned as we came; and this was called an *interview*. Mademoifelle Defportes, a ftrict obferver of punctilios, had fo ordered it, becaufe forfooth a man who has views of marriage ought never to fet his foot in a private houfe, where there is a daughter, until his propofals are accepted; but when once that is done, the marriage articles are directly to be drawn up, and the confummation is to follow immediately. This is the law and the prophets. A phyfician in the habiliments of his profeffion, is never a pleafing object to a young woman; nor could I indeed, at any period of life, figure to myfelf fuch a thing as love in a periwig. Gardanne with his three tails, his phyfical look, his fouthern accent, and his black eye-brows, feemed much more likely to allay than to excite a fever. But this I felt without making the reflection: my ideas of marriage were fo ferious, that I could not perceive any thing laughable in his propofals.—' Well,' faid my good mother to me, in a tone of tender inquiry, ' what think you of this man? Will he fuit you?'—' My dear mamma, it is impoffible

poffible yet for me to tell.'—' But you can certainly tell whether he has infpired you with diflike.'—' Neither diflike nor inclination: which of the two may come hereafter, I cannot fay.'—' We ought to know however what anfwer to give in cafe a propofal fhould be made in form.'—'.Is the anfwer to be binding?'—Affuredly, if we pafs our word to a decent man, we muft adhere to it.'— ' And if I fhould not like him?'—' A reafonable young woman, not actuated by caprice, after having once maturely weighed the motives that determine her in fo important a refolution, will never change her mind.'—' I am to decide then upon the ftrength of a fingle interview.'—' Not exactly that; the intimacy of M. de Gardanne with our family enables us to judge of his conduct and way of life, and by means of a little inquiry we fhall eafily come at a knowledge of his difpofition. Thefe are the principal points to found a determination upon: the fight of the perfon is a matter of much lefs moment.'—' Ah mamma! I am in no hafte to be married.'—' I believe it, daughter; but you muft fettle yourfelf in the world fome time or other; and you have now attained the proper age. You have refufed many offers from tradefmen; and they are the people from whom your fituation makes offers the moft likely to come: you feem determined never to marry a man in bufinefs: the match at prefent in queftion is fuitable in every external point of view.—Take care then not to

reject

reject it too lightly.'—' It appears to me there is time enough to think about it; M. Gardanne has, perhaps, made no decifion himfelf; for it is certain that he never faw me before.'— ' True; but if that be your only excufe, it is poffible it may not be of long duration: I do not, however, require an immediate anfwer. Revolve the matter in your mind, and two days hence let me know what you think about it.' On faying this, my mother kiffed my forehead, and withdrew.

Reafon and nature concur fo well in perfuading a prudent and modeft young woman that fhe ought to marry, that all deliberation upon the fubject is neceffarily confined to the choice of a mate. Now, as to this choice, the arguments of my mother were by no means deftitute of force. I confidered, befides, that my provifional acceptance, however it might be conftrued, could never amount to a pofitive engagement; and that it would be abfurd to fuppofe me under contract, becaufe I might confent to fee the perfon propofed at my father's houfe. I was fenfible too, if I fhould diflike him, no confideration upon earth could induce me to accept his hand. I determined then, within myfelf, not to fay no, but to wait till we fhould become better acquainted.

We were juft on the point of fetting off for the country, where we were to pafs a fortnight. I thought it would be improper to delay our journey in expectation of a fuitor, and my mother was

of

of the fame opinion; but when we were on the eve of our departure, Mademoifelle de la Barre came in great form to demand my hand in the doctor's name. My parents anfwered in the general terms that people employ when they wifh it to be underftood that their confent will depend upon further confideration. Permiffion, however, was afked, and granted, for the lover to pay his refpects in perfon. Mademoifelle Defportes, with her ufual formality, concluded it was her bufinefs to be his conductor; and a family collation, at which Mademoifelle de la Barre and one of my female relations were prefent, ferved to celebrate the gentleman's ceremonious entry into my father's houfe. The next day we fet off for the country, on purpofe to pafs there the precife time neceffary for inquiries. The fecond interview made no greater impreffion upon me than the firft; but I thought I could perceive that Gardanne was a fenfible man, with whom a rational woman might live upon good terms; and, like an unexperienced girl, I concluded that when once it was poffible to reafon and underftand one another, a fufficient provifion was made for matrimonial blifs.

My mother was afraid that he fhowed figns of an imperious difpofition; an idea that never came into my mind: accuftomed to watch over myfelf, to regulate my affections, and to keep my imagination within bounds, and impreffed with a ftrong fenfe of the rigour and fublimity of the duties of a wife,

wife, I could not underſtand what difference a diſpoſition, a little more or a little leſs indulgent,
could make to me, nor what more could be required
of me than I required of myſelf. I reaſoned like a philoſopher who calculates, or like a recluſe equally a
ſtranger to the paſſions, and to mankind. I took my
tranquil, affectionate, generous, and candid heart,
as a common meaſure of the moral qualities of
my ſpecies. I continued a long while to be guilty
of that fault. It was the only ſource of my errors.
I haſten to point it out: it is giving beforehand
the key of my ſcrutoire. I carried with me into
the country a ſort of inquietude: it was not that
gentle agitation with which the beauties of nature
uſually inſpired me, and which rendered its charms
ſtill more grateful to my feelings. I found myſelf
upon the eve of a new exiſtence: I was going, perhaps, to quit my excellent mother, my darling
ſtudies, my beloved retirement, and a ſort of independence, for a ſtate which I could not well define,
and which would impoſe on me the moſt important obligations. I thought it an honour to
have them to diſcharge, and was proud of being
able to undertake them; but the proſpect was
clouded, and I experienced all the hopes and fears
of incertitude. Mademoiſelle Deſportes had made
me promiſe to write to her; and I kept my
word: but, at the end of a fortnight, I heard ſhe
was very much afflicted. My father, who did
every thing by rule, would never have believed

that

that he had married his daughter properly, and fulfilled the duty of a parent, if he had not made his cuftomary inquiries in due form. Gardanne had been introduced by one of our relations, who knew his family, and was intimate with himfelf. All poffible information had been afforded, but it did not fignify; my father had written to three or four perfons in Provence, at the very beginning of the bufinefs, to inquire into the moft minute particulars of the doctor's family and habits. During our abfence, his vigilance did not even ftop there: he employed a variety of little manœuvres, in order to learn from fervants and tradefmen, the temper and way of life of his future fon-in-law. Nor was that all; he went to pay him a vifit; and, with an addrefs equal to that which he had made ufe of in his inquiries, when he let every body fee why he was making them, he affected to be very well informed. He mentioned to Gardanne in an awkward way, and as a man whom he ought to refpect, one of his countrymen with whom he was at variance, and added premature advice to his remarks in the authoritative tone of a father. Gardanne received at one and the fame time, letters from the country, rallying him upon the inquiries to which he gave occafion, intelligence of the inquifition carrying on concerning his private affairs, and the pedagogical exhortation of his intended father-in-law. Diftreffed, vexed, and irritated, he went

went to Mademoifelle Defportes, and complained with all the warmth of a native of the fouth, of the ftrange conduct of a man, whofe amiable daughter had no other fault than that of having fo fingular a father. Mademoifelle Defportes, fiery, as well as himfelf, and full of pride, was much difpleafed at his being fo little in love with her coufin as to complain of trifles like thefe, and gave him a very indifferent reception. The very moment thefe circumftances came to my knowledge, I eagerly embraced the opportunity of putting an end to my incertitude; and wrote to fay, that, on my return, I hoped to fee no more of my phyfical fuitor. Such was the *denouement* of a marriage which it was intended to hurry on with fo much fpeed, that Gardanne expected to conclude the bufinefs in a week after my return. I congratulated myfelf on efcaping ties, that my friends would fain have drawn clofely in fo fudden a manner; my mother, alarmed at the doctor's warmth of temper, felt as if delivered from fome dreadful danger, though grieving a little on other accounts; my father endeavoured to conceal his fhame and difappointment under the veil of lordly dignity; and my coufin preferved hers by forbidding the doctor to fet his foot in her houfe. Five years after, Mademoifelle de la Barre told her, that this marriage was written in heaven; that her friend kept himfelf free from all other engagements;

ments; and that the hand of Providence was preparing to bring us together, by means infcrutable to human eyes.

What an excellent prophecy! It was as good as Ninon's billet to the Marquis de la Châftre.

My mother's health began infenfibly to decline. She had had a ftroke of the palfy, which was reprefented to me as the rheumatifm, a pious fraud, in which, without flattering herfelf, fhe willingly joined, in order to prevent my taking any alarm. Serious and taciturn, fhe every day loft a portion of her vivacity; was fond of fecluding herfelf from the world; and obliged me, fometimes, to go out with the maid, réfufing to quit her apartment. She often talked of my changing my condition, and lamented I could not prevail on myfelf to clofe with any of the offers that were made me. One day in particular, fhe urged me, with melancholy earneftnefs, to accept an honeft jeweller who had demanded my hand: ' He has in his favour,' faid fhe, ' great reputation for integrity, habits of fobriety, and mildnefs of difpofition, with an eafy fortune, which may become brilliant; and that circumftance makes part of the merit of a man, who is not remarkable for his perfonal advantages. He knows that yours is not a common mind, profeffes great efteem for you, will be proud of following your advice, and fays already, that he would not object to his wife's fuckling her children. You might lead him

him any way you like.'—' Why, mamma, I do not want a huſband who is to be led; he would be too cumberſome a child for me.'—' Do you know that you are a very whimſical girl? for after all you would not like a maſter.'—' My dear mother, let us underſtand one another: I ſhould not like a man to give himſelf airs of authority : he would only teach me to reſiſt; but at the ſame time, I ſhould not like a huſband whom it would be neceſſary to govern. Either I am much miſtaken, or thoſe beings five foot and a half high, with beards upon their chins, ſeldom fail to make us perceive that they are the ſtronger. Now if the good man ſhould think proper to remind me of that ſuperiority, he would provoke me; and if he ſhould ſubmit to be governed, I ſhould be aſhamed of my own power.'—'I underſtand you ; you would like a man to think himſelf the maſter, while obeying you in every thing.'—' No, it is not that either: I hate ſervitude, but I do not think myſelf made for empire; it would only embarraſs me; my reaſon finds it quite enough to take care of myſelf. I ſhould wiſh to gain the affections of a man ſo completely worthy of my eſteem, that I might be proud of my complaiſance; of a man who would make his happineſs conſiſt in contributing to mine, in the way that his good ſenſe and affection might think meet.'—' Happineſs, daughter, does not always conſiſt in that perfect conformity of ideas and affections which you imagine;

if

if without that it could not exift, there would be hardly any fuch thing as a happy couple.'—' Neither do I know any whofe happinefs I envy.'— 'Perhaps fo; but ftill among thofe matches you do not envy, there may be many preferable to always living fingle. I may be called out of the world fooner than you imagine; you would remain with your father; he is ftill young, and you cannot imagine all the difagreeable things that my fondnefs for you makes me fear. How happy fhould I be, if I could but leave you united to an honeft man, when I depart from this world.' Thefe laft ideas afflicted me beyond meafure: my mother feemed to lift up the veil that concealed a fad and dreadful futurity, which I did not even apprehend. I had never thought of lofing her; and the mere idea of fuch an event, which fhe fpoke of as approaching, ftruck me with terror; a cold fhivering feized my whole frame; I gazed upon her with wild and eager eyes, from which her fmiles drew forth a flood of tears. 'What! you are alarmed? as if, in taking our refolutions, we ought not to calculate all poffible chances. I am not ill, though at a critical time of life, of which the revolutions frequently prove fatal; but it is in health that we ought to provide againft ficknefs, and the prefent occafion makes it peculiarly neceffary. An honeft and worthy man offers you his hand; you are turned of twenty, and will no longer fee fo many fuitors as have tendered you their homage

homage during the laſt five years. I may be ſnatched away—do not then reject a huſband, who has not, it is true, the delicacy on which you ſet ſo great a value (a quality very rare, even where we look for it the moſt); but he is a man who will love you, and with whom you may be happy.'—'Yes, mamma,' cried I with a deep ſigh, ' happy as you have been!' My mother was diſconcerted, and made me no reply, nor from that moment did ſhe ever open her lips to me about that or any other match, at leaſt in a preſſing manner. The remark had eſcaped me, as the expreſſion of an acute feeling eſcapes us when we have not taken time to reflect: the effect it produced convinced me that it was too true.

A ſtranger might have perceived at the firſt glance the great difference between my father and mother: but who could feel like me all the excellence of the latter? I had not, however, fully calculated all ſhe muſt have had to ſuffer. Accuſtomed from my infancy to ſee the moſt profound peace prevail in the houſe, I could not judge of the painful efforts it might coſt to maintain it. My father loved his wife, and was tenderly fond of me. Never—I will not ſay a reproach—but never did even a look of diſcontent break in upon the good humour of my mother. When ſhe was not of her huſband's opinion, and could not prevail upon him to modify it, ſhe appeared to paſs ſentence upon her own without the ſmalleſt reluctance.

It

It was only during the latter years of her life, that, feeling myfelf hurt by my father's mode of reafoning, I fometimes took the liberty to interfere in the difcuffion : by degrees I gained a certain fort of afcendance, and availed myfelf of it with confiderable freedom. Whether it was the novelty of my enterprife that confounded him, or whether it was weaknefs, I know not, but my father yielded to me more readily than to his wife; I always exerted my influence in her defence; and might not unaptly have been termed my mother's watch-dog. It was no longer fafe to moleft her in my prefence— either by barking, or by pulling the fkirt of the coat, or by fhewing my teeth in good earneft, I was fure to make the affailant let go his hold. It is worthy of remark, that, being no lefs referved than my mother in regard to her hufband, I never faid a word to her in private, and out of his hearing, that was not confiftent with filial refpect. I employed in her defence the force, I will fay even the authority of reafon, when addrefs did not fuffice; but when we were alone I fhould not have dared to utter a word relative to what had paffed. For her fake I could enter the lifts even againft her hufband ; but that hufband, when abfent, was no longer any thing but my father, about whom we were both filent, unlefs when any thing could be faid in his praife. I could perceive however, that he had loft by degrees his habits of induftry. Parifh bufinefs having firft called him from home ; fauntering abroad afterwards

wards became a paſſion. All public ſpectacles, and every thing that was paſſing out of doors, attracted his attention; a paſſion for gaming next laid hold of him; connexions made at the coffee-houſe led him elſewhere; and the lottery held out temptations which he could not reſiſt. The deſire of making a fortune having engaged him in ſpeculations, quite foreign to his profeſſion, and not always ſucceſsful, that deſire, when once he had loſt his aſſiduity, made him ſet every thing at hazard. In proportion as his art was leſs exerciſed, his talents diminiſhed; and by leading a leſs regular life, he impaired his faculties: his ſight grew weak, and his hand loſt its ſteadineſs. His pupils being leſs ſuperintended by their maſter, became leſs able to ſupply his place; and it was ſoon found neceſſary to diminiſh their number, becauſe the tide of buſineſs neceſſarily flowed elſewhere. Thoſe changes took place by inſenſible degrees, and their effect became very perceptible, before any one had calculated all its conſequences. My mother grew penſive, and began now and then to give me imperfect intimations of her uneaſineſs, which I was fearful of increaſing by ſpeaking of what neither ſhe nor I could prevent. I was careful to procure her every ſatisfaction that depended upon me; and as ſhe was grown averſe to walking, I ſometimes conſented to leave her, in order to go abroad with my father, whom I requeſted to take me out for a walk. He no longer ſought to have me with him as formerly; but he ſtill took a

pleaſure

pleasure in attending me, and I used to bring him back in a sort of triumph to that excellent mother whose tender emotions I could easily perceive whenever she saw us together. We were not always gainers by it; for my father, that he might neither refuse his daughter, nor be disappointed of his pleasures, would first see me safe home, and then go out again, for an instant, as he said; but instead of returning to supper, he would forget the hour, and not come home till midnight. In the mean time we had been weeping in silence; and if it happened to me, on his return, to represent to him our chagrin, he treated the matter lightly, parrying my gentle reproaches by raillery, or else retired in the silence of discontent. Our domestic happiness was buried beneath these clouds; but the peace of the family remained unaltered, so that an indifferent spectator would not have perceived the changes that were daily taking place.

My mother had suffered considerably, for more than a year, from a kind of obstruction in the respiratory passages, which resembled a cold in the head, but of which her physicians were totally unable to imagine the cause. After various remedies, they recommended exercise, which she was no longer fond of, and country air. That was just before Whitsuntide of the year 1775, and it was agreed that we should pass the holydays at Meudon. On the Sunday morning I did not wake, as I was accustomed to do when any of those rural excursions curfions were in agitation : I was overcome by broken and uneafy fleep, and tormented by ill-omened dreams. I thought we were returning to Paris by water, in the midft of a ftorm; and upon getting out of the boat, a corpfe that was dragging afhore impeded my way. I was terrified at the fight, and was endeavouring to find out whofe body it could be.—At that very inftant, my mother, laying her hand lightly upon my legs, and calling me with her foft voice, put an end to my dream. I was as much rejoiced at feeing her, as if fhe had faved me from the moft imminent danger; I ftretched out my arms, and embraced her with emotion, telling her fhe had done me great kindnefs by waking me. I got up; we made our arrangements, and fet off. The weather was fine, the air calm, a little boat conveyed us fpeedily to the place of our deftination, and the charms of the country reftored my ferenity. My mother was the better for the journey; and refumed a portion of her activity. It was on the fecond day we difcovered Ville-bonne, and the water-bailiff of the Moulin Rouge. I had promifed my Agatha to call upon her the day after the holydays; we returned on Tuefday evening; and my mother purpofed accompanying me to the convent; but being a little fatigued with the exercife of the preceding days, fhe changed her mind at the moment I was fetting off, and defired the maid to accompany me. I then wifhed to ftay at home; but fhe infifted on my

keeping

keeping my word; adding, that I well knew she had no objection to being alone, and that if desirous of taking a turn in the *Jardin du Roi*, I was free so to do.

My visit to Agatha was a short one: 'Why are you in such haste?' said she; 'does any one expect you?'—'No; but I am anxious to return to my mother.'—'Why, you told me she was well.'— 'I did so; nor does she expect me so soon; but I know not what it is that torments me: I shall not be easy till I see her again.' On saying this, I felt my heart swell, as it were, in spite of me.

It may, perhaps, be supposed these circumstances are added by the reflection of a sentiment, which lends its colour to preceding incidents.— I am no more than a faithful historian, and relate facts, which the event alone afterwards recalled to my mind.

It must certainly have appeared from the exposition of my opinions, and still more from the successive developement of the ideas I had acquired, that I was at that time no more infected with certain prejudices, than I am now with superstition. Accordingly, in reflecting upon what are called *presentiments*, I have often thought they are nothing more than rapid glances caught by persons of quick perception and exquisite feelings, of a multitude of things which are scarcely perceptible, which cannot even be described, which are rather felt than understood, and from which an affection results that is not to be accounted for, although it is afterwards juſtified by the event.

The more lively the intereſt any object inſpires, the ſtronger is our perception or ſenſibility in regard to that object, and the more we have of thoſe phyſical notices, if I may be allowed the expreſſion, which are afterwards called preſentiments, and which the ancients conſidered as auguries, or intimations given by the gods.

My mother was to me the deareſt object upon earth: ſhe was drawing near her end, without any external ſign that might ſerve to announce it to common obſervers: nor had my attention yet diſtinguiſhed any thing that clearly indicated ſo dreadful a blow; but doubtleſs ſome ſlight alterations muſt have taken place in her, by which I was agitated without knowing why: I could not ſay that I was uneaſy, becauſe I ſhould not have known why; but my mind was not at peace; my heart frequently ſunk within me while looking at her; and whenever I left her I experienced a diſagreeable feeling that made me impatient to return. When I was taking leave of Agatha there was ſomething ſo ſingular in my manner, that ſhe begged me to let her hear from me immediately. I hurried home notwithſtanding the obſervations of the maid, who was of opinion that a walk in the *Jardin du Roi* would be very pleaſant at that time of day. I came to the houſe, and found a little girl of the neighbourhood ſtanding at the door:—' Ah! Mademoiſelle,'

moiselle,' exclaimed she, on seeing me, 'your mamma is taken very ill; she has been for my mother, who is gone up stairs with her to her apartment.' Struck with affright, I uttered a few inarticulate sounds: I ran, I flew into the room; and there I found my mother in an armed-chair, with her head fallen on her shoulder, her eyes wild, her mouth open, and her arms hanging down. On seeing me her countenance brightened; she endeavoured to speak, but her tongue could with difficulty utter a few half-formed words: she wished to say, that she was waiting for me with impatience; she made an effort to raise her arms; one only obeyed the impulse of her will; she laid her hand on my face, wiped away the tears that bedewed it with her fingers; tapped me gently on the cheek, as if to comfort me; an effort to smile appeared in her countenance; she tried to speak:— vain efforts! the palsy tied her tongue, sunk her head, and annihilated half her body. Neither Hungary water, nor salt put into her mouth, nor friction, produced any effect. In an instant I had dispatched messengers for my father, and the physician; I had darted like lightning myself to fetch two grains of tartar emetic from the next apothecary's. The physician came; my mother was put into bed; and medicines were administered: the disorder notwithstanding made a dreadful progress. Her eyes were closed; her head, sunk upon her chest, could no longer support itself; and her short and convul-

five breathing indicated a general oppreſſion of the whole body. She heard however what was ſaid, and, when aſked if ſhe felt much pain, pointed out the ſeat of her ſufferings by putting her left hand to her forehead. I was inexpreſſibly active; I ordered every thing, and had always done it myſelf before it could be done by any other perſon: I appeared not to quit her bed ſide, and yet I prepared for her every thing ſhe wanted. About ten o'clock in the evening I ſaw the phyſician take my father and two or three women aſide; I begged to know what he had propoſed; and was told that they had ſent for the extreme unction:—I thought it was all a dream. The prieſt came, began to pray, and performed a ceremony I did not underſtand, while I held a light to him, in obedience to a mere mechanical impulſe. Standing at the foot of the bed without anſwering, or giving way to thoſe who wiſhed to take my place, with my eyes fixed on my adored and dying mother, and entirely occupied by a ſingle ſentiment, which at length ſuſpended all my faculties, I let the candle drop out of my hand, and fell ſenſeleſs on the floor. I was carried off, and found myſelf, ſome time afterwards in the parlour adjoining to my bed-chamber, ſurrounded by the family. I turned my eyes towards, the door; I roſe from my ſeat; and finding myſelf held back, made ſuppliant geſtures to obtain permiſſion to return. A ſolemn ſilence, and a mournful but conſtant oppoſition, counteracted my deſire. I regained my ſtrength; I begged; I inſiſted;

lifted; but they were inexorable; and I broke out into a fort of rage. At that inftant my father walked into the room, pale and fpeechlefs with grief; and anfwered to the filent inquiry that every one feemed to make, by a look which drew forth a general exclamation of forrow. The confternation of thofe around me gave me an opportunity of getting away; I rufhed forth impetuoufly: my mother —fhe was no more! I lifted up her arms; I could not believe it: I opened and clofed alternately thofe eyes that were never to fee me again, and that were wont to rivet themfelves upon me with fuch endearing tendernefs: I called her; I threw myfelf upon her bed in a tranfport of grief; I preffed my lips to hers; I feparated them; I endeavoured to inhale death: I hoped to draw it in with my breath, and inftantly to expire. I know not well what followed; I only remember, that towards the morning I found myfelf at a neighbour's, whither M. Befnard came, who had me put into a carriage, and conveyed me to his houfe. We alighted; my great aunt embraced me in filence; fet me down at a little table; offered me fomething to drink, and entreated me to take it. I tried to gratify her, and fainted away. They put me to bed, and there I paffed a fortnight, between life and death, in the moft dreadful convulfions. The phyfical fenfation, which I remember, was that of a continual fuffocation; and my refpiration, as I was afterwards told, was a kind of howling, that was heard in the ſtreet: I had ſuffered a revolution, which my ſituation rendered ſtill more critical, and from which I was only ſaved by a ſtrong conſtitution, and by the boundleſs attentions that were laviſhed on me. My reſpectable relations removed their beds into little cloſets, to afford me a more comfortable lodging: they ſeemed to have aſſumed new vigour, in order to redeem me from the grave; and would not permit any thing to be offered me by a mercenary hand. They inſiſted upon waiting on me themſelves, and would only conſent to be aſſiſted by my couſin, a young woman of the name of Trude, who came every evening to paſs the night with me, lying in the ſame bed, and careful to anticipate and relieve the fits of convulſion with which I was frequently ſeized.

Eight days had elapſed, and I had not ſhed a tear: great ſorrows, alas! are not relieved ſo eaſily.— (The ſcalding drops, at this moment, are ſtreaming down my cheeks; for I dread an evil ſtill greater than what I ſuffer. All my hopes and wiſhes were centred in the ſafety of what I love; and its fate is become more uncertain than ever! Calamities ſpreading like a dark and dreadful cloud, are ready to envelope all that was dear to me; and I labour, with difficulty and pain, to divert my attention from the preſent, by obliging myſelf to retrace the paſt.)—

An epiſtle from Sophy came to open the ſource of my tears; the ſoothing voice and tender expreſſions of friendſhip recalled my faculties, and ſpoke

con-

confolation to my heart. They produced an effect, which the warm bath, and the medical art, had courted in vain: a new revolution took place; I wept, and was faved. The fuffocation diminifhed; all the dangerous fymptoms abated, and the convulfions became lefs frequent; but every painful impreffion was fure to bring on a fit.

My father prefented himfelf to me in the fad apparel, that teftified a lofs, common to us both, but unequally felt: he undertook to confole me, by reprefenting, that Providence difpofed every thing for the beft, even in our calamities; that my mother had fulfilled the tafk affigned her in this world, the education of her child; and that, fince heaven had decreed I fhould lofe one of my parents, it was better the one fhould remain who could be moft ufeful to my fortune. My lofs was certainly irreparable, even in that refpect, as the event fully proved; but I did not then make the reflection: I only felt the inefficiency of this pretended confolation, fo little adapted to my way of thinking; and meafured, perhaps, for the firft time, the diftance that feparated my father from myfelf. It feemed as if he was tearing away the reverential veil, under which I had hitherto confidered him: I found myfelf completely an orphan, fince my mother was gone, and my father could never underftand me: a new kind of grief oppreffed my afflicted heart: and I fell again into the deepeft defpair. The tears, however, of my
coufin,

coufin, and the forrow of my worthy relations, ftill offered me occafions of tender emotion; they had their effect, and I was fnatched from the dangers that threatened my exiftence. Why, alas! at that period did it not terminate? It was my firft affliction; by how many others has it been followed?

Here concludes the ferene and fplendid era of that tranquil life, paffed in peace and in the enjoyment of blifsful affections and beloved occupations, and refembling the beautiful mornings of fpring, when the ferenity of the fky, the purity of the air, the verdure of the foliage, and the fragrance of plants and flowers, enchant all animated nature, develope exiftence, and confer happinefs by promifing it.

END OF THE THIRD PART.

AN

APPEAL

TO

IMPARTIAL POSTERITY.

PART IV.

PART THE FOURTH.

PRIVATE MEMOIRS.

SECTION III.

Prifon of St. Pélagie,
Aug. 9, 1793.

MY mother was not more than fifty years of age when I was deprived of her in fo cruel a manner. An abfcefs in her head, which proceeded from an unknown caufe, and which was only difcovered by a difcharge from her nofe and ears that took place at her death, accounted for the ftrange obftruction of the refpiratory paffages, with which fhe had been fo long afflicted: but for this incidental difeafe, it is probable that the fecond ftroke of the palfy would not have been attended with fatal confequences. Her cheerful countenance and frefh complexion did not announce fo untimely a death; her ailments appeared to be thofe of a time of life which women feldom attain without fuffering a confiderable change of conftitution;

and

and the melancholy, and even the defpondency that I had remarked for fome time before, were fufficiently accounted for by moral caufes, of which I was but too well aware.

Our laft excurfions into the country feemed to have given her new life: the very day fhe was torn from me I had left her in good health at three in the afternoon: I returned at half paft five—the hand of death was already upon her, and at midnight fhe was no more. Poor playthings of unpitying fate! why are fentiments fo lively, and fuch momentous projects, attached to an exiftence fo frail?

Thus was fnatched from the world one of the beft and moft amiable women that ever inhabited it. Nothing brilliant rendered her remarkable, but every thing tended to endear her the moment fhe was known. Naturally wife and good, virtue did not feem to coft her any effort; fhe found means to render it amiable and gentle, like herfelf. Prudent, calm, and tender-hearted, without being fubject to any excefs of fenfibility, her pure and tranquil fpirit purfued its even courfe like the docile ftream that bathes with equal gentlenefs the foot of the rock which holds it captive, and the valley which at once it enriches and adorns. Her fudden death made me experience the moft heart-rending pangs, and moft violent tranfports of grief.

'It

'It is a good thing to poſſeſs ſenſibility; it is unfortunate to have ſo much of it,' ſaid, mournfully at my ſide, the Abbé Legrand, who came to ſee me at the houſe of my aged relations. When I began to recover, they haſtened to invite, and to receive in ſucceſſion, the different perſons with whom I was acquainted, on purpoſe to familiarize me with external objects. I ſeemed not to exiſt in that world where I was placed: abſorbed by my ſorrow, I ſcarcely perceived what was paſſing around me. I did not ſpeak, or, if I did, my replying to my own thoughts, inſtead of attending to thoſe of others, made me appear like a diſtracted creature. Then again the beloved image which was always preſent to my mind, recalling by ſtarts the dreadful idea of my loſs, ſudden ſhrieks eſcaped me, my outſtretched arms ſtiffened, and I fainted away.

Although incapable of any application, I had lucid intervals, in which I perceived the ſorrow of my relations, their affection, and the kind attentions of my couſin; and in which I tried all I could to diminiſh their anxiety. The Abbé Legrand poſſeſſed ſagacity enough to judge that it was neceſſary to talk to me a great deal concerning my mother, in order to render me capable of thinking of any thing elſe. Accordingly he converſed with me about her, and led me inſenſibly to reflections and ideas, which, without being foreign to the ſubject, baniſhed the habitual recollection of my loſs. As ſoon as he believed me ſufficiently recovered to look at a book, he conceived the idea of bringing me the Héloïfe of *Jean Jaques Rouffeau*; and the perufal of it was in truth the firft alleviation of my forrow. I was then twenty-one years of age: I had read a great deal; I was acquainted with a confiderable number of writers, hiftorians, learned men, and philofophers: but Rouffeau made an impreffion on my mind fimilar to that which Plutarch had done when I was eight years old. It appeared that this was the intellectual food that fuited me, and the interpreter of ideas which I entertained before; but which he alone had the art of explaining to my fatisfaction.

Plutarch had prepared me to become a republican; he had called forth that vigour and elevation of mind which conftitute the character; and had infpired me with a real enthufiafm in favour of freedom and of public virtue. Rouffeau pointed out the domeftic happinefs to which I had a right to afpire, and the ineffable enjoyments which I was capable of tafting. Ah! while able to put me more effectually upon my guard againft what is called an *indifcretion*, why was it not alfo in his power to protect me againft a ferious attachment? I brought into that corrupt world in which I was doomed to live, and into the revolution which I was then far from forefeeing, a mind ftored long beforehand with all that could render me capable of great facrifices, and expofe me to great misfortunes. Death will only be the period of both. I expect

expect it, and I should not have thought of filling up the short interval which separates us with the recital of my own story, if Calumny had not dragged me forward on the stage, on purpose to make a more cruel attack upon those whom she seeks to ruin. I take a pleasure in publishing truths that interest not myself alone; and am determined not to conceal a single fact, that their connexion may serve to give them demonstration.

I did not return to my father's without experiencing the sensations always inspired by the sight of those places which we have been accustomed to inhabit in company with friends who are no more. The ill-judged precaution of removing my mother's portrait had been taken, as if the vacancy were not more calculated than the picture itself to awaken a painful recollection of my loss. I instantly demanded it, and it was restored.

Domestic cares devolving entirely on me, I made them my occupation; but they were not very numerous in a family consisting of only three persons. I never could comprehend how the attention of a woman who possesses method and activity can be engrossed by them, let her household be as considerable as it may; for supposing it great, there is a great number of persons to take part of them off her hands; and nothing is wanting but a proper distribution of employments, and a small share of vigilance. In the different situations of the kind, in which I have found myself, nothing has ever been done but by my orders: and yet when thofe cares gave me the moft occupation, they fcarcely ever confumed more than two hours a day. People who know how to employ themfelves, always find leifure moments, while thofe who do nothing are in want of time for every thing. Befides, it is not furprifing that the women who pay or receive ufelefs vifits, or who think themfelves badly dreffed if they have not devoted a great deal of time to their toilet, fhould find the days long and tirefome, and at the fame time too fhort for the performance of their duties; but I have feen what are termed notable women rendered infupportable to the world, and even to their hufbands, by a fatiguing pre-occupation about their trifling concerns. I know nothing fo difgufting as this ridiculous conduct, nor fo well calculated to render a man attached to any other woman rather than to his wife. She muft, no doubt, appear to him a fit perfon for his houfekeeper; but is not likely to cure him of the defire of feeking more amiable accomplifhments elfewhere.

I think that a wife fhould keep the linen and clothes in order, or caufe them fo to be kept, fuckle her children, give directions concerning the cookery, or fuperintend it herfelf, but without faying a word about it, and with fuch a command of temper, and fuch a management of her time, as may leave her the means of talking of other matters, and of pleafing no lefs by her good humour, than by the graces natural

to

to her fex. I have already had occafion to remark, that it is nearly the fame in the government of ftates as of families. Thofe famous houfewives who are always expatiating on their labours, are fure either to leave much in arrears, or to render themfelves tirefome to every one around them; and in like manner thofe men in power, fo talkative and fo full of bufinefs, a only make mighty buftle about the difficulties they are in, becaufe too awkward and too ignorant to remove them.

My ftudies became dearer to me than ever, and conftituted my confolation. Left alone ftill more than ever, and often in a melancholy humour, I found myfelf under the neceffity of writing. I was fond of rendering an account of my own ideas to myfelf, and the intervention of my pen affifted me in putting them in order. When I did not employ it, I was rather loft in reveries than engaged in meditation; but with my pen I kept my imagination within bounds, and purfued a regular chain of reafoning. I had already begun to make fome collections, which I have fince augmented, and entitled, 'The Works of Leifure Hours, and various Reflections.' I had nothing further in view than to fix my opinions, and to have witneffes of my fentiments, when on fome future day I might confront them with one another, fo that their gradations or their changes might ferve me at once as a leffon and a record. I have a pretty large packet of thefe juvenile works piled up in the dufty corner of my library,

library, or perhaps in a garret. Never, however, did I feel the fmalleft temptation to become an author: I perceived at a very early period, that a woman who acquires the title lofes far more than fhe gains. She forfeits the affection of the male fex, and provokes the criticifm of her own. If her works be bad, fhe is ridiculed, and not without reafon; if good, her right to them is difputed; or if envy be forced to acknowledge the beft part to be her own, her character, her morals, her conduct, and her talents, are fcrutinized in fuch a manner that the reputation of her genius is fully counterbalanced by the publicity given to her defects.

Befides, my happinefs was my chief concern; and I never faw the public intermeddle with that of any one without marring it. I know nothing fo agreeable as to be rated at our full worth by the people with whom we live; nor any thing fo empty as the admiration of a few perfons whom we are never likely to meet again.

Ah, my God! what an injury was done me by thofe who took upon them to withdraw the veil under which I wifhed to lie concealed! During twelve years of my life I fhared in my hufband's labours as I participated in his repafts, becaufe one was as natural to me as the other. If any part of his works happened to be quoted, in which particular graces of ftyle were difcovered; or if a flattering reception was given to any of the academic trifles, that he took a pleafure in tranfmitting to the
learned

learned focieties, of which he was a member; I part took of his fatisfaction, without remarking that it was my own compofition; and not unfrequently he brought himfelf to believe that he had been in a happier difpofition than ufual when he had written a paffage, which in reality proceeded from *my* pen. If, during his adminiftration, an occafion occurred for the expreffion of great and ftriking truths, I poured forth my whole foul upon the paper; and it was but natural that its effufions fhould be preferable to the laborious teemings of a fecretary's brain. I loved my country; I was an enthufiaft in the caufe of liberty; I was unacquainted with any intereft or any paffions that could enter into competition with that enthufiafm; my language confequently could not but be pure and pathetic, as it was that of the heart and of truth.

I was fo taken up with the importance of my fubject, that I had not a thought to throw away upon myfelf. Once only I was diverted by a curious coincidence of circumftances: That was while writing to the pope, to claim the French artifts imprifoned at Rome. A letter to the pope, in the name of the Executive Council of France, fketched fecretly by the hand of a woman, in the humble clofet, which Marat was pleafed to term a *boudoir* *, appeared to me fo ftrange a thing, that I laughed heartily after

* A private apartment decked out with all the refinements of Afiatic luxury, and confecrated to voluptuoufnefs.—*Tranf.*

I had

I had finished it. The pleasure of those contracts consisted in their secrecy; but that was necessarily less attainable in a situation which was no longer that of a private individual, and where the eye of a clerk surveys the hand-writing he is copying. There is nothing singular however in all this, unless it be its novelty. Why should not a woman act as secretary to her husband without depriving him of any portion of his merit? It is well known that ministers cannot do every thing themselves; and surely, if the wives of those of the old government, or even of the new, had been capable of making draughts of letters, of official dispatches, or of proclamations, their time would have been better employed in so doing, than in soliciting and intriguing first for one *friend*, and then for another: the one excludes the other by the very nature of things. If those who found me out had formed a right judgment of things, they would have saved me from a sort of celebrity, to which I never aspired: instead of now spending my time in refuting falsehood, I should be reading a chapter of Montaigne, painting a flower, or playing an ariette; and should thus beguile the solitude of my prison, without sitting down to write my confession. But I am anticipating a period which I had not as yet attained; I remark it without constraint, as I have done it without scruple: since I am the person to be described, it is necessary that I should be exhibited with all my irregularities. I do not conduct

my

my pen, it carries me along with it wherever it pleafes, and I let it have its own way.

My father ferioufly endeavoured, in the early part of his widowhood, to remain more at home than hitherto; but he was attacked by *ennui*: and when once the love of his profeffion proved infufficient to prevent that diftemper of the mind, it was not at all furprifing that my efforts to cure it fhould be of no avail. I wifhed to converfe with him, but we had few ideas in common, and it is probable that he already inclined to a fpecies of difcourfe in which he would not have wifhed to fee me an adept. I often engaged him in a game of piquet, but a game of piquet with his daughter was hardly interefting enough to keep him awake; befides, he well knew that cards were my averfion, and in fpite of my defire to perfuade him that they afforded me entertainment, and in fpite of my endeavours *really* to relifh the pleafure of amufing him, he perfifted in confidering my playing as the mere effect of complaifance.

I could have wifhed to render his home agreeable to him; but the means were not in my power. My only acquaintances were my aged relations, whom we fometimes went to fee, but who never ftirred out of doors. It would have been well if he had formed a little fociety at home; but unfortunately, he had found one elfewhere, and was well aware of the impropriety of introducing fuch company to his daughter.—Was my mother really in the wrong in fecluding herfelf from the world,

world, and in not making her houfe gay enough to captivate her hufband? This would be blaming her on too flight grounds, and it would alfo be unjuft to confider my father as very reprehenfible on account of a few errors of which he himfelf became the victim.

There is fuch a connexion between the evils which neceffarily refult from a firft caufe, that it always behoves us to revert to that original mifchief to account for all the reft.

The legiflators of the prefent day endeavour to form a general good, whence the happinefs of each individual is to fpring; but I am greatly afraid that this is putting the cart before the horfe. It would be more conformable to nature, and perhaps to reafon, to ftudy well what conftitutes domeftic happinefs, and to enfure it to individuals in fuch a way that the common felicity fhould be compofed of that of each citizen, and that all fhould be interefted in preferving an order of things, to which fuch bleffings would be due. However fpecious the written principles of a conftitution may be, if I behold a portion of thofe who have adopted it immerfed in grief and tears, I fhall confider it as no better than a political monfter; and if thofe who do not weep, rejoice in the fufferings of the reft, I fhall fay that it is atrocious, and that its authors are either weak or wicked men.

In a marriage where the parties are ill-matched, the virtue of one of them may maintain order and peace ; but the want of happinefs will be experienced fooner or later, and produce inconveniencies more or lefs to be deplored. The fabric of fuch unions refembles the fyftem of our modern politicians—it is defective at the bafe, and fome day or other muft needs tumble to the ground, in fpite of the art employed in its conftruction.

The perfons whom my mother would have naturally collected around her, would have been fuch as refembled herfelf; and thefe would not have tallied with the temper of my father; while, on the other hand, thofe whom he would have wifhed to receive as daily vifitors, would not only have been difagreeable to my mother, but incompatible with the manner in which fhe wifhed to bring me up. It therefore behoved her to confine herfelf to her own family, and to cultivate only thofe flight connexions which produce an acquaintance without creating an intimacy.

Every thing went on well, while my father, with an agreeable profeffion and a young wife, found all the employment and all the pleafure that were neceffary to his happinefs within his own walls. But he was a year younger than my mother; fhe began early in life to experience infirmities; various circumftances combined to damp his ardour for labour; and the defire of getting rich made him embark in feveral hazardous enterprifes:—from that moment all was loft. The love of labour is the principal virtue of focial man; it is more particularly

larly that of an individual who does not poffefs a cultivated mind; the moment that his induftry flackens, danger is at hand; if it totally fubfide, he muft become the prey of unruly paffions, which are always the more fatal in proportion as he is lefs informed, becaufe he is confequently lefs able to keep them within bounds.

Become a widower at the very period when he ftood in need of new chains to attach him to his home, my poor father kept a miftrefs, that he might not prefent his daughter with a mother-in-law; he gamed, to indemnify himfelf for his lofs of bufinefs, and for his expences; and though ftill an honeft man, and ftill fearful of wronging any one, he contrived to ruin himfelf by infenfible degrees.

My relations, who were plain honeft people, little verfed in pecuniary matters, and who confided in my father's fondnefs for his daughter, had negle&ed to demand an inventory * at the death of his wife; my intereft appeared to be perfe&ly fafe in his hands; and they would have thought fuch a requeft an injury to his honour. *I* had reafon to think otherwife; but as I fhould have deemed it indecent to reveal my fufpicions, I looked forward to the event in filent refignation.

* In France there was generally a claufe in the marriage contract, by which the hufband engaged to preferve his wife's fortune, and all her *perfonal effects*, for her children, or to reftore them to her relations in cafe fhe left no iffue.—*Tranf.*

I was

I was now become sole mistress of the house, and divided my time between my domestic occupations and my studies, which I sometimes quitted to give answers to those who were vexed at finding my father so frequently from home. The number of his apprentices was reduced to two, who were nevertheless able to do all his business: one of them only boarded in the house.

Our servant, a little woman, fifty-five years of age, thin, alert, lively, and gay, was extremely attached to me, because I rendered her life comfortable. When I was unaccompanied by my father, she always attended me in my walks, which did not extend beyond the residence of my aged relations or the church. I had not been seized with a new fit of devotion; but what was no longer due to my mother's peace of mind, was still due to the good order of society, and to the edification of my fellow-creatures. Actuated by this principle, I carried with me to church, if not the tender piety of former days, at least as much decency, and the same air of attention. I did not indeed follow the priest in his recital of the service; but read some christian work. I still retained a great liking for St. Augustine; and assuredly there are fathers of the church, as well as others, whom a person may peruse without being a bigotted christian: there is food in them both for the heart and for the mind.

I wished to go through a course of preachers, living and dead, the eloquence of the pulpit being

of

of fuch a nature, as to enable great talents to difplay themfelves in all their fplendour. I had already read Boffuet and Flechier; I took a pleafure in reading them again with a more experienced eye, and made an acquaintance with Bourdaloue and Maffillon. It was highly whimfical to fee thofe pious perfonages marfhalled on my little fhelves in the fame line with *The Syftem of Nature*, Raynal, and De Pauw; but a thing ftill more fo was, that by dint of reading fermons, the whim took me of writing one myfelf. I was vexed at our preachers always recurring to myfteries; it feemed to me that they ought to have compofed moral difcourfes, in which the devil and the incarnation fhould have been left totally out of the queftion: I therefore took up my pen to try what work I could make of it, and wrote a fermon on *brotherly love*. It ferved to amufe my little uncle, who was become a canon of Vincennes, and who faid it was a pity that I had not thought of that fpecies of compofition at the time he was obliged to deliver difcourfes from the pulpit, as in that cafe he would certainly have made ufe of mine.

I had often heard the logic of Bourdaloue highly extolled: I ventured however in fome meafure to differ from his admirers, and actually wrote a criticifm on one of his moft efteemed difcourfes; but I fhewed it to no one. I was fond of rendering an account of my opinions to myfelf, without feeling the fmalleft wifh to make a difplay of my learning

before

before any perſon whatever. Maſſillon, leſs lofty than Bourdaloue, and far more affecting, obtained the tribute of my praiſe. I was not then acquainted with the Proteſtant preachers, among whom Blair in particular has cultivated with equal ſimplicity and elegance that kind of pulpit oratory, of which I conceived the exiſtence, and which I could have wiſhed to ſee in vogue.

As to the preachers of my own time, I heard the Abbé l'Enfant, towards the end of his beſt days: politeneſs and reaſon appeared to me his leading characteriſtics. Father Elizée was already out of faſhion, notwithſtanding his excellent logic and the purity of his diction: his mind was too metaphyſical, and his delivery too ſimple, to captivate the vulgar for any length of time.

Paris in thoſe days was a ſingular place: that common ſewer of all the impurities of the kingdom, was alſo the focus of taſte and knowledge: preacher or comedian, profeſſor or mountebank, whoever in ſhort poſſeſſed abilities, was ſure to find followers in his turn; but the firſt abilities in the univerſe could not long fix the public attention, for which novelty was always neceſſary, and which was attracted by noiſe no leſs than by merit. A certain Ex-Jeſuit, who was become a miſſionary, and made a parade of his going to court, ſucceeded by thoſe means in obtaining great popular applauſe. I went alſo to hear the Abbé de Beauregard: he was a little man, with a powerful voice, who declaimed with uncommon impudence, and with a vehemence equally extraordinary, retailing common-place obfervations in a tone of infpiration, and fupporting them by geftures fo terrible, that he perfuaded a great number of people they were the fineft things in the world. I did not then perceive, as experience has taught me fince, that men, affembled in great numbers, rather poffefs long ears than great judgment; that to aftonifh is to feduce them; and that whoever affumes the authority of commanding, difpofes them to obey; nor could I find utterance for my aftonifhment at the fuccefs of this perfonage, who was either a great fanatic, or a great rogue, or perhaps both. I had not fufficiently analyfed the circumftances accompanying the harangues delivered from the tribunes of the ancient republics; if I had, I fhould have formed a better judgment concerning the means of working upon the paffions of the people. But I fhall never forget a low fellow who ftood directly oppofite the pulpit in which Beauregard was acting the pofture-mafter, with his eyes fixed on the orator, his mouth open, and involuntarily expreffing his ftupid admiration in the three following words, which I perfectly recollect: ' How he fweats!' Such then are the means of impofing upon the ignorant! and how much was Phocion in the right, when, furprifed at finding himfelf applauded

plauded in an affembly of the people, he afked his friends, if he had not faid fome very foolifh thing?

What an admirable *clubbift* would this M. de Beauregard have made; and how many members of the popular focieties, in their enthufiafm for brazen-faced babblers, have recalled to my mind the expreffion of the man above mentioned: ' *How he fweats!*'

The danger I had been in had made fome noife; it fhould feem that it was confidered either as very uncommon, or very meritorious, in a young woman to endanger her own life by her exceffive forrow at her mother's death. I received many marks of regard on this occafion, which were extremely grateful to me. One of the firft who beftowed them was M. de Boifmorel, whom I had not feen fince his vifits to my grandmother. I perceived the impreffion made upon him by the change that had taken place in my perfon fince that period. He returned at a time when I was abfent, and held a long conference with my father, who no doubt mentioned my ftudies, and fhewed him the little apartment in which I paffed my time: he looked at my books; my *works* were upon the table; they excited his curiofity; and my father enabled him to gratify it, by putting them into his hands.

Great was my difpleafure and heavy were my complaints, when I found, on my return, that my afylum had been violated. My father indeed affured me that he should never have done such a thing for a person of less gravity, or less worthy of consideration, than M. de Boismorel: but all his reasoning could not reconcile me to a proceeding which was an attack at once upon liberty and property; it was disposing, without my consent, of that to which confidence alone could lay claim. But the mischief was already done, and the next day I received a very handsome letter from M. de Boismorel, couched in terms too flattering not to procure his pardon for having availed himself of my father's indiscretion, and making me an offer of every thing his library contained   I did not receive it with indifference; from that moment we commenced a correspondence, and for the first time in my life I enjoyed upon reflection, all the pleasure which sensibility and self-love make us feel when we find ourselves prized by those on whose judgment we set a value.

M. de Boismorel no longer resided within the walls of Paris; his partiality for the country, and his wish not to remove his mother to too great a distance from the capital, had made him purchase *Le Petit Bercy*, a charming house, situated a little below Charenton, and of which the garden extended to the banks of the Seine. He pressed us much to take it in our walks, and testified the strongest desire to receive us there. Recollecting the reception formerly given me by his mother, I did not feel inclined to encounter it again, and long

resisted

refifted my father's entreaties. He infifted however; and as I did not wifh to object to the little parties he fometimes took it in his head to propofe to me, we fet off one day for Bercy, and found the ladies of the Boifmorel family fitting together in the fummer parlour. The prefence of the daughter-in-law, whofe amiable difpofition I had heard highly extolled, infpired me all at once with that modeft affurance, which was neceffary to prevent any alteration from taking place in mine. The mother, whofe haughty tone my reader will remember, and to whom increafing years had brought no increafe of humility, behaved, notwithftanding, with much greater politenefs to a young woman who feemed fenfible of her own importance, than fhe had done to the child whom fhe confidered as utterly infignificant. What a fine girl your daughter is, M. Phlipon! Why, do you know that my fon is quite enchanted with her? Pray tell me, Mademoifelle, don't you think of getting a hufband?—There are people, Madam, who have already thought for me upon that fubject; but as to myfelf, I have not yet met with fufficient reafons to induce me to change my fituation.—Your are very difficult, I fancy! Pray, fhould you have any objection to a middle-aged man?—An acquaintance with the perfon could alone determine my confent, my repugnance, or my diflike.—Matches of that fort are generally productive of the moft lafting happinefs; a young man often goes aftray, even when we think him the moſt attached to us.—And why, mother, ſaid M. de Boiſmorel, who was juſt come into the room, would not you wiſh the young lady to believe herſelf capable of captivating him entirely?—She is dreſſed with a great deal of taſte, ſaid Madame de Boiſmorel to her daughter-in-law. —Ah! very well indeed, and with ſo much decency! replied the young woman, with that gentle tone of voice peculiar to devotees; for ſhe was of that deſcription, and the little wings of her cap brought forward over an agreeable face, that had ſeen thirty-four ſummers, were in the ſtyle of that religious character. How different, continued ſhe, from the paltry feathers of giddy-headed girls! You don't love feathers, do you, Mademoiſelle?— I never wear any, Madam, becauſe it ſeems to me that they would announce a condition in life, and a fortune, that do not belong to an artiſt's daughter going about on foot.—But would you wear them if you were in a different ſituation?—I do not know; I attach little importance to ſuch trifles. I only conſider what is ſuitable to myſelf, and ſhould be very ſorry to judge of others from the ſuperficial information afforded by their dreſs.

The anſwer was ſevere, but its point was blunted by the ſoft tone of voice in which it was pronounced. A philoſopher! ſaid the young lady, with a ſigh, as if ſhe had diſcovered that I was not one of her way of thinking.

After

After a fcrupulous examination of my perfon, mingled with a great number of fine things like thofe I have juft related, M. de Boifmorel put an end to the inventory of my charms, by propofing a vifit to the garden and the library. I admired the fituation of the former, where he made me remark a fine cedar of Lebanon; I viewed the library with an eye of intereft, and pointed out the books, and even the collections that I wifhed him to lend me; fuch, for inftance, as *Bayle*, and the tranfactions of the different academies of fciences. From the ladies we received an invitation to dinner on an appointed day, of which we availed ourfelves; and I foon perceived, by two or three men of bufinefs, who, with ourfelves, made up the whole of the guefts, that care had been taken to provide fit company for my father, without attending to *me*. But M. de Boifmorel had recourfe, as before, to the library and the garden, where the converfation took an agreeable turn. A part was borne in it by his fon, a young man of feventeen, fufficiently ugly, and of manners rather fingular than agreeable. Nor did the fine company which came in the evening, and on which I caft an eye of obfervation, appear to me very engaging, in fpite of their titles: the daughters of a marquis, learned counfellors, a prior, and feveral antiquated dowagers, talked with more importance, but quite as infipidly as grey fifters, church-wardens, and fober cits. Thefe glimpfes which I ftole of the great world, difgufted me with it, and attached me more than ever to my own way of life. M. de Boifmorel did not lofe the opportunity, of keeping up a connexion, on which, perhaps, he grounded fome project for the future: he fo managed matters, that the two fathers and the two children formed a diftinct party. It was in this manner alfo that he carried me to the public affembly of the French academy, on the next anniverfary of St. Louis. Thefe affemblies were, at that time, the refort of the beft company, and exhibited all thofe ridiculous contrafts, which our manners and our follies could not fail to produce. On the morning of St. Louis's day, high mafs was chaunted in the chapel of the academy by the fingers of the Opera, after which a fafhionable preacher pronounced a panegyric on the fainted king. The Abbé de Befplas performed the office; and I liftened to him with great pleafure, notwithftanding the fubject was trite; for his difcourfe was interfperfed with bold traits of philofophy, and indirect fatire on the court, which he was obliged to cancel before he fent his fermon to the prefs.

M. de Boifmorel, who was acquainted with him, was in hopes of obtaining a faithful copy, which he might communicate to me; but the Abbé de Befplas, who was attached to the court, in quality of chaplain to *Monfieur*, thought himfelf very fortunate in purchafing a pardon for his audacity by the entire facrifice of the paffages it had infpired. In the evening, the fitting of the academy opened a fine

field

field for the firſt wits in the kingdom, by virtue of the feats they occupied; for the noblemen, who were proud of ſeeing their names infcribed on the liſt of members, and of exhibiting themſelves in their arm-chairs; for the *amateurs*, who came to liſten to the former, to gaze upon the latter, and to ſhew themſelves to the whole aſſembly; and for the pretty women, who were ſure of attracting their attention.

I took particular notice of *D'Alembert*, whoſe name, *Miſcellanies*, and writings on the *Encyclopedia*, excited my curioſity; his little face, and ſqueaking voice, made me think a philoſopher's works better worth contemplation than his perſon. The Abbé de Lille confirmed my remark as to men of letters, by reciting the moſt charming verſes in the moſt diſagreeable tone. The panegyric of *Catinat*, by Laharpe, bore away the prize, and was highly deſerving of its ſucceſs.

As free from affectation at the academy as at church, and as I have ever remained at the theatre, I bore no part in the noiſy applauſe beſtowed, with rapture, upon the moſt ſtriking paſſages, and not unfrequently with oſtentation on thoſe which every one wiſhed to have the credit of remarking. I was exceedingly attentive, liſtening without paying any regard to the obſervers; and when I was moved, I wept without even fuſpecting that my doing ſo would appear ſingular to any one. I had reaſon however to perceive that it was a

novelty;

novelty; for, on the breaking up of the affembly, while M. de Boifmorel was conducting me to the door, I faw feveral perfons pointing me out to one another with a fmile, which I was not vain enough to take for admiration, but in which there was nothing that indicated contempt; and I heard them faying fomething about my fenfibility. I experienced a mixed fentiment of furprife and agreeable confufion, which I cannot defcribe; and was very happy when I was at laft able to efcape from their fight, and from the crowd.

The panegyric of Catinat fuggefted to M. de Boifmorel the idea of an interefting pilgrimage. He propofed to me to pay a vifit to St. Gratien, where that great man ended his days in retirement, far from honours and the court. It was an excurfion perfectly fuited to my tafte. M. de Boifmorel came one Michaelmas day, with his fon, to call on my father and myfelf; and we all repaired together to the banks of the lake which embellifhes the valley of Montmorency. From the lake we proceeded to St. Gratien, and refted ourfelves in the fhade of the trees which Catinat planted with his own hands; and then, after a frugal dinner, returned to pafs the reft of the day in the delightful park of Montmorency, where we faw the little houfe that *Jean Jaques* * had inhabited, and enjoyed all the pleafure afforded by a beautiful country to

* Rouffeau.

feveral

several persons who contemplate it with the same eye. After one of those moments of repose, in which we consider the majesty of nature in silence, M. de Boismorel took a paper, in his own hand-writing, out of his pocket, and read to us an anecdote which he had copied, and which was then but little known. It was the trait of Montesquieu, when discovered at Marseilles by a young man whose father he had redeemed from slavery, endeavouring to escape from the thanks of those whom he had obliged.

Deeply impressed with a sense of Montesquieu's generosity, I did not exclusively admire his obstinacy in denying that he was the adored deliverer of a family transported with joy: the generous man does not look for acknowledgments; but however noble it may be to decline the testimonies of gratitude, it is not less the part of a great mind to receive its effusions. I even think it is a new obligation conferred on people of sensibility, to whom we have been of service; for it is to them a way of discharging their debt.

It must not, however, be supposed, that I was perfectly at my ease in regard to these frequent meetings of my father and M. de Boismorel: I saw with sorrow that there were no points of resemblance between them. His son looked at me a great deal; and did not please me at all. I thought that his manner rather indicated curiosity than affection; besides, the three or four years between his age and mine, placed us at a considerable distance

from

from each other. All this his father perceived, and I was afterwards told that he had one day faid to mine, with an affectionate fqueeze of the hand: Ah! if my child were but worthy of yours: I might appear fingular, but I fhould efteem myfelf one of the happieft of mankind!—I had no fufpicion of any thing of the fort: I did not even calculate the diftance between us; but I felt it, and it prevented any fuch idea from rifing in my mind. I looked upon M. de Boifmorel's conduct as that of a prudent and benevolent man, who honoured my fex, felt particular efteem for *me*, and, if I may ufe the expreffion, protected my inclinations. His correfpondence refembled him; its leading feature was a gentle gravity, and it bore the ftamp of refpectful friendfhip, and of a mind exalted above prejudices. By his means I became acquainted with what were called the *novelties (les nouveautés)* of the learned and literary world. I feldom faw him, but I heard from him every week. To prevent the frequency of meffages by his fervants to me, as well as to fave me the expence of carriage from Bercy, he ordered the books intended for my perufal to be left with the porter of his fifter, Madame de Favieres, whither I ufed to fend and fetch them. M. de Boifmorel, who had a great refpect for the republic of letters, and who fancied, in confequence of his prepoffeffion in my favour, that I might be ufefully employed in its fervice, or elfe was defirous of putting me to a trial, advifed me to choofe

the

the line of literature that suited me, and to sit down seriously to write. At first I took it for a compliment; but by returning to the advice, he gave me an opportunity of setting forth my principles on that subject, my well-founded aversion to coming forward in any manner on the theatre of the world, and my disinterested love of study, which I wished to make instrumental to my happiness, without aiming at any kind of fame that might tend to disturb it. After having seriously exhibited my doctrine, I changed the reasoning into verses, which flowed spontaneously from my pen, and of which the ideas were superior to the poetry. I recollect, that when speaking of the *gods*, and the way in which they have distributed our duties and rewards, I expressed myself thus:

> To man's aspiring sex 'tis given
>   To climb the highest hill of fame,
> To tread the shortest road to heaven,
>   To gain, by death, a deathless name.
>
> Of well-fought fields, and trophies won,
>   The mem'ry lives while ages pass,
> Extant in everlasting stone,
>   Or written on retentive brass.
>
> But to poor feeble woman-kind
>   The meed of glory is denied:
> Within a narrow sphere confin'd,
>   The lowly virtues are their pride:

Yet not deciduous is their fame,
Ending where frail exiftence ends :
A facred temple holds their name—
The bofom of furviving friends *.

M. de Boifmorel anfwered me fometimes in fimilar language, and in verfes fcarcely better than my own; but neither he nor I attached the fmalleft importance to our poetical effufions. One day he came to confult me concerning the means of reviving his fon's application to his ftudies, which of late had fuffered confiderable diminution.

That young man was naturally intimate with his contemporary, and firft coufin, M. de Favieres, a counfellor in parliament at the age of twenty-one, who joined to the ufual giddinefs of youth, all the confidence of a magiftrate, proud of his gown, without attending to his duties; and all the freedom of manners, perhaps even the licentioufnefs, of an only fon born to a confiderable eftate.

* *Aux hommes ouvrant la carrière*
Des grands et des nobles talents,
Ils n'ont mis aucune barrière
A leur plus fublimes élans.
De mon fexe foible et fenfible,
Ils ne veulent que des vertus;
Nous pouvons imiter Titus,
Mais dans un fentier moins penible.
Jouiffez d'être admis à toutes ces fortes de gloires;
Pour nous le temple de Mémoire
Eft dans les cœurs de nos amis.

The

The Italian theatre and the Opera employed the two coufins much more than *Cujas* and *Bartole* did the one, or the mathematics the other. I muft requeft you, faid M. de Boifmorel, to write a fevere letter to my fon, in terms fenfible and impreffive, fuch as your mind cannot fail to fuggeft, and fuch as may ferve to awaken his felf-love, and infpire him with generous refolutions.—Who, *I*, Sir ! Do you mean *me ?* (I could fcarcely believe my ears.) With what face, pray, can I preach to your fon? —You may adopt any mode you pleafe, with the certainty that your name fhall remain concealed. We will have the letter conveyed as if it came from a perfon who is in the habit of feeing him, who is acquainted with his proceedings, and who warns him of the danger that awaits his fteps. I will take care to have it delivered at a moment when it is likely to have its full effect : I only wifh him not to fufpect me of any hand in the bufinefs ; and in due time will let him know to what phyfician he is indebted for his cure.—Oh ! be fure you never mention my name !—but you certainly have friends who could do this better than I.—I think otherwife, and requeft it of you as a favour.— Well, then, I will lay afide my fcruples, to prove to you my defire to oblige ; and will make a rough draught, of which you fhall give me your opinion, and which I will beg you to correct.

That very evening I wrote a very pointed, and fomewhat ironical letter ; fuch as I conceived calculated to flatter the vanity, and to excite the thinking

thinking faculty of a youth, to whom it is neceſſary to talk of his advantages when you wiſh to recall him to ſerious occupations. M. de Boiſmorel was delighted, and begged me to forward it without altering a word. I ſent it to Sophia, requeſting her to put it into the poſt-office at Amiens, and waited with no ſmall degree of impatience to know what effect my ſermon would produce.

M. de Boiſmorel ſoon wrote me an epiſtle containing particulars which intereſted me exceedingly: he had brought together a number of circumſtances which rendered the thing infinitely ſtriking: the young man was affected; and fancying that the celebrated Duclos was the author of the remonſtrance, went to return him thanks: deceived in this conjecture, he next addreſſed himſelf to another of his father's friends, and found that he was not at all nearer the mark. Study, however, in ſome degree reſumed her reign.

It was not long after this tranſaction that M. de Boiſmorel, going with his ſon from Bercy to Vincennes, where he knew I was on a viſit to my uncle, and whither he was bringing me the *Georgics*, tranſlated by the Abbé Delille, was ſtruck by a *coup-de-ſoleil*. He made very light of it; but was ſoon after taken ill with a headach, firſt followed by a fever, and then by a lethargy; and died in the meridian of life, after an illneſs of a few days. Scarcely eighteen months had elapſed ſince we commenced our correſpondence: I grieved for his death, I believe, more ſincerely than his own ſon;

nor

nor does his image ever revert to my mind without my feeling that painful regret, and that sentiment of veneration and concern, which accompany the remembrance of a virtuous man.

When my sorrow was a little allayed, I celebrated his memory in a monody, which no one ever saw, which I sung to my guitar, and which I have since forgotten, and lost. I never heard any thing farther of his family, unless that one day, when my father went to pay an occasional visit, the young de Boismorel, who then bore the name of Roberge, told him in a very cavalier manner, that he had found my letters to his father, and thrown them by in a corner, in order to return them if required; and that among them he had discovered the original of a certain epistle which he himself had formerly received. My father, who was well acquainted with all that had passed, and who made him little or no answer, perceived the young man was piqued; whence I concluded that he was a blockhead, and gave myself no further concern about him: I do not know whether I guessed aright.

Some time after, Madam de Favieres came to my father to employ him in the purchase of some jewels, or in the execution of some work. I happened to be in my little cell, and could overhear all that was passing in the next room. 'Your daughter is a charming girl, Monsieur Phlipon: my brother used to say that she was one of the most sensible women he ever met with in his life; take care, however, that she does not set up for a wit: that would be very shocking indeed. Does she not, do you think, seem a little of the pedant? 'Tis to be apprehended; and, if I mistake not, I have heard something of the kind. She is a pretty-faced girl: a very good-looking girl indeed.' Upon my word, said I to myself, this is a very impertinent fine lady, and very like her mother: heaven defend me from ever seeing her face, or shewing her mine!

My father, who knew very well I was within hearing, did not think proper to call me, since I did not choose to shew myself; nor from that day to the present have I ever heard the voice of Madam de Favieres.

Hitherto I have scarcely mentioned my excellent cousin Trude. She was one of those kind souls, which heaven in its goodness formed for the honour of the human race, and the consolation of the unfortunate. Generous by nature, and amiable without art, I could never perceive any objection to her, but an excess of delicacy and virtuous pride. She would have thought herself defective in her duties, if she had left room to doubt her having fulfilled them. That was precisely the way to become completely the victim of a whimsical husband. Trude was a rustic, his ideas as extravagant as his temper was impetuous, and his behaviour brutal. He was engaged in the looking-glass trade, as all the Trudes have been, in regular succession, for

several

several generations. Of an active difpofition, laborious by fits, and affifted by the care and intelligence of an agreeable and prudent woman, he fucceeded tolerably in bufinefs, and was indebted to his wife's merit for the kind countenance fhewn him by his own family, who would have flighted him had he remained a fingle man.

My mother was very fond of her little coufin, who held her in fingular veneration, and was ftrongly attached to me.

She proved it, as my reader has already feen, on the death of my mother: taken up in the day with her houfehold affairs, and her hufband, fhe infifted upon being my nurfe during the night. She came from a confiderable diftance to perform the duties of a nurfe; nor had I any other as long as I continued in danger. That circumftance naturally increafed our intimacy, and we faw each other frequently. Her hufband took it in his head to come ftill more frequently, unaccompanied by his wife. At firft I bore with him on her account, in fpite of his tirefome converfation; but at length he became infupportable, and I made ufe of all the management neceffary with a wrong-headed man, to make him perceive that neither his quality of kinfman, nor that of hufband to my much-beloved friend, could authorize fuch frequent vifits, which would at any rate have been improper in the fickly and fuffering ftate to which my forrow had reduced me.

My dear cousin came less frequently, but he made tedious visits of three or four hours, notwithstanding my employing myself constantly, and even writing, to make him understand that I was in haste; and when I begged him in plain terms to retire, as I was at last forced to do, he went home in such a humour, and behaved so ill to his wife, that she entreated me to exert my patience for the sake of her domestic peace. On Sundays and holydays particularly, I was doomed to do penance: when the weather was fine I escaped, and appointed a meeting with his wife at the house of my aged relations; since the receiving her at home for a short time in his company, was not feeing her, but being a witness to the brutal behaviour of her surly husband. In the winter I managed another way: I gave a holyday to the maid, who locked, barred, and bolted every door; and I remained alone and quiet till eight o'clock at night. Trude came; could make nobody hear, came again, and sometimes walked for two or three hours round the house in the snow or rain, waiting for the moment of admission. To conceal myself when I was really there in company with any one, was almost impossible; and positively to forbid him the house by prevailing on my father to break off all connexion with this curious personage (which would have been difficult, because he had no children, and my father thought it prudent to preserve his good opinion), would have been coming to that

extremity

extremity which his wife dreaded, would have put an end to our intimacy, and would have expofed her to further afflictions.

I know nothing worfe than to have connexions with a madman: there is no way of dealing with him but by means of a ftrait waiftcoat; every thing elfe is of no avail. This brutal coufin was a plague to me, and I know nothing that can better prove the merit of his wife, than my refraining from having him thrown out of the window; but he would have returned by the chimney. To do him juftice, however, Trude was not without a certain fort of politenefs—rather a madman than a fool, he gave reafon to fuppofe he knew how far he could carry his extravagance with impunity; for his coarfe converfation was never indecent; and though for ever at variance with good-breeding and rationality, he never offended againft modefty, or wounded the moft delicate ear. When his wife was walking with me he watched us, and if we were accofted or faluted by any man, he became uneafy and furious till he found who it was. It will be imagined, perhaps, he was jealous of his wife, and that was in fome degree true; but he was ten times more fo on my account. In fpite of fo tormenting a life, Madam Trude's gentlenefs was not unaccompanied by gaiety; and fhe would pafs one day in weeping, and the next in making merry with her friends.

It was her cuftom to give family entertainments, which were followed by a dance, once or twice during the winter feafon. Her coufin was always the heroine of the feftival, and her hufband was more amiable than ufual for feveral days afterwards. At her houfe I became acquainted with two perfons whom I will mention here: one was the Abbé Bexon, a little witty hump-backed man, the great friend of François de Neufchâteau, and of Maffon de Marvilliers, and author of a hiftory of Loraine, that had but indifferent fuccefs. The celebrated Buffon fometimes employed his pen, as well as that of feveral others, to prepare materials and fketches, which he afterwards beautified by the vivid tints fupplied by his brilliant imagination. Bexon, affifted by the intereft of his protector Buffon, and by that of feveral women of quality, whofe relations he had known at Remiremont, his native place, where there was a chapter of noble canoneffes, became precentor of the holy chapel at Paris. He brought thither his mother and fifter, who would furnifh matter for an epifode, if I were inclined to introduce any not neceffarily connected with my fubject.

The poor creature died too foon for the happinefs of his tall fifter, with black eyes begging for adorers, and with beautiful fhoulders of which fhe was fond of making a difplay. He came twice to fee me at my father's, and was fo tranfported at finding Xenophon

nophon in folio on my table, that in the height of his ecftacy he would have kiffed me. But as in *my* opinion there was no good reafon for it, I calmed him fo effectually by my referve, that his wit ever after was unattended by raptures, nor did I fee him more, unlefs at my coufin's houfe.

The other perfon was the worthy Gibert; rigid in his morality, and infinitely gentle in his manners, he married at a very early age, a woman whofe beauty was greater than her good temper, and had a fon by her whofe education was his chief delight. He had an employ in the adminiftration of the poft-office, and devoted his leifure moments to painting and mufic.

Gibert had about him all the marks of a juft and fincere man; nor was his conduct ever at variance with them. His faults were thofe of his judgment: his friendfhip was a fort of fanaticifm; and we were tempted, while we lamented, to refpect his errors. Gibert had been connected from his infancy with a man for whom he profeffed equal veneration and attachment, in whofe praife he was loud upon every occafion, and of whofe friendfhip he was proud. Gibert was defirous of being acquainted with me; his wife and he came to my father's; I returned their vifit, and as they did not go out much together, he came alone from time to time to repeat his vifit. I always received him with particular pleafure, and in time we formed a connexion of a truly friendly nature.

ture. Gibert foon began to fpeak to me of his phœnix: it feemed as if he could not be happy till his friend and I had an opportunity of admiring each other; and at laft he invited him to meet me at dinner at his houfe. I met a man whofe extreme fimplicity bordered upon negligence. Speaking little, and never looking another in the face, it would have been difficult for one, who had never heard him mentioned, to form an opinion of him from a fingle interview; and I confefs, notwithftanding my particular tafte for modeft demeanour, I fhould willingly have taken him at his word in regard to his own importance. However, as he neither wanted fenfe nor information, people gave him the greater credit, whenever he happened to bring them to view; and, like Gibert, fuppofed him to have more than he actually poffeffed. His wife, who was rather infignificant, but by no means deftitute of fenfibility, brought to mind the *intentique ora tenebant* of Virgil, whenever her hufband opened his mouth to fpeak. He cannot, however, be a man altogether of a vulgar mind, who thus finds means to impofe, even upon thofe who fee him daily, in regard to his real merit: he muft be great in fomething; at leaft in diffimulation; and if circumftances induce him to carry it as far as poffible in important affairs, inftead of the falfe philofopher obtaining undeferved efteem, he may become a villain at the expence of his fellow-creatures. Hiftory will enable

able us to judge of him by the fequel. I feldom faw this friend of Gibert. He abandoned a lucrative place, and France itfelf, in order to fettle in Switzerland, whither liberty called him, and whither he was led by his tafte for a country life. Let him depart in peace: he will return too foon.—That was the manner in which I became acquainted with PACHE; for *Pache* was the man. My readers will fee how Gibert brought him to our houfe, ten years after, and introduced him to my hufband, who thought him probity itfelf; mentioned him at a moment when his fuffrage was fufficient to eftablifh a man's reputation; and was the caufe of his coming into adminiftration, where he diftinguifhed himfelf by nothing but follies, which procured him his removal to the mayoralty, where he authorized nothing but atrocities.

Madam Trude was extremely defirous of taking a journey, in order to vifit a relation to whom fhe was much attached, and propofed being abfent a fortnight or three weeks. Her hufband objected to his *counter*'s remaining fo long without its feminine ornament; but thought the thing feafible, provided I would confent to come now and then in the middle of the day to take her place. My coufin wifhed I would have the kindnefs to do fo: her intimating fo much, was quite enough to induce me not to refufe her; and my friendfhip made me willingly undertake the tafk. I went feven or eight times

to

to take Madam Trude's place behind the counter. Her hufband, highly delighted, and not a little proud, conducted himfelf with great propriety, attended to the external bufinefs, and feemed fenfible of the kindnefs of my behaviour. It was decreed, that at one time in my life, and in fpite of my averfion to trade, I fhould fell watch-glaffes and fpectacles. The fituation was not agreeable. Trude lived in the *Rue Montmartre*, near the *Rue Ticquetonne*, where his fucceffor muft now refide: I can conceive nothing fo dreadful as the noife of the carriages eternally rolling along, to a perfon ftanding in an open fhop. I fhould foon have grown deaf, as my poor coufin now is.—Let us quit this unfortunate couple, whofe fate we fhall fee hereafter, and return to my other relation.

I went to Mademoifelle Defportes' once or twice a week, on the days fhe was in the habit of receiving company; and fine portraits I fhould have to paint if the originals were worth the pains; but were I to pourtray counfellors of the *Châtelet*, like little *Mopinot*, whofe pretenfions to wit were grounded on epigrams; the bigotted *de la Prefle*, who had no other fault than that of being choleric, and a Janfenift; a widow who hid a love of pleafure under the mafk of commodious devotion, like Madam *de Blancfuné*; an old and rich bachelor, too difgufting to be named; a worthy man inceffantly *reafoning*, and as regular as clock-work, like Baudin,

Baudin, the cuftom-houfe officer; and a multitude of other individuals of different complexions, but of no greater value; it would only be throwing away my colours, and my time. I fhould like, however, to meet Father Rabbe, a very fhrewd Oratorian *, rendered refpectable by his age, and agreeable by his highly cultivated mind; and with Doctor *Cofte*, who amufed himfelf by imitating Perrault, without erecting a *Louvre*, and who fpoke ill of matrimony, as the Devil makes grimaces at holy water.

Mademoifelle Defportes had inherited from her mother much delicacy and pride, joined to the art of employing her little fortune in commerce, without appearing to have any concern in it, and of dealing on a footing of confidence and equality with the rich and titled individuals who bought her goods. But as fuch a mode of tranfacting bufinefs is quite foreign to the fpirit of trade, which fupports itfelf by active fpeculations, fhe found her little inheritance growing fmaller every day, and at laft bad adieu to commerce, reducing her expences at the fame time on a more moderate fcale.

Her difpofition, her manners, the fober way in which fhe lived, and the fondnefs fhe teftified for me, had made my mother wifh to fee me cultivate her acquaintance. Accordingly fhe often fent me

* The Oratorians were an order of monks.—*Tranf.*

to her houfe. A party of piquet was the rallying-point of the fociety, the other members of which either chatted or worked. Mademoifelle Defportes, probably with a view of exercifing my complaifance, often fet me down to play, which was my averfion; but the affiftance of a partner*, and permiffion to laugh at my own abfence of mind, rendered the trial of my patience lefs fevere.

Here, in his turn, I cannot help bringing forward on the ftage an old man lately arrived from Pondicherry, and with whom I kept up a frequent and agreeable intercourfe for little lefs than a year. My father, fome how or other (in the way of bufinefs I believe), had become acquainted with a reduced officer, metamorphofed into a clerk without a place, and had afterwards received him on the footing of a friend. His name was Demontchery. He was about fix and thirty, of polifhed manners and infinuating converfation, and was poffeffed of thofe graces which are derived from a knowledge of the world, and perhaps from tender connexions with the fair. Demontchery was attentive to my father; but feldom came into my mother's apartment, who would not have fuffered any man to pay his court to her. As to me, he frankly profeffed refpect, efteem, and fo forth, as well as an inclination to offer me his

* Four-handed piquet is played very commonly in France.—*Tranf.*

heart

heart if fortune fhould prove more kind—She fent him on a voyage to the Eaft Indies. He wrote to us, and did not conceal his wifhes for fuch fuccefs as might enable him to return with well-founded pretenfions; but being no more than a captain of fepoys, and too honourable a man to underftand any thing about making money, he had not, I believe, got very forward in the world, when he returned after feven years abfence, and learned that my hand had been difpofed of a fortnight before. I know not what is become of him, nor the fentiments he might have infpired me with, if my inclinations had been free. During his ftay at Pondicherry, he made acquaintance with M. de Sainte-Lette, one of the members of the council, and intrufted him with letters for my father, when the council difpatched Sainte-Lette to Paris, in 1776, to conduct fome important affair.

Sainte-Lette was more than fixty years of age. He was a man whom a gay turn of mind, and ftrong paffions, had led aftray in his youth, when he fquandered his fortune at Paris. He had gone over to America, and had remained thirteen years at Louifiana, as director of the Indian trade. Having afterwards removed to Afia, he was employed in the adminiftration of public affairs at Pondi cherry, and was endeavouring to amafs the means of living or of dying in France, on fome future day, with M. de Sevelinge, the friend of his youth,

of

of whom I shall hereafter make some mention. A grave and solemn voice, distinguished by that accent which is derived from experience and adversity, and supported by the ready expression of a cultivated mind, struck me in Sainte-Lette, the first moment I heard him speak. Demontchery had spoken to him of me; and probably made him desire our acquaintance. My father was civil; and I paid him much attention, because he soon prepossessed me in his favour. I found his company very agreeable; he was fond of mine, and during his stay, never suffered a week to pass without paying me a visit.

Persons who have seen a great deal, are always worth hearing, and those who have felt a great deal, have always seen more than any other persons, even when they have travelled less than Sainte-Lette. He had more of that kind of information which is derived from experience, than of that which is collected from books: with less pretensions to the title of a learned man, than to that of a philosopher, he reasoned from his knowledge of the human heart; and still retained a taste for the lighter kinds of poetry, in which he was no mean proficient. He gave me some of his productions; and I communicated to him in return some of my *reveries*.—'Mademoiselle,' said he repeatedly, in the tone of prophecy, or in that of conviction, ' you may do what you will to avoid it; but you

will

will certainly write a book.'—' It fhall be under another name then,' anfwered I, ' for I would fooner cut off my fingers than turn author.'

At my father's Sainte-Lette met a perfon with whom I was become acquainted a few months before, and who was fated to have a powerful influence over my future fortune, though I little thought fo at the time: I have already faid that Sophy, more taken up than I with paying and receiving vifits, was far from finding it conducive to her advantage. She had fpoken to me feveral times of a man of great merit, who had a place at Amiens, and was frequently at her mother's, while refident there; which, however, was not generally the cafe, becaufe he vifited Paris every winter, and in the fummer often made long journies. She had only mentioned him, becaufe in the infignificant crowd with which fhe was furrounded, fhe was pleafed to meet with an individual whofe inftructive converfation always feemed to contain fomething new, whofe auftere, but fimple manners, infpired confidence, and who was univerfally efteemed, though not univerfally beloved, becaufe his feverity, which bordered on the farcaftic, gave many people offence. Sophy had fpoken to him alfo of her beloved friend. Nothing indeed was talked of in her family but the intimacy and conftancy of a convent connexion, which acquired a certain degree of refpectability from time. He had alfo feen my portrait, which Madam Cannet

net had hung up in a confpicuous fituation. ' Why then,' he ufed to fay, ' do you not make me acquainted with this amiable friend? I go every year to Paris —Shall I never have a letter to deliver to her?' He obtained the commiffion he defired in the month of December 1775 : I was then in mourning for my mother, and in that ftate of tender melancholy, which follows violent grief. Whoever came on the part of Sophy, was fure of a good reception. ' You will receive this,' faid my beloved friend in her letter, ' from the hands of M. Roland de la Platiere, the philofopher you have fometimes heard me mention—an enlightened man, of fpotlefs reputation, who can be reproached with nothing but his too great admiration for the ancients, at the expence of the moderns, whom he undervalues, and with being too fond of fpeaking of himfelf.' This portrait can hardly be called a fketch; but the outline is well drawn. I found him a man confiderably turned of forty; tall, and negligent in his carriage, with that ftiffnefs which is often contracted by ftudy; but his manners were eafy and fimple, and without poffeffing the fafhionable graces, he combined the politenefs of a well-bred man, with the gravity of a philofopher. Want of flefh, a complexion accidentally yellow, and a forehead very high, and very thinly covered with hair, did not deftroy the effect of a regular fet of features, though it rendered them rather refpectable than engaging. There was befides great meaning in his

fmile;

smile; and a moſt lively expreſſion uſed to light up his countenance, and give him, as it were, a new face, whenever he grew animated in narration, or when any agreeable idea came acroſs his mind. His voice was maſculine, and his ſentences were ſhort (like thoſe of a man afflicted with a difficulty of breathing) : his converſation, which was full of intereſting matter, becauſe his head was full of ideas, occupied the mind more than it pleaſed the ear, his language, though ſometimes impreſſive, being always monotonous and harſh. An agreeable voice is, in my opinion, a very uncommon and very powerful accompliſhment: it does not depend upon the quality of the ſound alone; but reſults alſo from that delicacy of ſentiment which furniſhes a variety of expreſſion, and of tone.

(I am interrupted, in order to be told that I am included in the indictment of Briſſot, with other members recently apprehended. The tyrants are at bay: they think they ſhall be able to fill up the abyſs beneath their feet with the bodies of their virtuous adverſaries; but they will fall in afterwards themſelves. I am not diſmayed at being ſent to the ſcaffold in ſuch company; it is indeed diſgraceful to live among villains.

I am going to diſpatch this ſheet as it is. It will be only beginning a new one, in caſe I ſhould have it in my power.

Friday, October 4, the birth-day of my daughter, who is entering her thirteenth year).

This effect of the organ of speech, a thing very different from a strong voice, is not more common among professional orators, than among the multitudes that compose our social circles. I looked for it in the three national assemblies, and could meet with nobody possessed of it in perfection. Mirabeau himself, with the commanding magic of a noble delivery, neither spoke in a pleasing key, nor pronounced in the most agreeable manner. The Clermonts came nearer to the mark—Where then, I may be asked, is your model? I might answer like the painter, when asked whence he took the charming air, that he gave to the heads created by his pencil?—Hence, said he, putting his finger to his forehead—I should put mine to my ears. I was never a great frequenter of the theatre; but I thought I could perceive that the kind of merit in question was equally uncommon there. *Larive*, the only one perhaps who deserves to be mentioned, did not come entirely up to my idea.

When upon entering the period of adolescence, I experienced that agitation which the desire of pleasing produces in the bosom of young women, I was moved at the sound of my own voice, and was obliged to modulate it in order to please myself. I can easily conceive that the exquisite sensibility of the Greeks made them set a high value upon every part of the art of speech; and I can also conceive it natural for *sansculotisme* to make us disdain those graces, and to lead us to a barbarous rudeness,

rudeness, equally distant from the precision of the Spartans in their energetic language, and from the eloquence of the amiable Athenians.

But it is long since we parted with La Blancherie, either at Orleans, or elsewhere, and high time to give him his dismissal.

Returning shortly after my mother's death, he knew nothing of that event till he came to see us, and discovered a degree of surprise, and sorrow, that pleased and affected me; nor did I look upon him, in the repeated visits he afterwards paid me, with an eye of indifference. My father, who at first made it a rule to stay with me, when any one came, began to think the business of duenna was by no means amusing, and that it would be more convenient to leave me to myself, and the maid, and to shut his door against every body, whose age and gravity should not be such as to render his attendance unnecessary. He told me accordingly, that he intended to beg La Blancherie to discontinue his visits. I did not say a word in answer, although I felt some degree of pain. I reflected on that which I supposed my suitor would suffer from the prohibition, and determined to convey the intimation to him myself; for my father's manner made me fear he would give it in an unhandsome way. To tell the truth, La Blancherie had prepossessed me in his favour; and I thought it not impossible that I might love him: my head alone was working, I believe; but I was not in a fair way to get

get on. I wrote then a handsome letter, which gave La Blancherie his discharge, and which deprived him of all hope of my receiving his answer, but which was not calculated to destroy any other he might entertain.

The ice thus broken gave a free course to tender and melancholy ideas, by which my happiness was not materially disturbed. Sophy came to Paris, and made some stay there with her mother and her sister Henrietta, who finding herself on a level with us, by the addition to our age, and the sedateness she had acquired, became also my friend. Her lively imagination struck fire out of every thing, and animated every connexion in which she had a share.

I went often to the garden of the Luxemburg with my two friends and Mademoiselle d'Hangard, and there I sometimes met La Blancherie. He used to bow to me respectfully; and I returned his salute not without emotion.—' You are acquainted then with that gentleman?' said Mademoiselle d'Hangard one day, having at first supposed his bow was meant for her.—' Yes.'—' Do you chance to know him too?'—' Certainly I do, though I never spoke to him in my life; but I am in the habit of visiting the Miss Bordenaves, to the youngest of whom he paid his addresses.'—' Is it long since?'—' A year, or perhaps eighteen months. He found means to introduce himself; called there from time to time, and at last made a declaration in form: the young

ladies

ladies are rich, and the youngeft a pretty girl. He has not a fhilling himfelf, and is a candidate for an heirefs; for he made the fame propofal to one of their acquaintance, as they afterwards heard; he was difmiffed, and we have ever fince been accuftomed to call him the lover of the eleven thoufand virgins *'—' But, pray, how came you acquainted with him?'—' By feeing him frequently at Madam l'Epine's concert,' faid I, biting my lips, and keeping the reft to myfelf, not a little vexed at having thought myfelf poffeffed of the heart of a man, who, without doubt, had folicited my hand merely becaufe I was an only daughter; and ftill more fo at having written him a letter, which he did not deferve—Matter for meditation as to the exercife of my prudence on future occafions!

A few months had elapfed, when a little *Savoyard* came and told the maid fomebody wifhed to fpeak with her, I forget where: fhe went out, returned, and informed me that M. La Blancherie had defired her to beg me to receive his vifit. It was Sunday, and I was waiting for fome of my relations. ' Yes,' anfwered I, ' he may come, but let it be inftantly; and fince he is waiting for you at a little diftance from the door, go and bring him in.' La Blancherie came, and found me fitting by my fire-fide.—' I have not dared, Ma-

* In allufion to a legendary tale, which ftates the *miraculous* martyrdom of eleven thoufand virgins.—*Tranf.*

demoifelle,

demoifelle, to wait upon you, fince the prohibition you fent me, though exceedingly defirous of feeing you; nor can I exprefs all I fuffered from the dear and cruel letter I then received. My fituation has undergone a confiderable change fince that time; and I have now fome projects, to which you are probably not altogether a ftranger.' He immediately laid before me the plan of a work of morality and criticifm, in the form of letters, and in the manner of the *Spectator*, and propofed to me to hear fome of them. I let him go on without interrupting him, and even waited, after he had made a fhort paufe, in order that he might get to the end of his rofary. When he had faid all he had to fay, I took my turn to fpeak, and obferved to him, calmly and politely, that I had taken upon myfelf the care of requefting him to difcontinue his vifits, becaufe the fentiments which he had declared to my father, made me fuppofe he attached fome importance to their continuance, and I had wifhed to fhow him my gratitude by that mark of attention; that at my age, the imagination was bufy on all occafions, and fometimes dreffed up objects in very falfe colours; but that error was not a crime, and that I was fufficiently recovered from mine to render all concern on his part needlefs; that I admired his literary projects, without wifhing to bear a part in them, any more than in thofe of others; that I confined myfelf to good wifhes for the fuccefs of all the authors in the world; as well as for his, in all poffi-

ble

ble ways; and that it was to tell him fo I had confented to receive him, in order that he might fave himfelf in future all trouble of the kind; in confequence of which I begged him to put an end to his vifit. Surprife, grief, agitation, every thing, in fhort, that is becoming in like cafes, was about to be difplayed. I ftopped him by faying, I did not know whether the Mifs Bordenaves, and the other ladies to whom he had paid his addreffes, about the fame time, had expreffed themfelves with equal franknefs; but that mine was without bounds; and that the refolution it indicated did not admit of explanation. I rofe at the fame inftant, making a curtefy, and that motion of the hand which points out the door to troublefome vifitors. My coufin Trude came in; nor did I ever fee his rugged face with greater pleafure. La Blancherie in the mean time effected his retreat in filence, and I never faw him after; but who has not fince heard of the *Agent General of the correfpondence for forwarding the arts and fciences ?*

This hero having made his *exit*, let us return to Sainte-Lette and Roland.

We had reached the end of the fummer 1776; and during the eight or nine preceding months I had feen M. Roland feveral times. His vifits were not frequent; but he made long ones, like a perfon, who, not going to a particular place in order to fhew himfelf, but becaufe he has a fatisfaction in being there, ftays as long as he decently can. His

frank

frank and inſtructive converſation never tired me, and he was fond of ſeeing me liſten to him with attention; a thing which I am very capable of, even with thoſe who are not ſo well informed as Roland, and which has perhaps procured me ſtill more friends than the talent of ſpeaking with ſome facility. I had become acquainted with him on his return from Germany; he was then preparing to make the tour of Italy, and ſettling his affairs, a thing to which prudent people ſeldom fail to attend, when on the eve of a long abſence; he had choſen me for the depoſitary of his manuſcripts, which were to remain in my poſſeſſion in caſe he ſhould meet with any miſchance. I was much affected by this particular mark of eſteem, and received it with many thanks. The day of his departure he dined at my father's with Sainte-Lette; and on taking leave, begged permiſſion to ſalute me. I know not how it is, but that favour is never granted by a young woman without a bluſh, let her imagination be ever ſo tranquil.— ' You are fortunate to be ſetting off,' ſaid Sainte-Lette, in his grave and ſolemn voice; ' but make haſte to return, and aſk for as much more!'

During Sainte-Lette's ſtay in France, his friend de Sevelinge becoming a widower, he repaired to his reſidence at Soiſſons, to ſhare his grief, and brought him to Paris, in order to divert his attention from his loſs. They came to ſee me together. Sevelinge, whoſe age was about fifty-two, was a

gentleman

gentleman of small fortune: he held a financial situation in the country, and devoted part of his time to study, like a philosopher who is sensible of its charms. Having thus become acquainted, we kept up our intercourse after Sainte-Lette's departure, who used to say, that, on leaving France, he should feel a degree of pleasure at the thought of his friend's not losing the advantage of my acquaintance. He even begged permission to put into his hands for a short time some manuscripts, which, as I have already said, I had submitted to his inspection. This interesting old man embarked for the fifth or sixth time in his life. An ulcer in his head, of which some symptoms had already appeared, broke while he was at sea; he arrived sick at Pondicherry; and died there six weeks after he disembarked. We heard of his death by means of Demontchery. He was greatly regretted by Sevelinge, who continued now and then to write to me; and his letters, of which the style and the matter were equally agreeable, gave me great pleasure. They bore the impression of that mild philosophy, and melancholy sensibility, to which I have always felt myself so much inclined. I have remarked what Diderot says on this subject, with so much truth: 'that good taste implies good sense, delicate organs, and somewhat of a melancholy turn.'

My father, whose kindness was gradually diminishing, being of opinion it very unnecessary

fary to keep up an idle correspondence that put him to the expence of poſtage, I communicated my diſtreſs to my little uncle, and was authorized to have the letters of Sevelinge, whom he had ſeen at our houſe, addreſſed under cover to him. My manuſcripts came back to me with ſome critical obſervations, of which I was very proud; for I did not imagine that my *works* were worth the trouble of reviewing. They were in my own opinion ſenſible enough; but at the ſame time mere commonplace that any body might have written; nor did I conceive they had any merit, except the ſingularity of their being the productions of a little girl. I long retained that modeſt ſimplicity in regard to myſelf. Nothing leſs was neceſſary than the buſtle of the revolution, the various changes of my ſituation, and a frequent opportunity of making compariſons in a great crowd, and among perſons eſteemed for their merit, to enable me to perceive that the bench on which I was ſtanding, was not likely to break down with the throng. I muſt obſerve, however, and I haſten to do ſo, that all tended rather to prove to me the degradation of the ſpecies in my native country, than to give me a high opinion of myſelf. It is not wit that is wanting; you meet it at every turn: it is foundneſs of judgment, and a ſtrong temper of mind. Where theſe two qualities are wanting, I cannot recognize any thing deſerving to be called a man.—In truth, Diogenes
was

was in the right to take a lantern. But a revolution will ferve as well: I do not know indeed a better touchftone, nor a ftandard more exact.

The academy of Befançon had propofed the following queftion as a fubject for a prize: *How can the education of women be made conducive to the improvement of men?* My imagination was directly on the wing: I took up my pen, and wrote a *differtation*, which I fent anonymoufly, and which, as may eafily be imagined, was not deemed worthy of the prize. There was none indeed fo honoured. The fubject was propofed again for the following year, with what refult I know not; but I recollect that, in attemping to difcufs this matter, I felt the abfurdity of fixing a mode of education, without attending to the general manners, which depend upon the government; and thought it injudicious to attempt reforming one fex by means of the other, inftead of ameliorating the whole fpecies by good laws. Accordingly I found no difficulty in faying what I thought women ought to be; but I added, they could only be rendered fuch by a new order of things. That idea certainly did not correfpond with the intention of the academy: I reafoned about the problem without folving it.

I conveyed the differtation to M. de Sevelinge; but after having forwarded it to Befançon, he fent me nothing but a few remarks on the ftyle. The warmth of compofition was over; I found the plan of my production exceedingly defective; and amufed myfelf myself in writing a critique upon it, as if it had been the work of a person whom I should have been glad to ridicule. This may be compared to a man's tickling his sides, in order to make himself laugh, or flapping his cheeks by way of warming them; but most assuredly no one could laugh without company more heartily, or more innocently, than I did. Sevelinge, in return, communicated to me an academical discourse of his own writing, on the *faculty of speech*, which he had addressed to the French academy, and concerning which d'Alembert had written to him in handsome terms. If I recollect aright, there was in that work a great deal of metaphysics, and some little affectation. Six months, a year, and more, passed away in this mental intercourse, in the midst of which a variety of ideas occurred. Sevelinge appeared to be uneasy at my situation, and tired of living alone. He made many reflections on the pleasures of a *thinking* society. I thought it to be desired, and we reasoned at great length on the subject. I know not what fancy afterwards got into his head, but he made a journey to Paris, and came to my father's in disguise, as if upon business. The most whimsical part of the story is, that I did not know him, though I let him in. But the great air of mortification with which he left me, awakened in my mind the idea of his features; I thought after he was gone that the stranger was very like Sevelinge; and soon found by his letters it was Sevelinge

linge himſelf. This curious circumſtance made an impreſſion on me by no means agreeable, and which I cannot deſcribe; our correſpondence ſlackened, and at laſt ceaſed entirely, as I ſhall hereafter relate.

I went now and then to Vincennes: my uncle's canonical retreat was pretty, the walk delightful, and his company agreeable; but though he had the pleaſure of having his houſe very well managed by Mademoiſelle d'Hannaches, he began to perceive he muſt pay for it by ſuffering all the teaſing, ill-humour, and folly of a conceited old maid. The caſtle of Vincennes was inhabited by a great number of perſons to whom the court allowed apartments: *here* was Moreau de la Garve, an old cenſor royal; *there* a female wit, no other than Madam de Puiſieux; a little higher a Counteſs de Laurencier; a little lower an officer's widow, and ſo on to the end of the chapter; to ſay nothing of the king's lieutenant, Rougemont, whom Mirabeau made known to the world, and whoſe carbuncled ·face, and inſolent ſtupidity, rendered him a moſt difguſting character. A company of invalids, of which the officers' wives made part of the ſociety, amounted, in conjunction with the above motley crew, and the dean and chapter, to no leſs than ſix hundred inhabitants within the walls of the caſtle, without reckoning the priſoners in the tower. My uncle, though well received everywhere, was ſeldom aſſiduous in his

viſits,

vifits, and faw little company at home. But on our return from our walks, we generally ftopped in the evening at the pavilion of the bridge that overlooks the park, where the females affembled. Here I fhould alfo have portraits to paint if I had leifure; but time is treading clofe upon my heels, and the road I have yet to travel is long. I am therefore obliged to pafs over a great number of things. Very pretty things might however be faid concerning the dances in the robbers'-walk, d'Artois's horfe-races, the follies of Seguin, the Duke of Orleans's cafhier, whofe birth-day (Seguin's) was celebrated by illuminations, and who became a bankrupt fhortly after—and then the pleafant walks in the wood, and the beautiful profpect from the upper park, by the fide of the Marne, for the fake of which we ufed to climb over a breach in the wall; and the hermits in the wood, who were fituated in fo picturefque a fpot, and in whofe church was a picture admirably executed, and curioufly defigned, in which thoufands of devils were feen tormenting the damned in as many different ways; and my readings with my uncle, efpecially that of Voltaire's tragedies, of which we were one day rehearfing feveral of the parts, by turns, when, at the moment of the greateft pathos, Mademoifelle d'Hannaches, who had been fpinning in filence, fet up a loud outcry againft the poultry, to which we fhould have been glad to have fent her; and our lame concerts after fupper, when, upon

the

the table that had juft been cleared, muff-cafes ferved as a mufic-defk for the worthy canon Bareux, with his fpectacles on his nofe, and ftrumming his bafs-viol, while I fcraped on the fiddle, and my uncle played out of tune on the flute—Ah! I will come back again to thofe pleafing fcenes, if fuffered to exift; but it is now time to return home, after having fpoken however of a certain great romancer, who had obtained fome degree of fame.

A SKETCH

OF WHAT REMAINED TO BE TREATED OF;

Intended to ferve as a laft SUPPLEMENT *to the* MEMOIRS*.

THE manufcripts left with me by M. Roland made me better acquainted with him, during the eighteen months he paffed in Italy, than frequent vifits could have done. They confifted of travels, reflections, plans of literary works, and anecdotes in which he was perfonally concerned: a ftrong

---

* In my laft fheet I left off at Vincennes: I was going to fpeak of *Carracioli*, whom I met at the canon's, and whofe letters, under the name of *Ganganelli*, had made fome noife in the world, although they were often a repetition of what he had written in his numerous little works. But were I thus to go on ftep by ftep, I fhould have a long work to compofe, for which the limits of my life would not fuffice: I fhall therefore confine myfelf to a fketch.

mind,

mind, rigorous probity, ſtrict principles, learning, and taſte, were evident in every page.

Born in opulence, and deſcended from an ancient family, of the higheſt character for integrity in the law, he had ſeen, while a young man, all his hopes of fortune vaniſh, owing to a want of management on one the hand, and to prodigal expence on the other. The youngeſt of five brothers, four of whom were compelled to embrace the clerical profeſſion, he had left his paternal roof friendleſs, and alone, at the age of nineteen, that he might not take holy orders, nor enter into trade, from both of which he was equally averſe. His firſt flight carried him to Nantz.; where he ſtayed ſome time in a merchant's compting-houſe, in order to gain information concerning a variety of matters, with a view of going to India. His preparations were all made; when he was taken with a ſpitting of blood, and was forbidden to go to ſea, by the phyſicians, under penalty of death. He next repaired to Rouen, where his relation, M. Godinot, inſpector of manufactures, propoſed to him to enter into that department. He determined to do ſo; ſoon diſtinguiſhed himſelf by his activity and readineſs; and at laſt obtained a lucrative employ. Travelling and ſtudy divided his time, and filled up every moment of his life.

Before he ſet off for Italy, he had introduced to my father his beſt-beloved brother, a Benedictine monk, at that time prior of the college of Clugny

at

at Paris; a man of fenfe, of agreeable manners, and of an amiable difpofition. He came now and then to fee me, and communicated to me the notes which his brother tranfmitted to him; for wherever M. Roland went, he committed his obfervations to paper. They were the notes which at his return he publifhed in the form of letters, entrufting the care of printing them to fome friends at Dieppe, one of whom having a rage for the Italian, overloaded them with paffages in that language, by adding thofe of his own fabrication. This work, abounding in matter, wants only to be better digefted in order to hold the higheft rank among books of the kind. Ever fince our marriage, we have had the intention of putting it into another fhape; but I wanted to fee Italy alfo; and time and events led us another way.

On M. Roland's return, I found myfelf in poffeffion of a friend: his gravity, his manners, and his ftudious habits, all concurred in making me confider him as a perfon of no fex, or rather as a philofopher, who had only a mental exiftence. A kind of confidence grew up between us, the pleafure he took in my company making him feel a defire of coming more frequently. It was near five years fince my acquaintance with him began, when he firft made a declaration of his tender fentiments. I did not hear it with indifference, becaufe I efteemed him more than any man I had yet feen; but I had remarked that neither he nor his

his family were altogether indifferent to worldly confiderations. I told him frankly, that I felt myfelf honoured by his addreffes, and that I fhould be happy to make him a return for his affection; but that I did not think he would find me a proper match. I then expofed to him without referve the ftate of my father's affairs—he was a ruined man. By prevailing upon myfelf to afk him for an account of my fortune, at the rifk of incurring his difpleafure, I had faved five hundred livres a year, making, with my little moveables, all that remained of the apparent opulence in which I had been brought up.

My father was ftill in the vigour of life; his errors might lead him to contract debts, which his inability to pay might render difgraceful; he might marry imprudently, and add to thofe evils little beggars who would bear my name, &c. &c. &c. I was too proud to expofe myfelf to the malevolence of a family, which might feel its confequence hurt by the connexion, or to the generofity of a hufband who would find in it a fource of chagrin. I advifed M. Roland, as a third perfon might have done, to give up all thoughts of me: he perfifted; I was moved; and confented to his taking the neceffary fteps with my father. But as he preferred making his application in writing, it was agreed that he fhould not fend his letter till his return to his ufual place of refidence. During the reft of his ftay at Paris, I faw him every day;

confi-

considered him as the being with whom my future fate was to be connected; and conceived a real affection for his person. As soon as he returned to Amiens, he wrote to my father, making known his wishes and designs. My father thought the letter dry: he did not like M. Roland's severity, and felt no inclination to have for his son-in-law a man of rigid principles, whose very looks would wear the appearance of reproach. He answered in rude and impertinent terms, and shewed me the whole, when his letter was sent off. I came to a resolution immediately. I wrote to M. Roland, and told him the event had justified my fears in respect to my father; that I did not wish to be the cause of his receiving farther affronts; and that I begged him to abandon his design. I made known to my father what his conduct had induced me to do; and added, he could not be surprised if I should in consequence seek a new situation, and retire to a convent. But as I knew he had several debts of an urgent nature, I left him the share of plate that belonged to me, to satisfy his creditors; hired a little apartment in the convent of the Congregation; and there took up my abode, with a firm resolution to regulate my expences by my income. I did so; and curious particulars I should have to relate of a situation in which I began to avail myself of the resources of a strong mind. I calculated my expences to a farthing, reserving a trifle for presents to the perfons who did the menial offices about the houfe. Potatoes, rice, and dry kidney beans, dreffed in a pot with a fprinkling of falt, and a fmall bit of butter, varied my food, and were cooked with little lofs of time. I went out twice a week; once to vifit my aged relations; and once to my father's, in order to look over his linen, and take away with me whatever ftood in need of mending. The reft of my time, fhut up under my roof of fnow, as I ufed to call it (for I was lodged near the fky, and it was in the winter), and refufing to mix habitually with the boarders, I applied to my ftudies; fteeled my heart againft adverfity; and, by deferving happinefs, avenged myfelf on fate which denied it me. Every evening the kind-hearted Agatha came to pafs an hour with me, and accompanied the effufions of her foul with the confolatory tears of friendfhip. A few turns in the garden, when every body was out of the way, conftituted my folitary walks. The refignation of a patient temper, the quiet of a good confcience, the elevation of fpirit which fets misfortune at defiance, the laborious habits that make the hours pafs fo rapidly away, the delicate tafte of a found mind finding in the confcioufnefs of exiftence and of its own value, pleafures which the vulgar never know; thefe were my riches. I was not always free from melancholy; but even melancholy had its charms. Though I was not happy, I had within me all the means of being fo; and had reafon to be

proud

proud of knowing how to do without what I wanted in other refpects.

M. Roland, aftonifhed and afflicted, continued to write to me, like a man conftant in his affection, but offended at my father's conduct. He came at the expiration of five or fix months, and felt the flame of love revive on feeing me at the grate, where I preferved an appearance of profperity. He was defirous of taking me out of my confinement, offered me his hand again, and preffed me to receive the nuptial benediction from his brother the prior. I entered into a deep deliberation concerning what I ought to do. I could not help being fenfible, that a man under forty-five would not have waited feveral months without endeavouring to make me change my refolution; and I readily confefs that my fentiments were reduced by that confideration to a ftate which admitted of nothing like illufion. I confidered on the other hand, that his perfeverance, the fruit alfo of mature deliberation, proved his fenfe of my merit; and fince he had overcome his repugnance to the difagreeable circumftances that might attend the match, I was the more fecure of retaining his efteem, which I fhould not find it difficult to juftify. Befides, if matrimony was, as I thought, a rigorous tie, a partnerfhip, in which the woman generally undertakes to provide for the happinefs of both parties, was it not better to exert my faculties, and my courage, in that honourable ftation, than in the forlorn and afcetic life I was

leading

leading in a convent? Here I might ſtate at length the many prudent reflections, as I conceive them to be, that guided me; and yet I did not make all thoſe that the circumſtances might have warranted, but which experience alone can ſuggeſt. I became then the wife of a truly honeſt man, who continued to love me the more, the better he knew me. Married when my reaſon was matured, I met with nothing that could diſturb its ſerious courſe; and fulfilled my duties with an ardour that was rather the effect of enthuſiaſm than calculation. By ſtudying my partner's happineſs, I perceived ſomething was wanting to my own. I have never ceaſed a moment to conſider my huſband as one of the moſt eſtimable men in exiſtence, as a man to whom I might be proud of belonging; but I have often felt the diſparity between us. I have often felt the aſcendancy of an imperious temper, joined to that of twenty years more than I could count, rendered one of thoſe advantages a great deal too much. If we lived in ſolitude, I had ſometimes diſagreeable hours to paſs: if we mixed with the world, I was beloved by perſons, ſome of whom appeared likely to take too ſtrong a hold of my affections. I immerſed myſelf in ſtudy with my huſband, another exceſs by which I was a ſufferer: I accuſtomed him not to know how to do without me at any time, or on any occaſion whatever.

We paſſed the firſt year of our marriage entirely at Paris, whither Roland had been ſent for by the
Board

Board of Trade, who were defirous of making fome new regulations concerning manufactures; regulations which the principles of liberty that Roland carried with him wherever he went, made him oppofe with all his might. He was printing an account of fome of the arts, which he had written for the academy, and taking a fair copy of his Italian notes. He made me his copyift and the corrector of the prefs; and I executed the tafk with an humility, at which I cannot help laughing when I recollect it, and which feems almoft irreconcilable with a mind fo much cultivated as mine; but it flowed directly from the heart. I had fo fincere a refpect for my hufband, that I eafily conceived him to know every thing better than I could. I was at the fame time fo much afraid of a cloud on his brow, and *he* was fo tenacious of his opinions, that it was long before I acquired fufficient confidence to contradict him. I was then attending a courfe of lectures on natural hiftory, and another on botany: that laborious recreation was the only one I enjoyed after the employments of fecretary and houfekeeper; for living at ready-furnifhed lodgings, as Paris was not our ufual place of refidence, and perceiving that every kind of cookery did not agree with my hufband's delicate conftitution, I took care to prepare for him the difhes that fuited him beft. We paffed four years at Amiens; and there I became a mother and a nurfe, without ceafing to partake of my hufband's labours, who had engaged to write

a cona confiderable part of the new Encyclopedia. We never ftirred from the defk, unlefs to take a walk out of the gates of the town. I made a *hortus ficcus* of the plants of Picardy; and the ftudy of aquatic botany gave birth to *The Peat-digger's Art*. Frequent ficknefs alarmed me for Roland's life: my cares were not ineffectual, and ferved to ftrengthen the tie that connected us: he loved me for my boundlefs attention; and I was attached to him by the good I did him.

He had been acquainted in Italy with a young man, whofe gentle and kind difpofition he valued much, and who, after his return to France, where he applied to the ftudy of phyfic, became our particular friend. That was Lanthenas, whom I fhould have efteemed more, if the revolution, that touchftone of mankind, by drawing him into the vortex of public affairs, had not expofed to view his weaknefs and his mediocrity. Poffeffed of private virtues, without perfonal accomplifhments, he rendered himfelf very agreeable to my hufband, and attached himfelf to us both. I loved him; I treated him like a brother, and gave him the name. I could write largely concerning him, as well as feveral interefting connexions. I formed at that era, and who ftill exift.

Sophy married, during my refidence at Amiens, the Chevalier de Comicourt, who lived at fix leagues diftance from that place, and farmed his own eftate. Henrietta, who had been fond of M. Roland, and

would

would have found no difficulty in obtaining the confent of her family to marry him, made no fcruple of approving the preference he had given me, with that affecting fincerity which did honour to her difpofition, and with that generofity that made her fo much beloved. She married old *De Vouglans*, who was become a widower, and whofe confeffor and phyfician advifed him to take another wife, although at the age of feventy-five. Both are widows. Sophy is turned devotee again; and is reduced to a very weakly ftate by pectoral complaints, which endanger a life neceffary to the welfare of two charming children. The difference of our difpofition and opinions, added to abfence, and the cares of the world, have weakened our connexion, without breaking it. Henrietta, always frank, lively, and affectionate, has been to fee me in my captivity, where fhe would willingly have taken my place to infure my fafety.

Roland had defired, in the early part of our union, that I fhould be fparing of my vifits to my two friends. I complied with his wifhes; nor did I refume the liberty of frequenting their fociety till time had infpired my hufband with confidence enough to remove his fears of being rivalled in my affections. Thofe fears were injudicious : a married life is grave and auftere; and if you deprive a woman of fenfibility of the pleafures of friendly intercourfe with her own fex, you take away a neceffary comfort,

fort, and expofe her to dangers. How long a differtation would this theme admit of!

In 1784 we removed to the generality of Lyons, and took up our abode at Villefranche, in M. Roland's paternal houfe, where his mother, of the fame age as the century, was living with his elder brother, a canon and counfellor. Here I fhould have numerous pictures to paint of the manners of a country town, and their influence, of domeftic cares, and the life I led in the fociety of a woman rendered refpectable by her age, and terrible by her bad temper, and between two brothers, the younger of whom was paffionately fond of independence, and the elder accuftomed and inclined to domineer.

During two months of the winter we ufed to refide at Lyons, with which place I became well acquainted, and of which I fhould have a great deal to fay—a city beautifully fituated, and nobly built, flourifhing by its trade and manufactures, interefting on account of its antiquities and collections of curiofities, and refplendent with riches —a city of which the emperor Jofeph was jealous, and which had the air of a magnificent capital; now a vaft burying-place, filled with the victims of a government a thoufand times more atrocious than the very defpotifm, from the ruins of which it arofe.

We

We ufed to go into the country in the autumn; and after the death of my mother-in-law, Madam la Platière, fpent there the greater part of the year. The parifh of Thezée, at two leagues diftance from Villefranche, in which is fituated the *Clos** of La Platière, is a country of an arid foil, but rich in vineyards, and in woods; it is the laft region in which the vine is cultivable as you advance towards the lofty mountains of Beaujolois. It was there my fimple tafte was exercifed in all the details of rural and productive economy; and there I applied fome little knowledge I had acquired to the relief of my neighbours: I became the village doctor, and was the more revered becaufe I beftowed affiftance, inftead of requiring a reward, and becaufe the pleafure of doing good gave grace to my attentions.—How readily does the ruftic labourer grant his confidence to thofe who render him fervice! People pretend he is not grateful; and true it is that I was defirous of laying no one under obligations; but I was beloved; and my departure was lamented with tears. I have alfo had fome whimfical fcenes. Honeft country-women have brought a horfe for me two or three leagues, begging me to fave the life of fome individual given over by the phyficians. I fnatched

* The word *Clos*, in French, is particularly applied in France to a tract of vineyard inclofed, which is its fignification here. It is often ufed to diftinguifh the wines of different diftricts, as *Clos St. George*, &c.—*Tranf.*

my

my hufband from the embrace of death in 1789, when all the prefcriptions of the doctors would not have delivered him from a dreadful difeafe without my foothing cares. I paffed twelve days and nights without fleep, and without undreffing myfelf, and fix months in the uneafinefs and agitation of a precarious convalefcence; and yet I was not indifpofed: fo much does our ftrength and activity depend upon the heart. The revolution came, and the fame enthufiafm feized us both: friends to mankind, adoring liberty, and thinking it was regenerating the fpecies, and putting an end to the degrading mifery of that unfortunate clafs, which had fo often excited our compaffion, we welcomed it with tranfport. Our opinions difpleafed many people at Lyons, who, being accuftomed to commercial calculations, could not conceive it poffible to favour and applaud changes, only beneficial to others, from mere philofophy. For that fole reafon they became Roland's enemies; and that made the adverfe party prize him the more. He was elected one of the municipality at its firft formation; and exhibited in that fituation an inflexible integrity. He was dreaded, and calumny on one fide took the field againft him; whilft on the other he was defended by impartiality and affection. Being deputed in behalf of the interefts of the city to the conftituent affembly, he repaired to Paris, and there we remained the beft part of a year. I have related, in another place, how we became ac-

quainted

quainted with several members of that assembly, connecting ourselves naturally with those, who, like us, loved liberty, not for their own sake, but for her's, and who now share with us the fate common to almost all who have laid the foundations of freedom, as well as to the true friends of human nature; such as Dion, Socrates, Phocion, and other heroes of antiquity; and Barneveldt and Sydney in modern times.

My husband made me accompany him in a tour through England in 1784, and in another through Switzerland in 1787: we were acquainted with interesting individuals in both those countries, and continued to keep up a correspondence with several. It is not a year since I received a letter from *Lavater*, the celebrated clergyman of Zurich, so well known on account of his writings, his brilliant imagination, his affectionate heart, and the purity of his morals. The worthy and learned Gosse of Geneva certainly laments the persecution we undergo. I know not what is become of the able Dezach, formerly a professor at Vienna, who was lately travelling through Germany, whom I saw frequently at London, and with whom Roland got into an argument at the house of Banks, the president of the royal society, who used to assemble at his house the scientific of his own country, and the strangers who visited London. I travelled with the pleasure and profit derived from the company of a man who has been upon the spot, and seen

things

things with an attentive eye; and committed to paper the observations I made on every thing by which I was most forcibly struck. I also visited several parts of France; but the revolution came, and prevented the excursions which we meditated into the southern provinces, as well as the tour of Italy, which I had a longing desire to make. Fondly attached to the public happiness, it engrossed all our ideas, and superseded all our projects; the passion of serving it was, indeed, the only one we felt. The reader has seen in the article entitled, *Roland's First Administration*, how a share in the government was conferred upon him, unknown to himself, as it were; nor will his public conduct fail to prove to impartial posterity his disinterestedness, his knowledge, and his virtues.

My father, with whom we had no great reason to be pleased, neither married nor made any very ruinous engagements. We paid a few debts he had contracted, and by granting him an annuity, prevailed on him to leave off business, in which it was become impossible for him to succeed. Though suffering so much from his errors, by which my grandmother's little fortune had gone the same way as every thing else, and though he had reason to be highly satisfied with our behaviour, his spirit was too proud not to be hurt at the obligations he owed us. That state of irritated self-love often hindered him from doing justice, even to those who were the most desirous of pleasing him. He died,

aged

aged upwards of fixty, in the hard winter of 1787, of a catarrh, with which he had been long afflicted. My dear uncle died at Vincennes in 1789; and foon after we loft my hufband's much-beloved brother. He had made the tour of Switzerland with us, was become prior and rector at Longpont, and was nominated elector of his canton, where he preached liberty, and practifed the evangelical virtues. The counfellor and phyfician of his parifhioners, and too wife for a monk, he was perfecuted by the heads of his order, and had numerous moleftations, which, by their effect on his fpirits, contributed to haften his end. Thus, everywhere, and in all times, do the good fall victims: there muft be another world then in which they will live again, or it would not be worth while to come into this world!

Blind calumniators! follow the track of Roland, fift every action of his life, fcrutinize mine, confult the focieties in which we have lived, the cities in which we have refided, and the country where all diffimulation is laid afide: put us to the queftion, ordinary and extraordinary ...... and the more you fee of us, the greater will be your difappointment, and your rage: that indeed is the reafon why you wifh to fend us out of the world.

Roland has been reproached with having folicited letters patent of nobility: the truth is this.— His family had enjoyed all the privileges of that order, for feveral centuries, by virtue of offices,

which

which did not tranfmit them to their heirs, and of the opulence which enabled them to keep up all the *infignia*, arms, chapel, livery, fief, &c. Their opulence difappeared: it was fucceeded by circumftances tolerably eafy; and Roland had the profpect of ending his days on the only eftate which remained in the family, and which ftill belongs to his elder brother. He thought he had a right, by his labours, to infure to his defcendants an advantage which his anceftors had enjoyed, and which he would have difdained to buy. He accordingly fet forth his claims, in order to obtain either the acknowledgment of his nobility, or letters patent of creation. That was at the beginning of 1784; nor do I conceive any man at that period, and in his fituation, would have thought it unworthy of his wifdom to do the fame thing. I came to Paris, and foon faw that the new fuperintendants of trade, jealous of his long experience in a branch of adminiftration which he underftood better than they, and adverfe to his opinions concerning the freedom of commerce, of which he was extremely tenacious, in giving him the requefted certificates of his important fervices, which they could not refufe, did not lay that ftrefs upon them that was likely to infure his fuccefs. We therefore deemed it proper to let the matter fleep for a while, and made no further attempts. It was then that, becoming acquainted with the changes of which I have fpoken in the curious article of Lazowfki, I demanded and obtained

tained Roland's removal to Lyons, which brought him nearer home, and feated him in the midſt of his family, where I knew it had been his wiſh, ſome time or other, to retire. Patriots of the preſent day, you who ſtood in need of a revolution to give you conſequence, bring forward your good works, and, if you dare, compare them with his!

Thirteen years paſt in different places, in continual ſtudy, and in an intercourſe with a variety of perſons—years, the latter of which ſo cloſely connected with the hiſtory of the times—would furniſh the fourth, and moſt intereſting, ſection of my Memoirs. The detached pieces which will be found in the *Portraits* and *Anecdotes*, muſt ſerve inſtead of it. —I am no longer able to hold the pen in the midſt of the horrors that tear my country to pieces: I cannot live among its ruins; but chuſe rather to bury myſelf beneath them. Nature, take me into thy boſom!

At thirty-nine years of age.

DETACHED NOTES.

IF fate had allowed me to live, I believe I ſhould have been ambitious of only one thing; and that would have been to write the *Annals of the preſent Age*, and to become the *Macaulay* of my country. I have conceived, in my priſon, a real fondneſs for *Tacitus*;

Tacitus; and cannot go to sleep till I have read a part of his work. It seems to me that we see things in the same light, and that in time, and with a subject equally rich, it would not have been impossible for me to imitate his style.

I am very sorry to have lost with my Historical Memoirs, an answer I wrote to Garat, on the 6th of June. Charged with my remonstrances against my confinement, he had written me a handsome letter of four pages, in which he expressed his esteem, his sorrow, &c. At the same time he entered into a discussion of public affairs, and sought to impute the ruin of the *twenty-two* to themselves, as if they had acted, and spoken in the Assembly, in a way that accorded ill with the interest of the republic. I answered Garat with good reasons, expressed in a manner that makes me regret the loss of them; I represented his conduct as the consequence of that *weakness*, to which I attribute our misfortunes, a weakness common to a timid majority, who were obedient only to the impulse of fear; and I demonstrated, that both *he* and *Barrere* were fit for nothing but to ruin all the states in the world, by the obliquity of their proceedings. I have never been able to digest the silly declamations of a flock of buzzards, against what they called the *passions* of the *right side*. Men of integrity, steady to their principles, and full of indignation against guilt, exerted their powerful eloquence against the perversity of a few villains, and the
atrocious

atrocious meafures they dictated; and thefe eunuchs in politics reproached them with fpeaking with too much warmth!

Roland's retiring from the miniftry, very fhortly after he had faid he would defy the ftorm, has been imputed as a crime. People do not perceive it was neceffary for him to make known his refolution, in order to keep up the fpirits of the weak, and that in this manner he encouraged them on the fixth of January: but the fentence of Louis XVI. pronounced on the 18th, fhewing the weaknefs of the fober party, and the fall of their power in the Convention, he had no longer any fupport to hope for, nor any thing to do but to retire, in order that he might not fhare the difgrace of other people's blunders. Certainly Roland abhorred tyranny, and believed Louis guilty; but he wifhed to fee liberty fixed on firm foundations, and thought all was loft, when he faw that wrong-headed men had gained the afcendence. He is too well juftified in regard to thofe who are now about to be led to the block! As to every thing elfe, it appears to me I have been fufficiently explicit in the narrative entitled, *Roland's Second Adminiftration*. His going out of office was the fignal of *difcomfiture*; and that he forefaw.

My poor Agatha! fhe has left her cloifter; but fhe is ftill the fame gentle dove, and weeps for her daughter;

daughter; for that is the name by which she diſtinguiſhes me. I ſhould have had a great number of perſons to introduce into my hiſtory by way of epiſode: my worthy couſin Deſportes, who died at fifty years of age, after experiencing much vexation; my little couſin Trude, who has retired into the country, and is now ſuing for a divorce; our old maid, whoſe name was *Mignonne,* and who died at my father's houſe: ' Mademoiſelle,' ſaid ſhe, while expiring with reſignation in my arms, ' I never aſked any thing from heaven but to die in your ſervice: I am ſatisfied.'—And then that ſad connexion of my unfortunate father with the profligate Leveilly, for the fate of whoſe daughter I felt myſelf concerned. I made her the objeƈt of my bounty, her youth, her vivacity, and ſome ſhare of accompliſhments, exciting compaſſion; but ſhe debaſed herſelf; and having loſt all ſhame, obliged me in latter times to forbid her my preſence, while I continued to receive her brothers, and to render them every ſervice in my power.

A

COLLECTION OF LETTERS,

Addreſſed by MADAM ROLAND *to the* EDITOR,

At that Time Secretary to the Intendant General of the Poſt-Office *.

MY DEAR FRIEND!

I HAVE received a letter from M. Goffe, which, I think, you will be pleaſed to peruſe; and have therefore ſent it you incloſed. You will learn from it the way in which the combined forces of France, Savoy, and Berne behaved when they took poſſeſſion of Geneva.

I do not know whether you will agree with me; but I think that the poor Genevefe could not pof-

* I ſaid, in the advertiſement prefixed to Part I. that I ſhould ſubjoin theſe letters to the foregoing writings of Madam Roland, though ſeeming, at the firſt view, to be only intereſting to our friendſhip, becauſe I conſidered them as a neceſſary ſupplement to her private memoirs, and as a ſtandard that would ſerve to aſcertain the merit of that honourable victim of the late tyranny. I am ſorry to ſee ſuch a conſiderable *hiatus*; for it is in the effuſions of a regular and unaffected correſpondence that the whole heart is ſeen, and the inclinations, opinions, and acquirements exhibit themſelves in their true ſhape; but what remains will ſuffice, I believe, to make the writer known, and to ſerve as a ſpecimen of the eaſe of her epiſtolary ſtyle.

ſibly

fibly have managed worfe : one would take them for a company of blind men, committed with their own confent to the guidance of a few traitors, who betrayed them, and whofe manœuvres were evident. I was out of all patience, I know not how often, in reading it, and the very idea ftill makes my blood boil in my veins, I pity from the bottom of my foul, thofe who could not diftinguifh which was the wifeft way of proceeding, or rather, who had not influence enough to get it adopted; but it appears clear to me that Geneva, in general, was no longer worthy of liberty—we fee nothing like the energy it would have required to defend fo dear a property, or to die beneath its ruins. I have only the greater hatred for its oppreffors, whofe infectious neighbourhood had corrupted the republic before they came to put an end to its exiftence.

Goffe tells me, the friend who was with him at Paris is of the ariftocratic party; and that he has refufed to hold any intercourfe with him fince the overthrow of liberty, left the oppofite tempers of mind they are in fhould produce a difagreeable altercation. I would have laid a wager it would have taken place—It is a certain M. Coladon, whom I ufed to call Celadon, whofe only merit is that of being a pretty fellow, and whofe fervile air, and fupple demeanour, befpoke a flave at firft fight. I would not give a cripple, of the fame caft as Goffe, for a hundred of him.

Virtue,

Virtue, and liberty, have no longer any afylum, unlefs in the heart of a fmall number of honeft men: a fig for the reft, and for all the thrones in the world! I would tell a fovereign fo to his face—from a woman it would only be laughed at; but, by my foul, if I had been at Geneva, I would have died before they fhould have laughed at me.

February 9, 1783.

I WILL not fay, with the woman in the old ftory*, *Why, I chufe to be beaten, I tell you!* That would not be at all to my tafte. But I muft let you know that the word *loup* †, which appears to you fo terrible, is a term of endearment, a charming little name, which I have borne, not from time immemorial, but from the day after a certain fourth of February, which took place three years ago. I know not why nor wherefere, but my name in fhort it is, and I am called *loup* by fomebody, as perhaps you may be called *my lovely creature*, by fome fair lady, whom, like me, you do not care to mention. After that, judge of people by their words! Should we not be as much in the right to doubt their fignification, as Berkeley was to doubt the exiftence of bodies? But you have fomething better to do than to liften to ftories, and I than to write them.

* In the Medecin malgré lui of Moliere.—*Tranf.*
† A wolf.

Yefterday's quiet evening has no doubt fet you to rights again.—I have paffed the day in working harder than I have done for a great while. Health and pleafure attend you!

March 20.

YOU are a good creature, and deferving every body's love. Your letter is full of fenfibility and reafon; and is calculated to make you friends among worthy people, who fhould know nothing of you befides. Good inclinations, prudent projects, juft and natural fentiments; thefe are the materials of happinefs: you poffefs them; and no doubt the event will do juftice to your claims, and give accomplifhment to the wifhes of thofe by whom you are beloved. Among them we fhall never be the hindmoft.

I have no doubt that a fet of inftructions, with the leffons in queftion, would fuffice to carry you any length you pleafe; nor fhould I afk more if I had leifure; but I ftand in need of a mafter to fix an hour for that kind of ftudy, and my mafter is not punctual to his time: he is befides a mere machine, with whom it is impoffible to reafon, and who can only move his fingers in order to fhew what is to be done. I lofe all patience, and make but little progrefs. I cannot even play the mufic you felected for me, which is in general eafy; but the fimpleton likes better to make me ftudy what he is mafter of himfelf, and I am obliged

to

to submit, that my time and my money may not be altogether thrown away.

I believe the people who are afraid left the fine project for a reform in the administration of justice should fall to the ground, have great reasons for their fears: it would be a very singular phenomenon.

Adieu!—We are yours in all truth and friendship.

April 5.

IT is a nocturnal greeting I send you this time. It is half past eight, and the moment of a country supper cannot be far off; but I can always find time to devote to your service. Do not imagine, however, I am going to tire you to death with an endless epistle: you have no time to lose, and I will not spend mine in a way burdensome to any body, much less to my friends. This principle being established, nothing remains but to come to the point; and that is what I would still avoid doing to the end of the fourth page, by way of teasing *you* and amusing *myself*, if it were not right for such fancies to give way to reason.—The service of this Dame Reason is by no means an easy one. —Whatever truth there may be in my reflection, which you will take for the whim of the moment, you must know that Monsieur Maille, haberdasher of hard-wares, in the *Rue des Lombards*, deals in that famous *dogs'-grafs*, which has so much puzzled the doctors, yourself not excepted—the dogs'-grafs used

by

by bruſh-makers, which I, poor ignorant woman, often make uſe of without entering into an analyſis of its nature. But there muſt be food ſuited to every ſtomach; and people are ſo accuſtomed to look for ſcience in dictionaries, that it would occaſion a terrible outcry indeed, if none were to be put into a work of this kind, in which, by the way, there is now and then a want of it. Be good enough, then, to call on Monſieur Maille, and, like a philoſopher who knows how to extract information out of every thing, for once let a ſhop-keeper inſtruct you. You will aſk him whence he procures that commodity, what he thinks of its nature, and of the preparation it may have undergone, &c. &c. It is not neceſſary to teach you your leſſon; for you certainly are not one of thoſe, who, as the poet Sadi ſays, know not even how to inquire.—In ſaying this, I do not intend to pay you a compliment; but to expreſs a truth which flows ſpontaneouſly from my pen.

I believe it is now two or three long days ſince we have been favoured with any thing from you in the ſhape of a letter. We ſhould be glad to know whether you have received *The Peat-digger's Art*: the deſire of the author muſt have been ill complied with, if the work was not delivered to you on Wedneſday laſt: you were the firſt perſon to whom it was diſpatched.

We have been very buſy theſe two days in digging, hoeing, and ſowing our little garden. We mean to fill it with flowers, not with pretty
ones

ones, according to the general idea, but with such as are interefting in the eyes of the botanist. We are doing great things, I affure you!

Adieu!—It is a great deal later than I imagined.

April 14.

IS it not enough to leave the poor women difconfolate, without fending them to the devil into the bargain? Young man, you are not tolerant; but as there is fomething laughable in your malice, it is forgiven you, and we only infer, that you would rather come in the way of all the *prickly hollies* in the univerfe, than in that of Madam Maille. After this, very poffibly, your friends may beg you to wander about the fields and bufhes for information, but nothing more. They find, however, your difinterefted nefs much to their advantage; and while that is the motive of your conduct, have the greater reafon to depend on your perfeverance.

Your giving me a defcription of your laborious life anfwers very little purpofe: I do not pity you at all. In my opinion, to be bufy is to be halfway towards happinefs, efpecially when it is a mean of preferving our liberty; for when once we can get rid of the empire of habit, we are little expofed to that of love. Flutter then, at your eafe, about the woods and fhrubberies, like a coquettifh fparrow, yet a ftranger to flavery: it may be long avoided by fuch a way of life, and the mind will gain proportionable ftrength. I only pity you

for

for not being able to divert yourſelf theſe enſuing holydays, and ſhall think of you every time we go to take our walk, in which you will be our ideal companion.

April 17.

YOU are ſad, and we are quite afflicted at it! Nobody, moſt certainly, can better conceive how much reaſon, with your delicate way of thinking, you muſt have to be ſo. It is painful to ſee the ſeeds of malevolence, or of any thing like it, growing in the hearts of thoſe about us; and a generous mind regrets it the more, when it is owing to ſome external advantage. It would be eaſier for ſuch a man to ſet himſelf above poſitive injuſtice, than to overcome the vexation of afflicting the perſons around him, by any ſuperiority not intrinſically his own. That very diſpoſition, however, ought to procure him his pardon for many advantages; and, indeed, it ſeldom happens, the ſelf-love of rivals and competitors is much hurt by thoſe of which the poſſeſſor does not avail himſelf in an overbearing manner. That kind of diſcontent that many perſons feel at the promotion of a fortunate individual, is, beſides, one of the evils attendant on ſociety; and in theſe caſes, a man muſt reſolve to bear what he cannot avoid.

Our friend has written you a letter to-day, which will be delivered by Monſieur de Vin, whoſe departure for Paris is fixed for this evening. He

is

is an excellent man, of a truly honeſt and feeling heart, whoſe friends reproach him with nothing but indolence, which prevents his ſhewing what he is worth, and availing himſelf of his talents. But I could willingly reproach him with talking too much on newſpaper politics, which tire me to death, and keeping to himſelf all he knows on the *belles lettres*, of which I am ſo fond : but every one muſt follow his inclinations. I am glad you have all thoſe of a found mind, and all that can ſatisfy an active difpoſition. It is having materials for happineſs, and arms againſt melancholy, from which the indolent cannot deliver themſelves with equal advantage.

April 23.

YOU have too much foul for anyone to reproach you with having ſenſes: it would at leaſt be an abſurdity. It is extremely natural at five-and-twenty to forget Ariſtotle, for the fake of a pair of fine eyes ; and it would be very ſtrange, if, at a female tribunal, you were not held pardonable for ſuch an offence. I am well content likewiſe, to make up all our other quarrels.

I could not help ſmiling at your earneſt deſire to ſee M. de Vin. Your active friendſhip meaſures that of other people by itſelf; but the worthy M. de Vin is the laſt man in the world to perceive all thoſe little things which intereſt you, becauſe your heart ſets a value upon them ; nor do I doubt but you

would

would learn more from our brief correfpondence, than he would by vifiting us day after day. I fhould not be aftonifhed if he were to pafs three weeks at Paris without feeing you, although he really defires it; for he is a man likely to fpend one half of his life in planning the very contrary of what he will execute in the other: a kind honeft-hearted creature notwithftanding, and well calculated to make a fenfible woman happy.

Your maidens of Poitou do not at all refemble our young ladies of Amiens. The latter have all the affurance of a woman with whom bafhfulnefs has long been out of the queftion; talk quite as loud in company; game as foon as they are in their teens; and at that early time of life, play off all the airs and graces of damfels hackneyed in the ways of the world. It is truly farcical; but there are luckily a few remarkable exceptions.

I would almoft lay a wager that you are an adept at ninepins. We have already played fome famous matches with my daughter; but the little fimpleton throws the bowl on one fide: in fober fadnefs, if fhe never takes better aim, fhe will be a poor creature; but patience is neceffary for every thing; as you have occafion for it to bear ftudy, confinement, and the rain when it overtakes you in the fields. But God be praifed! fince you ftill have time left to fay a few words on the fubject of friendfhip, and an inclination to retain that fentiment, in fpite of the roguifh tricks

tricks of the urchin who gives you fuch mental abfences, when you are in company with the Abbé's fifter.

Adieu!—We good folks, who have made the voyage of Cithera, love you with all our hearts, and without partaking of your abfence of mind.

April 25.

YOU are an excellent man, and we greet you moft heartily. Your fenfibility, and your goodnefs of heart, difcover themfelves without your endeavouring to fhew them, in a manner highly gratifying to your friends, and well calculated to infure you their lafting affection. Defend M. de Vin as much as you pleafe: you will give us great pleafure, as you would do him a great deal of good, if it were poffible for you to infpire him with activity like your own: it is energy that is wanting to his happinefs, as well as to his mind: he is fenfible of it, and perhaps would acquire more, if he were always with people whofe fenfibility might ferve as a *ftimulus* to his own.

I fancy you would like thofe to whom he belongs exceedingly. It may be faid his family are worthy people, in the full force of the term.

I wifh you a Eudora, becaufe you are formed to enjoy the fimple pleafures which fhe affords us, and which we hope fhe will fome day or other more widely diffufe. For our fakes, I wifh fhe may be fuch, that a man like you may reafon in the fame

way

way eighteen years hence. I should then be almost ready to say *Nunc dimittis*.

Adieu!—May your health be equal to our friendship.

May 5.

WE received your last letter yesterday with much pleasure: this indemnification for the absence of our friends is a great satisfaction.

Are you indebted for the recovery of your liberty in the evening to a decrease of official business, or to the kindness of one of your colleagues? The latter cause would be the more agreeable, as well as the more lasting.

Thanks to your information, we know what to think of the translation of Aristotle. However estimable the work may be, the present edition is above our purchase: we have no occasion for the Greek text, and can do very well without a cumbersome *quarto*. We shall therefore wait for a modest *octavo* without the text, which will probably be published hereafter, and which will suit us a great deal better. I am very glad to hear you say so much in favour of the herbal in question: we shall place that work among those of the pleasing science to which it relates, and which will be one of our dearest recreations, when we shall have assumed the patriarchal style permanently.

I accept your happy augury concerning my little Eudora; nor shall it be any fault of mine if the
event

event do not convert it into a prophecy. I enjoy at leaſt every moment of the preſent time by aſſuring myſelf that ſhe is in poſſeſſion of all the health and all the happineſs that belong to her time of life: I have occaſion for this conviction, in order to congratulate myſelf on her exiſtence; and I have occaſion for it alſo to aſſiſt me in ſupporting the loſs of her, in caſe I ſhould meet with ſuch a misfortune. My health does not improve very faſt. Our friend will almoſt tell you that I am no longer worth looking at, and that I am withering on my ſtalk. He is alarmed at my unpleaſant feelings, as I am at his growing thin. In this way do we make one another uneaſy. Content, and permiſſion to eat ſtrawberries, which Linnæus deems ſo ſalubrious, and which, without being of a wonderful quality in this country, are here, as well as every where elſe, in my opinion, the moſt agreeable fruits, becauſe they pleaſe the ſmell and the taſte alike; an advantage that many others cannot boaſt of*.

It ſeems to me that you were obliged to ſhut your eyes while conſulting the Abbé. But tell me .... Do thoſe of his ſiſter make war on you in good earneſt? Have a care of the winged boy, who ſtrikes and eſcapes like an aſſaſſin! Adieu!—Health and joy attend you.

* Something is wanting to complete this ſentence.

May 13.

THERE was fo much agreeable chit-chat in your laft, that I could not help thinking we had you fitting by our fide. I admire you for placing to the account of coldnefs what would feem to be the fruit of wifdom; for furely it is the higheft property of it to fee no more than what is vifible, and to keep reality clear of all illufions: the circumftance that carried you to that height fignifies little—fo much the better, if, in order to reach it, you had no occafion for efforts and trials: your mind has received no fhock, and your energy has not been wafted. Whatever courfe we purfue, we may go a great length, provided imagination does not come acrofs our way, but remains fubordinate to reafon.

M. de Vin told us fomething about the parliamentary fatires. It muft be confeffed that Paris is a curious place: puns and pamphlets are there the refult or the caufe of the moft ferious affairs; and good and evil are turned into ridicule alike, as fome kind of confolation for the exiftence of the one, and the impoffibility of the other.

You would no longer then make one in a game at prifon-bars? But if a Sophy were to be the prize of contention in the race, could you not find legs as good as thofe of *Emile* ? I am not at all forry for the rain which made you leave off botanizing, and take up your pen; but I wifh you would avail yourfelf of the prefent fine weather, and fet off on another

other excurſion. It is in my opinion one of the moſt charming occupations poſſible: it calls forth the activity of youth; favours the reveries of the penſive mind; enables us to enjoy all the pleaſures of the country, and all the agreeable ideas it in‑ ſpires; and affords gratification alike to tender melancholy, and to ſportive gaiety. We ſtrolled yeſterday along the ditches of the city, and found a few plants; but I am as yet ſo unſkilful; I have ſo little time to rub away the ruſt of ignorance; and the neceſſity of conſulting books which are not portable, and which I have little leiſure to turn over at home, occurs ſo often, that I ſhould be out of all patience if my taſte for the ſtudy did not overcome the difguſt occaſioned by my miſtakes.

Sailly, near Corbie.

I DO not know what is the day of the month: all I can tell you is, that we are in the month of June, that yeſterday was a hólyday, and that, accord‑ ing to our reckoning here, it is three o'clock in the afternoon. On Sunday I had a viſit from my good man, who left me again yeſterday evening. I paſſed a very bad night, and was ſo ill this morn‑ ing, that I could not write to you, although it was very much my intention. I do not give you this ſucceſſion of events as neceſſarily reſulting from one another; but I relate things fairly and honeſtly as they are. Your letters were communicated to me, becauſe we number the receipt of them among our enjoyments, and becaufe we cannot tafte any pleafure without fharing it between us. I have nothing to fend you in return for your news: I do not trouble my head about politics; I am no longer in the way of picking up any of another kind, and can only entertain you with an account of the dogs that wake me, of the birds that confole me for not being able to get to fleep again, of the cherry-trees that are oppofite my windows, and of the heifers that graze before the door.

I refide under the roof of a woman, whom the want of fome object on which I might fix my affections, made me diftinguifh, when, at eleven years of age, I was in a convent, with forty other girls, who thought of nothing but romping, to difpel the gloom of the cloifter. I was devout, like Madam Guyon in days of yore; I attached myfelf to a companion, who was a little myftical alfo; and our friendfhip was fed by the fame fenfibility that made us love God Almighty to diftraction. That companion, after her return to her own country, made me acquainted with M. Roland, by intrufting him with the delivery of her letters. Judge whether what has followed ought not to make me love and cherifh the accidental caufe which gave it birth.

This friend, in fhort, is lately married; and I had fome fhare in inducing her fo to do. I am now vifiting her in the country, which I have often reprefented to her as the abode beft fuited to a virtuous mind. I walk over her eftate; I count her

poultry;

poultry; we gather the fruit her garden produces; and are of opinion that all this is well worth the gravity with which fashionable folks sit round the card-table; the important business of dressing, in which it is necessary to pass half the day, in order to spend the rest in tiresome company; the prittle-prattle of petit-maîtres, &c. &c. But notwithstanding all this, I feel a longing desire to return to Amiens, because only one half of me is here; my friend forgives me, because her husband being absent, she is the better able to judge of my privations by her own; and although we find it very comfortable to condole with one another, we are perfectly of opinion, that to be at a distance from the dovecot, or to be there alone, is a very miserable thing. I am, nevertheless, to pass the whole of next week here: I do not know whether my health will be as much benefited by it, as my good man was inclined to hope. I have, however, laid all study aside for these three days, without feeling yet any wonderful advantage. I was pretty well satisfied with the looks of our friend: I dread his closet, as I dread fire; and the week I have yet to pass here, seems an eternity, on account of the mischief he may do himself in the mean time.

Must I not have great confidence in your indulgence, to entertain you with such rustic prate? I expect you, however, not to be obliged to me for it, but to take it as an act of friendship per-

fectly

fectly sincere, and perfectly free from vanity. I am very heavy; and notwithstanding my taste for every thing about me, my fondness for rural details, and those soft emotions which the sight of nature in her simple state never fails to excite in my bosom, I feel my faculties benumbed, and my mind in a state of stupefaction.

I have brought plants home with me from all my walks; and have found out what several of them are: the rest got dry before *Murray* could help me to form a judgment of them. In the mean time day succeeds to day, without restoring me my animation. Women, however, are as changeable in their physical temperature, as the air they breathe: I write according to the impulse of the moment; and it is not impossible that this letter would have been lively and gay, if I had postponed it till to-morrow.

Farewel, and remember your friends. I include a friend of mine in the number, because all our affections are in common, and because you are one of the objects on which we have the greatest pleasure in fixing them.

Amiens, July 29.

IT is enough that you lay down your arms: I do not require you to give them up: I will not suffer any one to impose laws upon me; nor do I wish to domineer. You were not mistaken as to the pretensions of your sex, I will even say as to

their

their rights; but you were much miftaken in the way you took to defend them. Neither did you lay them open to my attacks; for it is not my intention to attack any one of them: you forgot the *mode*, that was all. What elfe is the deference, the refpect paid by your fex to mine, but the indulgence fhewn by powerful magnanimity to the weak whom it protects, and to whom it does honour at the fame time? When you affume the tone of a mafter, you make us immediately think that we are able to refift you, and perhaps to do more, notwithftanding all your ftrength. (The invulnerable Achilles was not invulnerable every where.) Do you pay us homage? It is Alexander treating his prifoners, who are not ignorant of their dependence, with the refpect due to queens. In this fingle particular, perhaps, our civilization goes hand in hand with nature: the laws place us in a ftate of almoft conftant fubjection; while cuftom grants us all the little honours of fociety: we are nothing in effect; in appearance we are every thing.

Do not then any longer imagine that I form a falfe eftimate of what *we* have a right to require, or of what it becomes *you* to claim. I believe, I will not fay more than any woman, but as much as any man, in the fuperiority of your fex. In the firft place you have ftrength, with all the advantages that belong to it, and all that it confers; courage, perfeverance, extenfive views, and great talents:

talents: it belongs to you to make political laws, as well as scientific discoveries. Govern the world; change the surface of the globe; be magnanimous, terrible, skilful, and learned: you are all this without our assistance; and this, no doubt, makes you our masters. But without us you would be neither virtuous, nor kind, nor amiable, nor happy: keep then to yourselves glory and authority of every kind; we neither have nor desire any empire but over manners, nor any throne but in your hearts. Further than this I shall never extend my claims. I am sometimes sorry to see women contend with you for certain privileges which become them so ill: there is not one of those privileges, even to the title of author, that does not seem to me ridiculous in female hands. Great as their powers may be in certain respects, it is not to the public that their talents or their knowledge ought to be exhibited.

To make a single person happy, and to bind a number together by the charms of friendship, and by winning ways, is, in my mind, the most enviable destiny that can be conceived. Let us have no more contention; no more war: let us live in peace. Only recollect, that to keep the high ground you stand upon, in relation to womankind, you must be cautious of making them feel your superiority. The war in which I have engaged you for the sake of amusement, and with all the freedom of an old acquaintance, would be carried on in a more serious manner by an artful coquet; nor would you

leave

leave the field without a wound. Protect always, that you may only submit when you pleafe; that is the fecret of your fex. But what a pretty fimpleton am I to be telling you this, and all the reft of it, which you know fo much better than I do! You wifhed to make me prattle; well! we are even. Adieu!

May 23, 1784.

I CHARGE you with a commiffion, which you will naturally fuppofe to be an act of charity, that requires your co-operation. The matter in queftion is, to take the inclofed ticket to the *Mont-de-Piété**, to pay the needful, and to take out the effects: you will afterwards put the faid effects into the parcel with our books and other things, fo that they may be delivered without farther expence.

Your going to take petticoats out of the *Mont-de-Piété* is an excellent joke; but, all joking apart, you feem to be come to a critical moment, and to be much occupied in taking a final refolution. It is an age fince you wrote to us; and I am going to fend to the poft-office before I clofe my letter, to fee if you have as yet given any figns of life.

Our friend is in an indifferent ftate of health, by no means a pleafant one: a fwelled face, a pain in his limbs, fhivering fits; mere trifles, in fhort.

---

* A public eftablifhment at Paris, which lends money upon pledges at very low intereft.—*Tranf.*

Eudora

Eudora is well; but has not recovered the brilliant complexion of perfect health. Have you heard any thing lately of our friend Lanthenas? I know he has been in the country some time. Adieu! —Ere this you will have received our little matters. Our best wishes attend you.

June 7.

IT is long, my worthy friend, since I had the pleasure of conversing with you through the medium of the post; but I have so much to do, and so much rest to take, that I begin a thousand things without finishing one. The days passed at Crespy were completely filled up by friendship, in the first place, and afterward by visiting, and excursions in the country. Of our excursions, that to Ermenonville was not the least interesting: much taken up with you, and with the things to be seen, we enjoyed the latter, while regretting the want of your company. The place in itself, the valley in which Ermenonville is situated, is the most miserable thing in the world; sand on the high grounds, a morass below; black and muddy water; no prospect; not a single view from the fields of any thing like a rich and cultivated country; woods in which you are in a manner buried, and low marshy meadows: such is the nature of the place. But art has conducted, distributed, and confined the water, and cut avenues through the woods, and from both there result a me-

lancholy

lancholy and affecting scene, pleasing points of view, and parts highly picturesque. The island of poplars, in the midst of a noble piece of water, surrounded with trees, is the most agreeable and most interesting spot in all Ermenonville, independently even of the object that has so much attraction for feeling hearts and pensive minds. The entrance into the wood, the manner in which the castle offers itself to the eye, and the laying out of the water in front of it, compose the next piece of scenery by which I was most forcibly struck. I was pleased to find inscriptions engraved on stones scattered here and there; but the ruins, and edifices erected in a variety of places, have, in general, the defect with which I reproach almost all those imitations in the English gardens: it is that of being constructed on too small a scale, by which means the illusion is destroyed, and they produce an effect that borders on the ridiculous. Ermenonville, in short, does not display those splendid beauties that astonish the traveller; but I think it must please the inhabitant who frequents it every day. If *Jean-Jaques* however had not given it celebrity, I doubt whether any one would have gone out of his way to pay it a visit. We went into the master's room, which is no longer inhabited, and in which Rousseau must have been very badly lodged, or rather buried alive, without either air or prospect. He is now more handsomely accommodated than he ever was while in existence.

ence. He was not fit to live in this unworthy world.

It would be a tedious ſtory if I were to tell you all I have experienced from my leaving Paris to my arrival here. Poor Eudora did not remember her afflicted mother, who expected to be forgotten, and who wept neverthelefs like a child on finding it the cafe. Alas! faid I to myfelf, I am like the mothers who do not fuckle their children. I have deferved, however, more than they, and yet I am no better off. The fufpenfion of the habit of feeing me, has broken that of affection, by which this little creature was attached to me.......Whenever I think of it, my heart is ready to burſt. My child, however, has refumed her cuftomary manners, and careffes me as before; but I dare no longer believe in the fentiment, from which thofe careffes derived their value. I wiſh ſhe were ſtill in want of milk, and that I had milk to give her.

Do you, whom we count among the dearcſt of our friends, remember thofe whom you are no longer in the habit of feeing? Adieu!—I muſt conclude: we falute you affectionately.

June 9.

I HAVE this moment received your kind epiſtle, the letters-patent, and the *accompaniment*. It was already my intention to write to you; thefe matters add

add to what I had to fay; and I know no longer where to begin. Our friend receives proof-sheets; we have abundance of letters to anfwer, and to write; I did not rife till near ten o'clock, becaufe I had paffed a bad night; our good brother* Lanthenas is come; and M. Roland's fucceffor is here to receive his inftructions: we are all, as you may fuppofe, in a great buftle, and our time is very much engaged. Obliged to attend to bufinefs himfelf, in preference to epiftolary chit-chat, however agreeable it may be, our friend defires me to affure you, that he will fhortly fend an anfwer to the academy, to which you have juft had the kindnefs to make him known. At the fame time that he tranfmits you his letters, he will inform you where you may get copies of his works, in order to prefent them to that learned body. In charging you with a commiffion, I forgot to fay any thing of the money requifite for its execution: in a few days, however, a perfon will fet off from hence, who will reimburfe you all you advance. Another thing, affuredly, highly interefting. You introduced me to the acquaintance of M. Brouffonnet; and I recollect perfectly what you told me, and what I faw, of his unaffected learning, of his politenefs, and of that amenity which is fo ftrong a characteriftic of thofe whofe manners are foftened by the cultivation of their minds; nor do I forget your encou-

* Brother was the ufual appellation by which Madam Roland diftinguifhed Lanthenas, as appears by the preceding memoirs.

raging

raging me to hope that from him we might procure letters of recommendation for England. In that refpect I folicit the interference of your friendfhip, and truft to it to plead my caufe with M. Brouffonnet, on whom I cannot myfelf have any particular claim. I afk, however, for thefe letters with a confidence, which I fhould not have ventured to affume, had we been going to undertake the journey without having M. Roland in our company; in that cafe, I fhould have been perfectly fenfible, that not one of the party, and myfelf lefs than any, would have been properly qualified to cultivate the acquaintance of the fcientific people to whom M. Brouffonnet can introduce us. In a lafting connexion, we may fometimes hope to make good humour and tafte ftand in the ftead of learning, even with the learned themfelves; but when we only fee them *en paffant*, it is neceffary to be able to pay them in their own coin. Now, as you know our fecurity, I have nothing more to fay, unlefs to beg you will recall me to the recollection of your friend, by faying a thoufand handfome things in my name. We are making preparations for a fpeedy departure; time runs like a thief; the time for us to ftart alfo is very near; a thoufand things come preffing on us together; and although I am in the midft of my own houfe, and of my own family, I am only on a halt, or like a fox-hunter at the place of turning out.

I am

I am doing my duty, and executing your commiſſion: the kiſs on my own account is given ſoftly on the lips, the place reſerved for the friend of our heart; yours I give, where I ſhould have received it, upon the cheek; but very affectionately notwithſtanding. Sentiment accompanies them both, *voilà la reſſemblance**: yours has all the livelineſs of hearty friendſhip; mine, the inſinuating ſoftneſs of a more intimate union: *voilà la différence*, to make uſe of the words of the ſong, and all for your more perfect information, and in compliance with your requeſt.

I am not at all like Eudora; your dear little ſiſter has taken a place in my remembrance, and in my heart, whence nobody can diſlodge her. Let me know how ſhe is, and give her a kiſs on my account. Our friend Lanthenas has ſo many kind things to ſay to you, and the other friend, and I ſo many more, that I know not how to expreſs them all: I am almoſt *choking* with them, like Monſieur Sage.

Adieu! my good friend; our kindeſt wiſhes attend you!

---

* *Voilà la reſſemblance*, and *voilà la différence* (that is the reſemblance, and that is the difference), were alternately the burden of a French ſong, in a comic opera, much in vogue when this letter was written.—*Tranſ.*

June

June 17.

I RECEIVED your moving and melancholy epiftle yefterday, without having it in my power to anfwer it immediately. My brother-in-law was juft gone by with two friends, who could not delay their journey to London, where we fhall probably be in time to overtake them; my good man was fetting off himfelf, with his fucceffor, to make the circuit of the department; and I remained at home with the bachelor, and all the buftle of a great wafh, a thing of no fmall importance in country houfe-keeping. I did not think our friend had left you in doubt as to the deftination of the copies: there is a complete one of all his works for the academy; another of his letters only for the Count de Saluces; and a third, I believe, of thofe letters alfo for M. Lamanon. I have inquired and endeavoured to find out, to no purpofe yet, whether there be any uncommon kinds of fifh in our rivers and pools: the people of this country poffefs no more fcience in that refpect than their cooks; and although I intend to make farther refearches, I have no hopes of furnifhing any thing for your friend's Ichthyology. He will have the goodnefs not to make the information we fend him ftandard for the length of his letters.

The painter and his miftrefs who have fet every body talking about the pleafures they have enjoyed; the Marquis d'Arlandes, who alfo publifhes with-

out

out referve his pretenfions and his forrow; all that multitude of people, in fhort, who are obliged to fay they are happy, in order to be fo, appear to me very unworthy of fuccefs in their amours, and very incapable of relifhing the pleafures of love: much good may it do them! I neither envy nor efteem their mode of proceeding.

But tell me, my friend, where is your reafon and your philofophy? How can you fee a fituation in which your amiable fifter may find fo many means of becoming more amiable ftill, in fo gloomy a point of view? If fhe enjoy the income which you expected to be able to fecure to her, fhe will not lofe the hope of a fuitable match, and may wait for it in comfort. I confefs to you, that the *non ignara mali* makes me, on the contrary, look on the fituation in queftion as advantageous, and that is the way in which I fhould fpeak of it to the dear little girl, now that the forrow of the firft moment muft be fomewhat difpelled. But, alas! the fenfation occafioned by our own loffes, is an evil which a third perfon can never eftimate; nor is it always by the nature of grief, that we ought to calculate its amount! Remember, my good friend, thofe who love you, who fhare in all you fuffer, who would wifh to alleviate it, and who bear your image impreffed on their hearts.

Adieu!—I take leave of you to attend to the little matters that call for my care, and beg you to believe

believe in the truth of my affection. My brother*
defires to be remembered to you moſt kindly.

You will fee what is the deſtination of the parcel that accompanies this, and will have the goodneſs to forward it accordingly. I bid you once more farewell, without ceafing to be with you in heart and fpirit.

June 24.

YES, we love you ſtill; and I am confident ſhall always love you: you muſt undergo a great change indeed for it to be otherwife; and you are not made of ſtuff likely to diminiſh in value. Receive then, my good friend, thefe fincere profeſſions, of which I know very well you do not ſtand in need, and which I only make for the pleaſure of repeating them. We undertake your commiſſion with great pleaſure, and ſhall execute it in the beſt way we are able. Try then and find out fome means of forwarding the mufic that M. Parault is defirous of fending to London. I ſhould be very happy to execute any commiſſion for him alfo: tell him fo in my name, and affure him of my refpect and good wiſhes until I have an opportunity of doing fo in perfon. You would oblige us much by finding out and letting us know what the *Genera Plantarum*, and the *Philofophia Botanica* of Linnæus, coſt bound and new. We bought

* Lanthenas.

them,

them, but have forgotten the price, and are now about to spare them to M. d'Eu, who wants them. We shall buy them again in our way through Paris, and shall take them with us. I believe I have already sent you word that Achates set off on Tuesday: my good man is going on Saturday to finish his excursion on the coast of Calesis*, and I am to take my departure on the Thursday following. We are all, as you see, on the wing, and are only held to Amiens by a single thread. But Eudora will still remain in this same Amiens; and heaven knows how dear it will be to me as long as it is my little girl's abode! How does your good sister go on? How is her health, her disposition of mind, and her habitation? Say every thing to her in my name, that you can conceive of my feelings, and that *I* cannot express. My best and most affectionate wishes attend you.

June 28.

WHY now, would not any one suppose that it is *you* who are setting off, by your declaring that you will not write till the journey is over? If I had time, I would make you change your note; but, unfortunately, it is also the last time I shall write to you before I go. I am always doing something, and always find something to be done; the

* The district round Calais.

hours

hours fly; that of our departure will foon ftrike; and then, adieu, good night to you!

I have already heard feveral times from Achates, whom contrary winds forced to make fome little ftay at Boulogne, whence he did not fet fail till yefterday. I do not fend you the famous differtations, of a girl of twenty, on the underftanding: I fhould be obliged to look for them among a heap of dufty old papers, and have not time; but when I leave this country, I promife to pack up a few clothes with the trafh in queftion, which you fhall afterwards fee in my way through Paris, if you ftill remain in the fame mind. That is all I can do for the honour of my word; but as I perceive it is no joke to give it you, I promife nothing as to the journal. I would rather you fhould owe the obligation to my complaifance, provided I fhould have modefty enough to fhew you my fcrawl: this is pretty plain, I take it! I am called; I am in hafte; and embrace you affectionately.

Auguft 7.

WHY, truly, you have a very lively imagination, and draw moft terrible conclufions. You did not figure to yourfelf travellers arriving only to fet off again, in the midft of a thoufand embarraffments, writing in hafte, and faying but a fingle word, though their hearts dictated a hundred affectionate things. We had agreed that I fhould write to you to-morrow morning, for we devote the afternoons to packing up; and certainly you will never divine for what reafon I have taken up the pen at this moment. I will tell you at the end of my letter, and in the mean time will give you an account of your commiffions.

Dollond, the moft celebrated optician in London, fpeaks French nearly as well as I fpeak Englifh; but we went to his fhop with Monfieur Dezach, and I not only explained your intentions, but communicated to him your own words concerning the diameter, the focus, and the magnifying power of the *lens*. Dollond replied, that it was very difficult to combine thofe proportions with the effect required; that he had nothing of the kind ready made, but that he would do it in the beft way he was able. It took him feveral days, at the end of which he gave us your magnifier, as the refult of his labour, to guide him in which, the properties required had been left with him in Englifh. I fend you thefe particulars, not with a view of proving that I have done my beft, for that I am fure you will not doubt; but to confole you for what is, by the impoffibility of its being otherwife. On the other hand, I have to inform you for your fatisfaction, that Eudora knew us on our return, although fhe was in bed, and though we appeared to her as if in a dream. She kiffed me with a kind of gravity mixed with affection; and then uttered a faint cry of furprife and joy on perceiving her father. She had been in great health, and had not met with the fmalleft accident during our abfence; but next morning, while running about, fhe fell, and rolled down ftairs in fuch a way that I thought her dead, and was little better myfelf. I found at laft that fhe was not at all hurt, and foon got the better of my fright. In the mean time our friend, for whom the journey had done wonders, found himfelf much fatigued on his return, and has fince been tormented by an unfortunate tumor, which has made me very unhappy. To-morrow I mean to make him take phyfic, with ptifans, according to the old prefcriptions. I never think of him who gave them to us, of the neceffity of recurring to them, of my friend, of you, and of all the circumftances this brings to mind, without being much affected. Another perhaps would be filent on the fubject, for fear of affecting you alfo; but I feel I partake too much of what my friends fuffer, not to make them partakers in all that concerns me, efpecially in things that are almoft reciprocal.

By way of changing the theme for fomething more agreeable, I muft tell you that while making our arrangements, and packing up, a *Chevalier* defired to fpeak with me. He was come to fee the houfe, and according to military ufage, took the opportunity of paying his refpects to the miftrefs of it. He is a good kind of man; but his compliments, and all the infipid things which fuch

people

people call gallantry, put me ſo out of patience, that I ſat down to write to you by way of getting rid of him, and turned him over to our friend, who will not have done with ſuch a chatterbox in a hurry. It is but fair, however, that in all well-regulated families, each perſon ſhould take his ſhare of the burden, and this is one that I reſign to abler hands.

This reminds me of an Engliſh comedy I ſaw repreſented at London. A French *petit-maître* was introduced, and occaſioned a hearty laugh, in which we were ready to join. I ſend you no account of a journey that has given me great ſatisfaction: we will talk it over when we meet, which will be infinitely preferable. We employed our time as you may imagine; I ſeized a few haſty moments to write, and ſhall ever remember with pleaſure a country of which Delolme taught me to love the conſtitution, and where I have witneſſed the happy effects which that conſtitution has produced. Fools may chatter, and ſlaves may ſing; but you may take my word for it, that England contains men who have a right to laugh at us. I have it in my power to tell you ſome curious particulars of Lavater, with whom M. Dezach paſſed a conſiderable time.

At length we live under the ſame ſky with you, and love you as much as ever, like true friends, whoſe device you know is, *far* and *near*, *ſummer* and *winter*.

Auguſt

August 13.

INDEED you would have been very much mistaken, if you had thought I attach so much importance to my journal, as to have any objection to your seeing it. As I know you will look on it with the partial eyes of friendship, it is very much at your service; but at the same time, as it cannot be worth the attention of any but a friend, I beg you to keep it to yourself. I take the first opportunity of forwarding it to you. I thought I should give you real satisfaction by annexing to it the observations made in a journey to the same country, by my good man, in the year 1771, and written *currente calamo*. I became acquainted with him in 1775, and shortly after he communicated to me this and several other journals, with manuscripts of different kinds. It was during the perusal of them, at the time he was making the tour of Italy, that I wrote the loose sheet which you will find inclosed, and which, strange as it may appear, he has not yet seen. You will probably be of opinion, that the young solitary maid, who thus studied his character while reading his works, began by not hating him; and you will not be deceived. But it may appear singular that you should be the first to whom, after such a length of time, I have communicated the opinion I formed of him in 1777.

I was reading at the same period a work of Delolme upon the English constitution, and would
send

fend you the abstract I made of it, if it were to be found.—By the way, the author has juft publiſhed a new edition, which I faw at London, and which I advife you to read as the beft book, in the opinion of the Engliſh themfelves, that was ever written upon their conftitution.

Auguſt 25.

WITH one leg on a chair, the other foot on the ground, and my arms on the corner of a defk, which is no longer mine, I once more, my worthy friend, write you a few lines from this place. I am about to leave it, certainly for a great while, perhaps for ever; and am happy to mark every era of my life by a particular attention to the duties of friendſhip. Receive then a renewal of the affurances I have fo often given you in this place, and which I ſhall be happy to repeat wherever I may be.

Every thing is ready, and our effects are in the carriage. It is going to Monſieur d'Eu's, where we are to dine, and whence we ſhall fet off. Adieu!—I am about to increafe the diftance between us; but it is in order to ſhorten it afterwards, and in the hope of embracing you ere long. In the mean time our beſt wiſhes attend you. Adieu!— We ſhall ſhortly meet.

Longpont,

Longpont, Thursday Morning, Sept. 13.

YOU left me diſtreſſed and affected beyond meaſure, at the moment when we were about to be ſeparated by an interval of a hundred leagues; at the moment, perhaps, of taking an everlaſting leave; at the moment when, in the effuſion of my ſoul, and with the hands of my huſband and my daughter joined in yours, I was renewing the ſacred compact of friendſhip, a compact which was the more ſolemn, becauſe accompanied by a ſilence which none of us could break; at that moment you tore yourſelf away, and fled from our preſence!........I remained motionleſs on my ſeat, with my child in my arms, and my eyes, ſwimming with tears, fixed upon the door through which you had juſt paſſed. In what ſtate were you then yourſelf?

Your image has purſued us hither, and will follow us everywhere; and our ſouls, ſteeped in the bitterneſs in which we ſaw you plunged, will refuſe to welcome the pleaſures that ſurround us, till we are aſſured that you confide in your friends, that you love them, and that you are perſuaded of their affection; till confidence, in ſhort, ſhall reſtore the intimate union of former days. Would you, my young and kind-hearted friend, puniſh thoſe who love you for an act of diſcretion which their ſenſibility thought due to yours? Search to the bottom of your own heart, and judge of ours, and then tell me if it be poſſible for us to be any

thing

thing but what we profefs to be. Return, my good friend, to the bofom of confidence: it is made for your honeft heart. The injury your fenfibility did us by believing that we had done you one, was an error of fentiment, proceeding from its excefs. Write to us, my worthy friend, unbofom yourfelf, receive our affectionate embraces, and let us renew our oath of eternal friendfhip.

My heart is full, I am in hafte, and have a crowd ftanding round me. Adieu!—Come here on Sunday.—Herewith you will receive the tranflation you defired: the beft wifhes of our friend Lanthenas, and of *my* friend, and my own, attend you!

Clos la Platière, Oct. 3.

TELL me then, my good friend, what is become of your affection for thofe who continue to feel for you the moft tender attachment, the trueft efteem, and friendfhip the moft fincere? I wrote to you from Longpont; and our friend Lanthenas has by this time repeated to you the expreffions dictated by our hearts. We flattered ourfelves, I confefs, we fhould find a letter from you here, or receive one foon after our arrival, for we wrote to you from Dijon alfo; and are as much diftreffed by your filence now, as we were afflicted by your tears. Obdurate man, whofe imagination does us all fo much harm, why do you refufe to open your heart to truth, to confidence, and to friendfhip, fo long tried? It is in vain you oppofe to them

the

the illufions by which you fuffer yourfelf to be deceived: the franknefs of our affection cannot fail to bring you back to our arms. I fhould, indeed, no longer know what to think of any thing, if your error could hold out long againft the truth, and the energy of the fentiments of which, in our connection with you, we have ever obeyed the impulfe. Open your eyes, my good friend, and turn them on the worthy people who love you; who could never find any thing but reafons to love you more and more, and who defire nothing fo much as the renewal of your attachment. We arrived here without accident, but much fatigued: our brother was come to meet us, and we immediately fet about opening trunks, and packing up anew, in order to go into the country, where we now are. I have not the heart to fpeak to you of any thing relative to the perfons I have about me, till you have given me figns of life. You have learnt from our friends that we have feen M. Maret, M. de Morveaux, and M. Durande; and that we have bought your fkins, which we have with us, and which we wait for your directions to forward, unlefs we fhould in the mean time find a favourable opportunity. The letter written at Dijon was put in the poft-office at Beaune, becaufe we fet off early in the morning, and did not wifh to leave it at the inn. To-morrow our friend will take this to Villefranche; and I fhall quarrel with you in good earneft if he do not find a letter there. Tell our friend Lan-

thenas

thenas that we are well, and that we shall wait to embrace him without flinching. He has certainly been at Vincennes to fee my Agatha, &c. I shall thank him for all his care whenever he will add that of coming to fee us. Say a thoufand civil, kind, and affectionate things for me to M. Parault.

Adieu, my good friend!—Tell me, is it a matter of indifference to you to receive frequent affurances of our loving you as much as ever? My beft love to your dear fifter.

Villefranche, Nov. 7.

AT length we have received a letter from you, my good friend: on our part, it is ftill with the fame joy as in times paft: what is the reafon that, on yours, it is not written with the fame pleafure and friendfhip? Be it as it may, you will find us ever the fame, and the day perhaps will come, when you will fay, that people whofe attachment to you had been of an ordinary kind, would not have been capable of taking fo much trouble, and fo conftantly to perfevere in it, to perfuade you to the contrary *. What intereft, but that of the heart, could be our inducement? You will become fenfible of it; you will open your heart to confidence, and will indemnify us by its intenfity for that interruption in its duration, which was occafioned by the unfortunate cloud that hangs over your mind. I am perfectly fatisfied of it, becaufe a fenfe of our

* This feems inaccurate; but it is rendered exactly from the original.

claims

claims on your friendship is inherent in the love we bear you, and carries with it the affurance of being able to bring you back to truth. This is the laſt time I ſhall ſpeak to you on the ſubject. I ſhall continue our correſpondence on that footing which we have no reaſon to change, and you ſhall perceive that, ſo far from avoiding our ſick friends, we renew, on ſuch occaſions, the ſacred vows of friendſhip, which unite us to them for ever.

My good man is juſt ſet off for a circuit in the mountains of his department, and is afterwards to make a ſhort ſtay at Lyons, ſo that I ſhall be ten days at leaſt, perhaps a fortnight, without ſeeing him. The houſe is full of workmen; and my apartment is nearly finiſhed; but much remains to be done to the Inſpector's ſtudy. We ſhall have things of this kind to attend to for a long while; and I am ſadly afraid leſt the maſons, over whom it is neceſſary to keep an eye, ſhould prevent our going in the ſummer to botanize on Mount Pila. Our friend Lanthenas, who left us the third of this month, muſt have mentioned us to you more than once, and has a great deal to ſay ſtill, if he means to execute the whole of his commiſſion. My little Eudora prattles more than ever, and I am extremely pleaſed to ſee that ſhe grows more and more fond of my company, and will no longer conſent to leave me. She called to me to-night to aſk where you were, and whether you were not to come and ſee us. In playing about us ſhe has already learnt a part

part of her alphabet, and whenever I take up a book infifts upon looking at it. I have had little leifure fince my arrival here; for you muft know it is the cuftom to vifit the new comers; and I fhould already have had the whole town with me, if several perfons were not ftill in the country, which prevents their vifits from being over quite fo foon as they would otherwife have been: befides, my mother-in-law keeps a great deal of company; but I flip away the moment they fit down to cards to our good brother's ftudy, and there we read the journals, or whatever elfe comes to hand; converfe on literary fubjects, or concert plans for the future, with fo much friendfhip and unreferve, that fupper always comes too foon. I muft beg you to procure me Bemerzrieder's Leffons of Harmony for the Harpfichord, in quarto, of which you once bought a copy for a friend of mine; but I am in no hurry; for I have no harpfichord, and it is an acquifition not quite fo eafy to make. My hufband will have other matters to communicate to you on his return. We left the country at the moment when an untimely fall of fnow had produced a great change in the fcenery around us. If the neceffity, however, of making our arrangements had not called us to town, we fhould have been in no great hafte to come here. The news of the war gives me pain, becaufe I always confider thefe quarrels of kings as ruinous to the people; and I regret it the more, fince it gives you particular caufe of uneafinefs.

Send

Send us an account of every thing new that relates to the fciences, to authors, to the academies, or to intrigues. I fhould have afked you firft for particulars of your prefent ftudies and occupations, if your obfervations on thofe fubjects did not oblige me to wait for the moment when it will be agreea ble to yourfelf to mention them. My beft compliments to M. Parault, whom you have no doubt the pleafure of fometimes feeing. We have been long in expectation of news from Amiens, and are almoft doubtful of the fate of a parcel, in confequence of the filence of a man who is interefted in its contents, and to whom it was to be given by M. d'Eu.

Adieu!—Do not forget thofe who love you, and whofe attachment to you is unalterable. I embrace you in the name of my little family.

November 21.

IN a parcel addreffed to us by our friend Lar- thenas, I found the enclofed letter to you, and embrace with pleafure this opportunity of writing you a few lines. Happy as I am always in doing fo, I frequently reprefs my defire for fear of tiring you: you cannot imagine the pain this idea gives me! But after all, I am too much your friend, either to leave you to your unfortunate prejudices, or to combat them in a troublefome way.

You muft put thefe forrowful expreffions to the account of impreffions of the fame nature, which I cannot help feeling at this moment. It was not

my

my intention to fay any thing more on the fubject; but my heart overflows in fpite of me. I was much affected by your dear fifter's letter, which I fhall anfwer immediately. It came to me with the direction in your hand-writing; but not another word. What then is the matter with my friend? Forgive me once more for recurring to complaints: I pardon every thing that proceeds from your fenfibility; and you will readily excufe fome little effects of mine. I am once more a widow: my good man returned from the mountains, and juft fet off again for Lyons; my brother-in-law is in the country, directing pioneers, ftone-cutters, &c. My dear Eudora has a very bad cold, for the firft time in her life: when fhe coughs it goes to my heart, and alarms and torments me beyond defcription. The dear little girl remembers you perfectly; but recollects lefs of your playing with her, than of the ftate fhe faw you in at our departure. ' *Mamma,*' faid fhe this morning, in her foft tone of voice, which already befpeaks fentiment, ' *M. d'Antic cries!*' She brought the tears into my eyes alfo.

My health is but indifferent. I am looking over a prefcription that I brought with me from Paris, and making comments on it in my own way. When I recollect that it is for this paper, and a vifit made and received on account of a man, of whom I have never heard any thing fince; when I recollect, I fay, that on fuch a foundation your friendfhip has built

built I know not what monſtrous chimera, I cann
help ſaying to myſelf, either you muſt be very mad
or I muſt be very fooliſh, not to underſtand any
thing about the matter; or rather, I neither know
what to ſay, think, or do.

Harkye, my good friend; we ſhall be conſtantly
harping on the ſame ſtring, if you do not recover
your reaſon. I promiſe you, however, not to return
to this again, and I promiſe you above all, that my
friendſhip for you ſhall be unalterable: this is what
I know, what I underſtand, and what pleaſes me
beſt. Take a box on the ear, and an embrace,
equally hearty and ſincere; for ſuch is the way in
which I muſt vent the mixture of good and ill-humour that conſtitutes my feelings at this moment.
Adieu!—I long to receive a letter from you in the
old ſtyle. Burn this, and let us ſay no more on ſuch
a nonſenſical ſubject.

December 15.

I HAD rather you would confeſs the ill you
think of us, than have merely the right of believing that you think well, without receiving the
aſſurances of it from your own mouth. Take us,
at leaſt, my good friend, for the confidantes of your
ſentiments and opinions in every thing that concerns us: we ſhall be ſufficiently ſatisfied with what
we are, to bear every thing you may believe us to
be without imputing it to you as a crime. Do not
tear the letters you may have written to me in
the

the fulnefs of your heart; every thing that iffues thence is as grateful and as dear to me as it ever was. Your error is the effect of a degree of fenfibility, which attaches us more ftrongly to you; and the caufe alone would cancel a great deal of injuftice. I underftand the ftate of your mind much better fince I have had a converfation *tête-à-tête* with our friend Lanthenas, concerning the reafons you had to complain of the perfon in queftion; but your ideas are not the lefs falfe in regard to us. I fhall lament as long as I live, a piece of falfe delicacy which has proved fo prejudicial to a friendfhip I thought unalterable; but what am I faying! it will triumph over that obftacle; and if the filence of a moment (although proceeding from excellent motives on our part) muft needs appear fo terrible an offence in your eyes, you cannot at leaft help forgiving and forgetting it, for the fake of friends whofe regret well deferves fuch a facrifice. The day will come, when you will love us the better for having borne with this fally of ardent youth, and confidered it in a proper point of view; our tears, my good friend, flow refponfive to yours. Is it not very ftrange, that being fo well agreed, and fo entirely attached to one another, fo much fhould yet be wanting to our happinefs? Until the defired revolution take place in your mind, as I fully expect it will, let me preferve and correfpond with the friend of Eudora: you will not vifit the fins of her parents upon her head; and my heart will be grateful to you for the exception, which, in fpite of your error, you are ftill juft enough to make. The friend of my child has great claims on my affection: I will fpeak to you of her on your own account, and of ourfelves on hers; and you fhall find me as fincere, as full of confidence, and as much attached to you as ever. The dear little girl has recovered all the vigour of full health, at the expenfe of two dofes of phyfic. Is it not dreadful to be fo foon obliged to employ thefe falutary poifons? But fuch is the effect of fociety, and the fedentary life of towns! Her mind continues to develop itfelf more and more, and I truft that her heart will be no ftranger to foft and virtuous affections.

If you knew how angry I am with myfelf, on account of an opportunity I have loft, I think you could not help pitying me. A friend whom we had at Rome, came and paffed four and twenty hours with us on his way to Paris, where he means to fettle; and I was to have given him the fkins we bought for you at Dijon. But his fellow-travellers carried him off fooner than he expected, for his intention was to ftay at leaft two days; the fkins were left behind, and I was angry at my forgetfulnefs an hour after the poft-chaife had driven off. If you knew of any other channel, I imagine you would point it out to me; but I cannot defcribe to you the rage I was in.—We talked of you, of Lavater, and of a thoufand agreeable things. Monfieur

fieur Le Monnier, who, if I miſtake not, is to alight at M. Vincent's, of the academy, is quite full of him, which he has juſt viſited the ſecond time. He is a man of gentle and agreeable manners; is acquainted with Monſieur Rome de l'Iſle; and like all thoſe who know that worthy character, holds him in the higheſt eſteem: the children of the arts are allied by nature to thoſe of the ſciences.

I hear pretty frequently from our friend Lanthenas, without knowing any more, than yourſelf how his projects go on. Perhaps he does not know himſelf: he muſt neceſſarily be much dependent on circumſtances.

I take it very kindly of you to have been at the pains of procuring me certain accounts of Agatha. I do not return you thanks for it, becauſe I place all your attentions to the account of friendſhip; they are engraven on my heart, though my mouth paſſes them over in ſilence. My good man is ſtill at Lyons. Arriving at that place on horſeback, he ran againſt a carriage, and hurt his leg. The miſchief, however, is now over; and he writes and runs about at a terrible rate. My health has been deplorable in the full force of the term; but I have been recovering remarkably within this laſt week, and begin to think myſelf no longer ſick. Say a thouſand kind things for me to your ſiſter: I attach myſelf to all that belongs to you; and beg you to repay my affection to my daughter, if you cannot make a return of it to myſelf.

self. In that case I shall stifle half my complaints, and utter the rest in a low voice. Adieu, my dear friend! move about, and mix with the world; and may you meet with beings as sensible of your worth, and as affectionate as ourselves.

It is an age since I wrote to Amiens; visits upon visits, and study, and various odd jobs besides, and then repose, which is so delightful in the unreserved intimacy of a brother......Time flies, and a thousand things are forgotten—You will never be forgotten.

December 20.

WELL! my good friend, how are you going on? In what state are your health, business, connexions, and study? Are all these things as you could wish, as we should desire, and as we could contribute to make them, as far as relates to friendship at least, if our hearts were known to you? But why should I again make a doubt of it? Let us say no more on the subject, but act with confidence in each other.

I have received the inclosed draft from Lyons, in order to transmit it to Paris; and you are the person I have pitched upon, because there is nobody to whom we would sooner be under an obligation. I beg you to receive the amount, and to procure in exchange a good bill, upon Lyons or Villefranche, of equal value. I suppose you will get one more easily on the former town; or what perhaps would be better than applying to the merchants, you may send to the custom-house or

post-

post-office, for a rescription on me of the receivers of Lyons.

Eudora is perfectly well: her strength and gaiety are as brilliant as ever, and her mind makes a considerable progress. I am better also; and am in daily expectation of seeing my good man. We have no news here, except the effervescence in the minds of the Lyonnese, on account of the election of a new Prévôt des Marchands, and the intrigues and satires customary on such occasions. The weather is horribly cold; our roads over the mountains are unpassable; and the others are not much better.

Our friend is at present much taken up with the academy at Lyons.—The academy has, as you may suppose, numbered him among its associates. The study is not yet arranged; and a sad thing it is to have any thing to do in so rigorous a season. It is some time since I heard from our friend Lanthenas. He is returned to his father's, and owing to his having a great deal of occupation, is a little in arrears in his epistolary correspondence: he regrets it much in regard to you, and desired me to tell you he would make amends the first opportunity.

Say a thousand kind and affectionate things for me to your dear sister; and as many more to the excellent Monsieur Parault. The shepherd Sylvain has been sadly treated on account of his work saved from the deluge: the *Année Literaire* has lashed him terribly.

terribly. It is a fhame for the critics thus to hurl Jove's thunder againſt a few wild flowers. What are all your ſcientific friends ſaying and doing? Tell me who is advanced to the academy of ſciences? and whether M. Brouſſonnet be ſtill at the door. Adieu, my good friend!—Let us end the preſent year, and begin the new, under the auſpices of hearty and affectionate friendſhip: I renew that which I have vowed to you, in the fulneſs and ſincerity of my heart.

February 9, 1785.

YOU ſee I pay you in your own coin; if not with my own hands, at leaſt through the medium of a third perſon, and that I have ſent you *a little quality* alſo. It appears to me that you *lavaterize* perfectly well with the *Countefs*, and that you have a vaſt field for obſervation to go over. You ought by this time to be an adept. Tell me then what you have diſcovered or recognized in our portraits. I wiſh much to know whether you will divine aright, and more eſpecially what my countenance beſpeaks. Your idea of the original is perhaps a little confuſed: you were not a doctor of phyſiognomy when you had an opportunity of examining it, and the veil is now a hundred leagues thick; but I ſhall be the better able to judge whether our portraits be well drawn. Speak to me frankly on the ſubject: I cannot, however, help telling you beforehand, that either you are a very bad diſciple of

Lavater,

Lavater, or the portraits in queſtion are very little like, if you do not find in them the lines that characterize true friends. I thought I had written you word that our friend Lanthenas was very buſy, and that he had commiſſioned me to tell you not to be ſurpriſed, if you ſhould be ſome ſhort time without hearing from him: he has ſuffered twelve long days to paſs without writing us a line. We have received the two tranſlations of the worthy M. Parault. The firſt I underſtand very well; but as to the other, I am quite loſt in it: it would be neceſſary to be able to ſay with Swedenborg, *I have ſeen* this ſame intellectual world. A-propos of ſeeing—our family is very ill provided with the means: we have all bad eyes. Thoſe of the grandmother, the two ſons, and the daughter-in-law, are all inflamed, and we all complain alike of a burning and ſhooting pain. What is ſtill worſe is, that we have not been laughing like you: we are not very gay when we cannot ſee why, and are almoſt tempted to be melancholy.

You may make the moſt you can of this ſtyle, one half proper, and one half figurative: I am ſometimes inclined to write nonſenſe, as well as the Counteſs.

I muſt tell you, however, in plain language, that you are beginning to grow amiable again; you are a little of the braggadocio neverthelefs; but at your age it is pardonable; and then if at a hundred leagues diſtance one were bound to take notice of

every

every thing !........At the end of the reckoning, and all joking apart, we love you dearly, and embrace you moſt affectionately. I do not know how you have paſſed your carnival; but as to me, I am ſober enough to edify the whole town; and lucky it is that I am; for the ſiſter-in-law of a very regular canon, who bears no reſemblance to thoſe of the capital, is obliged, under pain of public and private ſcandal, to be very regular alſo.

Our Eudora, our little delight, grows, and entertains us with her prattle. At this moment ſhe is putting out her little mouth, and trying to kiſs us, after having received from papa a tap upon her fingers, which were overturning every thing upon the table. She repeats your name, and ſometimes deſires to ſee what you have written about her. You tell me nothing of your dear ſiſter: recall us to her recollection, and do not forget in the midſt of changeable Paris, your unalterable friends,

March 16.

EQUABILITY and conſtancy you are ſure of finding in us at all times, and you will one day or other, perhaps, value them more than you do at preſent. Return to ſuch friends without fear: they will never bear you any ill will for having ſhewn yourſelf ſuch as you are. You would wiſh then for long letters? while I, conſidering the diſpoſition of mind in which I thought you would obſtinately perſevere, had reſolved to write to you very briefly,

briefly, until time should render you such in respect to us, as I always hoped you would become. Glory to heaven, and peace upon earth, if it be true that I am no longer bound to act according to that resolution which I had but just taken! Have you received all the letters I have written you? A very old one, inclosing another for your sister; and one of recent date, with a note addressed to my father.

I send you this time some papers for *M. Le Monnier, painter, at the Little St. Anthony, Rue du Roi de Sicile*. I have been thinking, if you were not desirous of knowing a man, with whom we are connected by the ties of friendship, you would at least be pleased to see an estimable artist, of mild and agreeable manners, lately returned from Italy, where he made a long stay. But why do I express an unpleasant and fleeting doubt, without avowing the sentiment that serves as its corrective? Yes, I still believe that a person who has lately seen us, and with whom we are in habits of intimacy, is for that sole reason not altogether uninteresting to you. Eudora improves in strength much more than in learning and discretion: she is very lively, and very giddy, although brought up alone. She is, in short, a perfect romp, whose violent animal spirits will stand in need of a strong mind to govern them. She has all the intelligence that can be expected at her time of life, and can put up with any thing, even with dry bread, when doing penance.—Beaumarchais, at *St. Lazare*, sounds like a ludicrous antithesis. He

is

is puniſhed like a ſchool-boy, and will revenge himſelf like a fox.

I am called: adieu!—I thank you for your good
wiſhes, and conclude like you, *toto corde.*

March 23.

I HAD a great mind to make my daughter
ſpeak; but I have too much to ſay on my own
account; and ſhall content myſelf with ſending you
a ſheet of paper, which ſhe has ſcrawled over in her
own way. You made me weep with your ſtories,
after having made me laugh with the grave ſuper-
ſcription of your letter. Eudora was much pleaſed
to hear that you had written to her. In ſhort, I
read her the letter; and when ſhe heard the name
of mother, and the recommendation to kiſs, ſhe ſaid
with a laugh, 'Why, that's for me now.' You have
no need of a pardon, I aſſure you, on account of
the matter that makes you aſk it. Do you think
I ſtand in need of proteſtations and aſſurances as
to things of that ſort? The two following lines
would apply perfectly well to the preſent caſe:

Il ſuffit entre nous de ton devoir, du mien,
Voilà les vrais ſermens, les autres ne ſont rien*.

If I had ever any thing to forgive you, it would have
been the unfortunate idea, of which the traces are
not yet effaced; but my attachment left generoſity
nothing to do: it enabled me to form a juſt eſti-
mate of the errors of yours, in which I could ſee

---

* Between us, your duty and mine will ſuffice: theſe are the
beſt oaths; the others are nothing.

nothing but marks of its ſtrength, and perhaps I love you better than if you had not done me the wrong of aſcribing one to me that I do not feel myſelf guilty of. In proportion as time ſhall reſtore all its ſplendour to truth, you will perceive that you have loſt nothing by the diſtance you regret, becauſe you will ſee it has operated no change in the affection of your friends; nor will the pleaſure of a friendly correſpondence ſeem to be impaired by a few leagues further to travel over in idea.

You aſk me what I am about, and do not ſuppoſe I have the ſame occupations as at Amiens: it is true I have leſs leiſure to devote to them, or to intermingle them with agreeable ſtudies. Houſe-keeping is now my principal employ, and the trouble it gives me is of no ſmall account. My brother was deſirous of my taking charge of the houſe, which his mother for many years had ceaſed to ſuperintend, and which he was tired of directing, or of leaving to the care of the ſervants. —This is the way in which I paſs my time. On riſing, I buſy myſelf about my child and my huſband. I make the former read, and get breakfaſt for them both, and then I leave them together in the ſtudy; or if the father be abſent, the little girl remains with the maid, while I go and inquire into the houſehold affairs, from the cellar to the garret: the fruit, the wine, the linen, and other details, contribute each their part to my ſtock of daily cares. If I have any time left (obſerve,

we

We dine at noon, and are obliged to be then in decent drefs, becaufe there is a chance of our having company, which the old lady is fond of inviting), I pafs it in the ftudy, in the labours which I have been accuftomed to fhare with my hufband. After dinner we ftay a little while together, and I remain pretty conftantly with my mother-in-law till company comes. I am then at liberty, and go up ftairs to the ftudy in order to begin, or to continue to write; but when the evening comes, our good brother joins us, and we read the newfpaper, or fomething better. Male vifitors fometimes come up. If I am not the reader, I fit down modeftly to my needlework, and liften, taking care to prevent the child from interrupting; for fhe never leaves us, unlefs on occafion of fome formal repaft. As I do not wifh her to be troublefome to any one, or take up the attention of the company, fhe then ftays in her own room, or goes to take a walk with her maid, and does not make her appearance till the end of the deffert. I never pay vifits unlefs they are abfolutely neceffary. I go out sometimes, though yet it has been but feldom, to take a walk with my good man and Eudora. Bating thofe little differences, every day fees me go over the fame ground, and turn in the fame circle. The Englifh, the Italian, and mufic, which is fo much my delight, remain far behind. They are talents and inclinations which lie hidden under the afhes, but which I fhall know where to find in order to inftil them into

my

my Eudora in proportion as she grows up. Order and peace in every thing that furrounds me, in the matters entrufted to me, and among the perfons with whom I am connected, added to the intereft of my child, of which, amid my various cares, I never lofe fight; thefe conftitute my bufinefs, and my pleafure. This kind of life would be very auftere, were not my hufband a man of great merit, whom I love with all my heart; but, with this *datum*, it is moft delightful. Tender friendfhip, and unbounded confidence, mark every inftant of it, keep an account of every thing, and ftamp a value upon every thing, which nothing without them would have. It is the life the moft favourable to the practice of virtue, and to the fupport of all the inclinations and of all the purfuits that infure focial and individual happinefs in the ftate of fociety wherein we live. I am fenfible of its worth; I congratulate myfelf on enjoying it, and exert my beft endeavours to make it laft. I pleafe myfelf with the hope that the world, on fome future day, will bear witnefs to my deferving what I once expreffed to M. d'Ornay:

>*Heureufe la mere attendrie*
>*Qui peut dire avant d'expirer;*
>*J'ai fait plus que donner la vie,*
>*Mes foins l'ont appris à l'aimer*.*

My brother-in-law, of an extremely gentle temper, and of great fenfibility of mind, is very reli-

* Happy the tender mother who can fay before fhe expires, I have not only given life, my cares have rendered it agreeable.

gious

gious alfo. I leave him the fatisfaction of thinking his articles of faith appear as evident to me, as they feem to be to him; and act outwardly as becomes the mother of a family in the country to do, whofe conduct ought to be edifying to every body about her. Having been very religious in my early youth, I am as well acquainted with the fcriptures, and even with the church fervice, as with the heathen philofophers, and willingly avail myfelf of my facred erudition, which pleafes him exceedingly. Truth, the bent of my difpofition, and the facility with which I conform to every thing that is agreeable to others, while it is no violation of honour or decorum, makes me what I ought to be naturally, and without the fmalleft effort. Keep this effufion of confidence to yourfelf, and do not anfwer it, unlefs in fuch a vague way as may fuit the fubject. I am ftill alone: my good man is at Lyons, whence he will not return till after Eafter: he writes that his eyes are getting better; and I have had a frefh affurance of it from his fervant, who came here to execute a few commiffions, and who is fince returned to his mafter. You may judge by thefe effufions of friendfhip, whether I believe in yours, to which I truft for your fetting a due value on this teftimony of mine.

It was my intention to have faid fomething of the academy, of Beaumarchais, and of that attractive fyftem of chymiftry which engages your attention; but I have taken the time of writing to you out of the interval that remains between my morning bufinefs and dinner. I have only ten minutes to drefs, which are precifely as many as it generally takes me. I embrace you with all my heart.

Give me fome account of academic and fcientific matters; and more efpecially of your own perfonal concerns.—Once more adieu.

March 26.

YOUR ftory of the pointed nofe puts me out of all patience; it feems to me that mine is not fo, and that, unfortunately perhaps, I could at leaft enter into competition with all the fharp nofes in the univerfe. But you are quite filent as to the portrait, and the *Lavateric* obfervations which you have made upon the fubject. What care I for your fkill in phyfiognomy, if it teach me nothing concerning my own face? Anfwer me then, fpeak without difguife, and we will difpute afterwards, if we fee occafion. You will find Le M. an agreeable man, whom you would wifh perhaps to poffefs a little more energy; and above all, a little more of that turn of mind that borders upon madnefs, and that does fuch wonders in his art. I fhould be at no lofs to find excellent means to juftify my delay in bringing you acquainted with him; for in the point of view in which you exhibited yourfelf to me, I had reafon to fear it might look like importunity, if I made too frequent calls on your attention,

tion; but fuppofing I was in the wrong in that refpect, I freely confent to give you this fubject of forgivenefs, by way of eftablifhing a perfect equality between us.

April 9.

I WILL now confefs that I applaud your acquaintance for not choofing to employ themfelves for any body but you, and hold myfelf obliged to them for acting and thinking in that manner. I can eafily conceive that your excellent heart makes you defire ftill greater means of being ufeful to your friends; but you ought not to regret the want of thofe you do not poffefs. Your true friends have no occafion for proofs of intereft and power, to make them believe in the return of the tender friendfhip they have fworn to you. Thofe friends will always be greater gainers by your availing yourfelf of all the means that ftudy and philofophy furnifh for your perfonal improvement, than by the multiplicity of your connexions, and a fuperior degree of influence. Do not then go in fearch of dinners and *ennui* for the fake of advantages, which it is eafier to do without, than to be contented with. If ever you turn your mind to ambition, it will increafe with your fuccefs, and engrofs your whole foul to the very end of your career. But enough of moralizing. I am out of fpirits, however —my Eudora is not very well: her cold indeed does not increafe; but her cough refembles the one that

is

is the forerunner of the meafles: fhe is a little drowfy, and laft night appeared to me to have a fever. To-day I am to take advice. Her father is no better; his cough is no longer relieved by expectoration; and he feels himfelf ftuffed up, and ill at his eafe. May heaven fend you better health! Adieu!—We embrace you with all our hearts. Say a thoufand kind things for us to M. Parault.

It is not true that Eudora has been told not to love you a dozen years hence; but only to hold her tongue about it, and let you find it out.

April 20.

I AM much more eafy in regard to Eudora; and without daring to flatter myfelf fhe will efcape the prevailing difeafes, I hope, in cafe fhe catches, fhe will get fafe over them. They propofe giving her a dofe of phyfic; but as I wifh to fpare her the naufeous draught, we are at prefent temporizing. The poor child is fadly altered! You cannot figure to yourfelf my regret at feeing fo tender a little being forced already to fubmit to difgufting and racking remedies. It would feem that medicine ought only to be calculated to relieve the infirmities of age, or the violent diforders which our phyfical and moral exceffes produce. But that amiable infancy fhould ftand in need of a fallacious art, is a perverfion of all order, and a real fubject of lamentation. Happy thofe who in fuch circumftances can find motives of confidence in a man of abilities! There is not here a single physician on whom I can venture to depend. I have however sent for one; and have got into a fine quarrel with another. We are so alarmed for what we love, that we are always seeking for opinions, without daring to follow our own.—But let us return to the academies, of which you have sent us such entertaining accounts. My good man would wish to know a great deal more of Quatre-mere's Treatise upon Sheep, or rather of Berthollet's, upon *The Theory of Bleaching:* I recollect it is the latter which, when setting off, he desired me to mention to you, in order that you might communicate to him all the information you possess, or may be able to procure, on the subject. He affirms also, you have said nothing concerning the oily and farinaceous feeds, unless that you cannot discover any grounds for a system: now *the tall meagre man, with a tenor voice,* is not at all satisfied with such a result: he will have a system, even if it be brought from the moon, like so many other hypotheses.

The weather is at last grown milder; but I do not recover my strength; and if it were not for the activity of my mind, I should bear a great resemblance to the silkworms, when they are about to spin their cocoons, and drag themselves languidly along. I cannot discover that I have any particular ailment, but always feel as if I were much fatigued; and notwithstanding my endeavours to preserve a sprightly appearance, lassitude announces

itself

itself by drawing a hollow circle round my eyes. If my Eudora, however, recover her health, and our friend find himself the better for the country, the pleasure I shall feel at their welfare will make me forget my own trifling complaints.

April 22.

YOU gave me a scolding in your short epistle which I received yesterday; and I cannot deny you might have some reason; but I was so taken up with my child, and so fatigued in body and mind, that perhaps I was not very much to blame.

Eudora, though better, is not exactly what I could wish: she is so livid, so........I do not know what, that I am alarmed, without well knowing why. We have really and truly the smallpox in our horrible house, where we are obliged to have two lodgers, because we are not able to fill it ourselves, although our family is tolerably large. We are here a hundred years behind Paris in building and fitting up our houses, at least as far as relates to the laying out of apartments, and still more in the little matters of ornament: it would seem that we are quite as far behind Lyons, although we are only at the distance of five leagues. True it is, that owing to local circumstances, wood, and all other carpenter's materials, are very dear in this little town, where the principal luxury is that of the table. At the house of every little citizen, who is at all above the common, more fumptuous repafts are given than in the richeft houfes at Amiens, and even than in many very fubftantial ones at Paris.

Uncomfortable houfes, a luxurious table, elegant dreffes, and continual play, fometimes for large fums; fuch are the principal features of a town where all the houfes are flat-roofed, and where the fmall ftreets ferve as drains for the privies. On the other hand, the inhabitants are by no means ftupid: they fpeak pretty well, without any provincial accent, and even without ufing incorrect expreffions. Their manners are alfo genteel and agreeable; but they are a little, that is to fay, *very deficient*, in information. Our counfellors are looked upon as very important perfonages; our advocates are as proud as thofe of Paris, and the attornies are as great rogues here as every where elfe. In another refpect, it is quite the reverfe of Amiens: there the women are generally fuperior to the men; at Villefranche they are the contrary, and in the women it is that the ruft of the country is the moft perceptible.

I do not know why nor wherefore I have thus undertaken to do the honours of my adoptive country. I confider it as my own, and treat it accordingly, as you may perceive.

La Blancherie then has got his head above water again? I faw the opening of his rooms advertized in the *Journal de Paris*. Why, by my faith, thefe

mufeums

muſeums are like the phœnix: they riſe every year out of their own aſhes. Were you at the fitting of the academy when the panegyric of Gebelin was pronounced? Adieu!—Our males are ſtill in the country, for which they find themſelves the better: one of them is to return immediately to the dove-cot: I leave you to gueſs which.

April 28.

THE poſt does not ſet off till to-morrow; I wrote to you yeſterday; it is only nine o'clock in the morning, and I have a thouſand things to do; but I have received your agreeable chit-chat of the twenty-fifth, and am ſitting down to pay you in kind. I need very little provocation to induce me to enter into this friendly warfare with thoſe I love.

I have juſt received accounts of the male part of our family, by one of the vine-dreſſers, who brings us every Thurſday a proviſion of butter, eggs, vegetables, &c. Are not theſe pretty things to put in a letter? but they are of great uſe in a family; they recall rural occupations to our minds, and in that point of view are very agreeable. My poor turtle-dove is quite frozen with the cold winds that prevail; I ſhall not ſee him, however, in a hurry; for his brother is to return on Saturday to confeſs the nuns, and he muſt ſtay behind to ſuperintend the operations of the cellar. All our ſervants are gone down, or rather, up there; there is nothing but *caps* in the houſe,

house, and only think of my simplicity! I have not sent for a single *beau* to divert me. It is not because there is any want of beaux in town; but they are not tempting. The young men of this place are not agreeable; and it is no wonder; for the women do not underſtand their buſineſs. Travels, and obſervation, are neceſſary to give them a poliſh; and accordingly they return home more amiable men; while the women remain in their corner, with their little airs and graces, by which nobody is impoſed upon.

I believe my experience would be of great uſe to your *Lavaterian* knowledge, if I were to enlighten your obſervations on the face which you are ſtudying, and of which the lips diſpleaſe you. Nature has made her good, and has endowed her, not with wit, but with ſound ſenſe: her faculties are not enlarged, or improved by education; nor muſt you expect to find in her either ideas above the common, or taſte, or delicacy, or that exquiſite ſenſibility that proceeds from an organization peculiarly happy, or from a well-cultivated mind. Add to this on one hand, that eaſe of manners which a knowledge of the world generally confers; and on the other, an inclination to command, and the habit of doing ſo, though without knowing how to keep people properly in their places, or, if you will, in their ranks, and you have the key of every thing. The reſult of all is a tolerably agreeable companion, with whom every one is at his eaſe;

eafe ; a woman truly eftimable, becaufe her heart is perfectly honeft, although fhe is a little wanting in dignity; and a perfon worth knowing, becaufe fhe does not exact too much, and does juftice to herfelf, as well as to others.

With thefe *data*, ftudy and improve. If we were making our obfervations together, I have the modefty to think my infpiration would affift your fcience: there are things which you cannot get hold of but by dint of labour, and others concerning which I might fay of you, and of almoft all other men, what Clara faid of Volmar: 'He might have fwallowed all Plato, and all Ariftotle, without being able to divine it.'

The day before yefterday, Eudora took a dofe of kermes, with a ftrong infufion of burrage and fyrup of violets. Her cough is entirely gone ; but fhe cannot be faid to be entirely recovered: fhe is as full of mifchief as a monkey : my brow is knit like that of a pedant in a college, and I am quite hoarfe with fcolding her. I was juft now horribly fcandalized at hearing the brat utter a great oath, and infifted on knowing where fhe picked it up: ' Lord, Mamma, Saint-Claude fays fo as well as I.'—Saint-Claude, one of our fervants, is an honeft fellow, who takes care never to fwear in my prefence ; but makes amends for it, I dare fay, when I am out of the way. What admirable aptitude! She does not pafs an hour in a

fortnight

fortnight with the fervants; nor do I ever ftir a ftep without her.

May 7, or 8.

I SHOULD be very happy to have a little converfation with you, although your projects* have ftruck me dumb for feveral days. I am now in great hafte; and can only fay a few words, by way of announcing to you, that the Infpector will write immediately, in anfwer to feveral particulars of your letter.

I dare not exprefs my fentiments to you concerning your intended voyage; for it would be impoffible for my obfervations to be difinterefted. With the ftrongeft defire to talk the matter over like an indifferent perfon, my forrow, at the idea of fo long an abfence, would be bufy unknown to me.

If you had a nearer profpect of promotion in your office, I fhould contend with advantage. You have activity enough for the enterprife which tempts you; but you have not that iron conftitution which feconds the energy of the mind, and fits a man to encounter the hardfhips of fuch a voyage. I know we have a right, even at the rifk of our lives, to run hazards that may have a fortunate event: it is a lottery, in which fentiment holds the balance

---

* I had been appointed naturalift to attend La Peyroufe in his voyage round the world.

and regulates reafon; but friends have a different compafs to fteer by: their mind approves while their heart is repugnant: they have nothing then to do, but to be filent. This is what we are reduced to, while weeping like children, whenever you are the fubject of our converfation. Why does not content retain in the fame place, thofe whom friendfhip connects fo clofely with one another?— Eudora is better. Our friend Lanthenas defired me to fay a thoufand kind things for him; but he muft have written to you himfelf fince he commiffioned me to do fo.

Adieu!—I have half a mind to be angry with you on account of the pain you give me; but the thing is not poffible; and fo I am forced to embrace you.

May 18.

AND I alfo take upon me to fend you plants; not to make experiments in dying; but to know their names; and to give you an idea of the *Flora* of this country. I am become grofsly ignorant on the fubject; and have fo many things to do, that I prefer your telling me what they are, to fpending my time in looking for them in books. The lichen, or mofs, in my little parcel, was gathered from the walls of a fountain, whither Eudora often goes to reft herfelf, and to drink the excellent water it contains. This fountain is called Belle-Roche, from the domain in which it is fituated; a domain, with

a little

a little château, in the poffeffion of the dean of this chapter, with whom we paffed the whole of yefterday. The yellow flower belongs to a thorny fhrub, very common in the woods round the town, and faid to be good for cattle when the thorns fall off, which happens by degrees as the flower fades away. The two other little plants were formerly of my acquaintance; nor is any thing more common in the woods. I had them once at my fingers ends; but have forgotten them, and fhould like to know what they are, without being obliged to learn them over again: fo tell me quickly their names, furnames, clafs, genus, &c.

La Blancherie then has opened his rooms when I am no longer at Paris, and when I was going to Amiens *parimente*. As to the laft article, it fignified little; but I am forry not to have feen thofe famous rooms before I removed to fuch a diftance. Adieu! —Good night, or good morning: I am in hafte, and going away.

Lyons, June 19.

YESTERDAY evening, on coming home, we found your letter of the thirteenth; and although I have little time to fpare, and although you have ere this received one of ours, informing you of our proceedings, and confequently accounting for our filence, I cannot refift the longing defire I feel to anfwer the kind expreffions of your anxious friendfhip.

I long

I long ago perceived the flackness of my correspondence, and have been defirous of an opportunity of making amends, by writing with the leifure fo dear to fenfibility. Houfehold affairs, and occupations in the ftudy, have fo taken up my time, that my little excurfion was delayed by them, notwithftanding the fpeed with which I haftened to bring them to a conclufion. Though we have been here fome days, time paffes away, as you know it does on a journey, when we have only a few minutes to ourfelves, which we endeavour to employ to the beft advantage.

We have taken up our abode in an apartment which my good friend hired for himfelf, and with which the whole of our little family can make fhift upon occafion. I have brought with me our Eudora, the maid, and a man fervant; and every thing goes on to our perfect fatisfaction. We are in a handfome houfe, and in a good quarter of the town, quite clofe to the hotel of the Intendant *(l' Intendance)*, though very far from our acquaintance; but the moft diftant of them lends us his carriage, of which I make as much ufe as I pleafe. I went yefterday to fee Mademoifelle St. Huberti in Dido, her favourite part, which I had never feen her play at Paris: I thought her fublime. Our friend has a great deal of bufinefs on his hands: a compliment to the academy as an affociate; another fitting at the agricultural fociety, to which he alfo belongs; profeffional cafes; and information to be obtained

for

for the continuation of his labours in the Encyclopedia. If he were to ſtay here three months, he would find ſufficient employment,; and I could ſtay as long without being tired of the place. I have taken a maſter for the forte-piano, and ſtudy muſic every morning, but little, it is true; for viſits, dinners, &c. engroſs a great part of my time. The other day I met *M. Juſſieu*, the younger, at his ſiſter's, whom I was viſiting, and whoſe huſband has a very excellent cabinet of natural hiſtory.

Eudora gave me ſome uneaſineſs yeſterday. She ſeemed to have a ſlight attack of a fever; but is pretty well this morning.

We ſhall receive your Perſian traveller with a twofold intereſt: if he had only the recommendation of having ſeen a great part of the world, he would be welcome: what will he be as your friend!

Write us longer letters. I had a thouſand things to ſay to you about your laſt revolution, which prevents our loſing you; but it is preciſely on the things of which the heart is the fulleſt, that we keep ſilence, when we have not time to expreſs the whole of what we feel. If you could not, however, divine the greateſt part of it, you would not deſerve an explanation. Believe me, of all thoſe to whom you are dear, nobody is more happy than ourſelves at your being preſerved from the great hazards, which we do not love to ſee thoſe perſons run,

run, to whom we have, in a manner, attached our exiftence.

Adieu, my friend!—We embrace you with all the franknefs, and all the unreferve, of that tender friendfhip which we have fworn to maintain to the end of our lives.

Villefranche, July 4.

WE returned two days ago, and have been ever fince in a great bufile. We are employed in a variety of things; in letter-writing, and feveral others that have got a little into arrears, and in houfehold affairs, which call for my accuftomed vigilance, to fay nothing of thofe little troubles, of which every one in this world has his fhare.

I am far from enjoying that agreeable tranquillity in which it is a pleafure to hold converfe with our friends, efpecially when they are in the difpofition and circumftances you are in at prefent. I fhould wifh to talk with you at my eafe, concerning the hazards and the advantages of the two fituations, between which you have made a choice; concerning the folly of confuming life in vain regret, when we had good reafons for our determination, and concerning the inanity of that glory for which we make fuch facrifices, which almoft always betrays us, and never leads to repofe; the end every one has in view, and which he is only endeavouring, though generally to no purpofe, to render more comfortable. I fhould wifh to put into your head

a few

a few more grains of philofophy, in exchange for that excefs of active heat, which produces good effects, and great torments. I think all this, adminiftered by the kind hand of friendfhip, might be of fome ufe to you, and certainly would be a very agreeable office to me; but a thoufand things prefs on me together, and the tide of time carries me away.

I add to this a flower with which I am unacquainted, and which, for want of the *Genera*, I cannot make out. It has eight ftamina; the plant is herbaceous, and fix inches high, more or lefs. The flowers proceed from the *axillæ* of the leaves; are borne by a *petiolus* enlarged at the bafe, and grow up along the ftalk, at the top of which they meet in a clufter.

Auguft 2.

HERE I am at laft, having before me the half hour it wants to dinner-time, and meaning to devote that fpace of time to your fervice, that you may not repeat, ' It was well worth while to retire into the country.'

You muft know, in the firft place, the day before yefterday I was dying, yefterday I was in a languifhing ftate, and to-day I am as gay as a lark.

Afk me why? I cannot tell; but fo it is; and if any one will figure to himfelf a continual fucceffion of great activity, and of extreme languor, he will

have

have a complete idea of my health. My good man has taken to fpectacles, as, perhaps, I have already told you: his eyes are better, without being perfectly well. He has been bathing for fome days; but bufinefs upon bufinefs comes inceffantly to harafs him; fometimes it is the blind and groping adminiftration, building up with one hand, pulling down with the other, and always afking for advice, without ever taking it: fometimes the academies, to which he muft addrefs fome elaborate compofition or other, at the time perhaps when leaft inclined; fometimes it is a ufeful connexion; fometimes a friendly correfpondence which muft be kept up with equal care; and then the great work above all, the continuation of the Encyclopedia, to which it is become neceffary to return. You may expect in confequence to be tormented like a poor foul in purgatory. Heavy complaints are already made of you, becaufe you no longer fpeak to M. Audran; becaufe you appear to neglect him, &c. You muft fee him, follow him up, hurry him, get a great many things from him, urge him for a great many more, and fo on. You have had memorandums of queftions concerning furs; try to procure anfwers to them, and fend them to us; for we are thinking in good earneft of that important work. Every wheel muft be put in motion, every engine muft be fet to work, to collect and complete the materials: take your meafures accordingly; join your love for the fciences to your friendly zeal, and ferve us, as you are fo well able to do.

I have another thing to beg of you, Mr. Naturalift, Chemift, &c. and that is, that you will employ your talents for the good of mankind. You muft know that we have vipers in the *Clofe*, and that a child of twelve years of age was lately bitten by one, and died in lefs than four-and-twenty hours. Find out a *certain and eafy* remedy, which we may always have at hand, and even carry about us. It will be rendering a fervice to the world, and, perhaps, to your friends. On my firft vifit to this place, five years ago, we found in our own little domain, near the houfe, a viper, which my Roland killed, even though he was without his *durindana**; I have now a Eudora, who may flip away from me into the garden, and may meet with that terrible reptile under the grafs, in fome unfrequented walk. —Good heavens! my heart fails me, and I deteft the *Clofe!* It is very true, I affure you: more reafons than one put us out of humour with this country-houfe; we have laid afide the idea of rebuilding it; and if you, who know every thing, fhould chance to hear of a fnug box to be fold, with a good garden, good water, a fine profpect, and pleafant grounds about it, near Villefranche, or on the road between this and Lyons, pray let us know, that we may make the purchafe. Now, is it not a fine piece of folly to defire you to look out

---

* The fword of the famous Orlando, who in French is called *Roland.—Tranf.*

for

for fuch a thing? It is becaufe, to our forrow, it is a thing very fcarce, and very hard to come at.

So, poor Lanthenas is at liberty again? We fhall fee him I hope ere long: I am heartily rejoiced at it. My poor Eudora grows thin, and waftes away, without my knowing to what to attribute it. I fancied our water was not good, and fent to fetch fome from a fountain without the town. I next fuppofed fhe had worms, and gave her a vermifuge mixed up with honey, and afterwards lemon-juice and oil. They operated violently, without her voiding any worms, unlefs fomething that looked like a fmall one, about which I am not fure. Her tongue is loaded, her breath has a faint and bilious fmell, her complexion is pale and wan, her eyes are hollow, and her flefh is flabby; but fhe is ftill gay and lively, and very gentle and patient when in pain. This is her prefent ftate; and this it is that torments me, and breaks my heart. While my uneafinefs on her account quite wears me out, I am teafed and tormented by other cares; and in the midft of all this, I have fometimes the courage of a lion, and fometimes I weep like a child. Adieu.—I wifh you health, ftrength, peace, and happinefs: we embrace you with all our hearts.

Auguft 8.

I AM going, Sir, to begin my day with you, by order of my lord and mafter, who gave me your letter

letter the moment I awoke. It is ten o'clock however; but I bathed at seven, went to bed again, and enjoyed that sound and refreshing sleep which is so necessary to health. I was yesterday at a ball given by one of our lodgers, and danced two cotillons. Take notice, that it was the first time I had danced since two years before my marriage. I found that a relish for that agreeable exercise is not so speedily lost; and notwithstanding my matron-like age of one-and-thirty, I was rather induced to withdraw at midnight by prudence, than by satiety.

I do not know what to make of the story you tell me of your man of a superior kind: do I know him, or do I not? It appears to me hardly possible to receive his homage at my feet on the first interview, if I have not beforehand some notion of what he is. In good truth, you have no pity for a poor rustic, whose imagination naturally grows cold under the influence of every thing around her. I do not mean that our country ladies are more scrupulous than those of your great town; but for my part, I think our country gentlemen stupid; and if I had not been already virtuous from habit and principle, I should have been made so by disgust, or the want of knowing how to better myself. In sober sadness, there is nothing here to make it worth while to lose the honour of the field. Accordingly my habits are formed, and your wonderful man will not make me change them:

them: so much the worse for him, if he is not satisfied. But if he be a traveller, by the diligence, the notice you have given us will be altogether useless: that carriage does not stop on the road; if otherwise, I expect to see some good sort of a man in your own way.

I send you a plant, which from its first appearance I took for a kind of valerian; but I think I can discover a specific difference. It is very common here on the banks of a beautiful little river. Adieu!—I have at this moment old father *Renard* by my side. He tells me his son has seen you three times; but you are so busy, that he is afraid of being troublesome. Farewell! Our best wishes attend you.

August 19.

WHILE you were dining with your literati, we were at dinner here with the widow of an academician, and with counts and countesses of the neighbourhood, as well *sacred* as *profane*; for among them was a canoness and a count of Lyons*: only think what holy personages! The widow is the relict of the Count de Milly, and rejoices with reason at her widowhood.—If you are not acquainted with her history, I will treat you with it on some future day. We had not an interesting

* The counts of Lyons constituted a noble order of religious.— *Transf.*

hortus ficcus to vifit, like that which made you fo happy; but we had officers with us, who were both polite and tolerably well informed, a thing too uncommon among military men, not to be very agreeable; and we concluded the day by taking a walk to a *vogue:* fuch is the name given here to certain feftivals, to celebrate which, the populace affemble in the country, and dance and drink in a meadow to their hearts' content. In one place are fiddles; fifes in another, and a bagpipe in a third. Thofe who have no inftruments make amends with their voices; others fit under tents, and guzzle new wine as four as that of Surenne; and fometimes the fair ladies make up a country dance. But to return to our own affairs; you are a perfect romancer; a great promifer of nothings; you always announce people who never come. It was well worth while to make my mouth water for a *quiefbet* *! Three times we have already calculated, and waited impatiently for the moment, when, according to the notice you gave us, fome great perfonage was to arrive: nobody has yet appeared. I confole myfelf, however, for the non-arrival of the gallant you have found out for me, fince I have been informed that he is only fifteen : he would want tutoring, and I am not old enough to undertake his education, or

---

* This is fome cant word, neither in common ufe in France, nor to be found in a dictionary. It is in italics in the original French —*Tranf.*

to

to seek my fortune among school-boys. I am not afraid, let me tell you, Sir, to encounter a connoisseur. I wish to heaven I had you in England: you would fall in love with all the women. I was very near doing so, although a woman myself. They bear no resemblance to ours; and have in general that oval form of countenance which Lavater commends. I am not at all surprised that a man of sensibility, who has seen the English women, should feel a longing desire to visit Pensylvania. Take my word for it, that the individual who does not feel some esteem for the English, and a degree of affection mixed with admiration for their women, is either a pitiful coxcomb, or an ignorant blockhead, who talks about what he does not understand.

As to you, Sir, you are an impertinent fellow, and a coxcomb too; for I only suspected it to be *valerian* by its manner of growing; but the very great specific differences convinced me it was another plant, and made me ask you the name. The inference may be easily drawn. You are much mistaken, if from this sportive style you suppose me to be in good spirits. I am heartily vexed, as you will easily believe when I add, that I am not to go into the country at all this year; and that I shall see no more of *the Close* than yourself. The only difference is, that I shall eat some of the fruit; but they must be brought two long leagues; their bloom

bloom will be gone off; and, befides, they will not be gathered by my own hands.

I fhall conclude with this lamentation, wifhing you all joy and health.

Auguft 27.

THE poft does not fet off till the day after to-morrow; but I have a few moments of leifure, and haften to tell you, that you have not the merit of being the firft perfon from whom I heard of La Blancherie. I had already been told that he was at Lyons, and from that moment made no doubt but he was the man of whom you meaned to fpeak. I am, however, very glad to find that you did not mention Mademoifelle Phlipon to him. His negligence appears to me the more excufable. *How very modeft I am!* But what I have to tell you is, that La Blancherie having waited upon M. de Villers the director of the academy of Lyons, in order to requeft he would take him to a fitting, that gentleman afked him, out of attention and politenefs, whether he fhould like to become a member. ' *No*,' faid La Blancherie, ' *I ought not to belong to any academy.*'—' And why fo, pray?'—' *Becaufe, if I did, I fhould be obliged to belong to all the academies in Europe.*' The grave M. de Villers, who is poffeffed of both energy and fpirit, contented himfelf with replying, ' You told me, Sir, that you were to dine with M. ——: you may beg him to conduct

duct you to the academy alfo.' At a fitting of ours, I met two or three men of merit from Lyons, who all agreed in faying, that La Blancherie is a moft unfufferable coxcomb. Between ourfelves, I was not much furprifed at hearing it; for ten years ago he feemed to have a turn that way, which fo great a length of time employed in intriguing in the world, cannot fail to have wonderfully improved.

Let us return to our academical fitting, which was very agreeably filled up, in the opinion of every body prefent. I give you their teftimony, becaufe my own might appear fufpicious to you, in two different points of view. In the firft place, my good man read a difcourfe that was much applauded, upon *the influence of the cultivation of letters in the provinces, compared with their influence in the capital.* There was a good deal in it concerning the women, which feveral prefent had good reafon to apply to themfelves, and they would tear my eyes out, perhaps, if they imagined that I had any fhare in the production.

The director entertained us with an account of the difcoveries of the prefent age; and a ftranger very agreeably explained his opinion, that plants are not deftitute of fentiment. This author is a Swifs, fettled at Lyons, and a proteftant minifter. He is arrived from England, after taking a doctor's degree at Oxford, and is lately married to a young woman of eighteen, who is a native of Sedan, and whom he brought with him. We kept them
with

with us the day after the fitting, and became very intimate. A high-vicar of Lyons, whom we knew before, read fome pieces of excellent criticifm, tranflated from the German. The fecretary recited an epiftle in very pleafing poetry, congratulating our friend on his return to his country, accompanied by a helpmate, of whom the poet fpoke as poets are accuftomed to do. It is pretty certain this did not tend to recommend me to the favour of the women. Not daring, however, to fay any thing againft it, they would fain have it in their power to criticife the difcourfe of an academician, whofe wife was the fubject of a public panegyric. But, unfortunately, although it contains fome fevere truths that regard them, the language is exceedingly polite, and even elegant.

Now for a word or two of your Meffieurs Ducis and Thomas, who are at Lyons, and who puff each other off like the two affes in the fable. The latter has thought proper to print fome poetry, addreffed to Jeannin, whom you know, and whom every body ridicules. In his verfes, the academician praifes the charlatan in the moft extravagant terms, and to make the matter more moving, has inferted an epifode about Ducis, who in paffing the mountains of Savoy in an old crazy carriage was overfet, and frighted out of his wits. Thomas fees in his brother academician the Sophocles of France, whofe furious horfes are dragging him along like Hyppolitus, and dafhing his chariot to pieces. A country

try gentleman, tired of this learned jargon, and sick of such fulsome flattery, has answered him in verses which I inclose, sincerely regretting that I cannot join in your opinion concerning my countrymen; but if the judges of your Parnassus make such blunders, how will you defend the herd of our *badauds* * ? Independently of the bad subject chosen by Thomas, his verses are not even worthy of a writer of panegyric. These, however, are the great men who are to shine on Tuesday at the public sitting at Lyons, where one of them is to read a canto of his Petreide: you will have an account of it from La Blancherie, who is to return immediately. I do not imagine he has met with many subscribers at Lyons.

October 12.

WELL, my good friend! how do you do? It is a long time since I wrote to you; but the truth is, that for this month I have scarcely taken up my pen. I verily believe I am imbibing some of the inclinations of the beast whose milk is restoring me to health. I am growing *asinine* by dint of attending to the little cares of a *piggish* country life. I am preserving pears, which will be delicious; we are drying raisins and prunes; are in the midst of a great wash, and getting up the linen; make our

* The Parisians are called *badauds* in derision, as our Londoners are called cockneys.—*Transf.*

breakfast

breakfaft upon wine, and lie down upon the grafs to let the fumes of it go off; overlook the people who are bufied in the vintage, and reft ourfelves in the woods and meadows; knock down walnuts, and after gathering our ftock of fruit for the winter, fpread it in the garrets. Heaven knows how we make the doctor work!—You make us kifs him! Upon my word, you are a ftrange fort of creature.

We were much entertained by the charming narrative you fent us. You ought, indeed, to be always moving about for the amufement of your friends, particularly that you may not forget to pay them a vifit.

Adieu!—There is a talk about breakfafting, and going afterwards in a body to gather almonds.

The Clofe, October 15.

YOU fee I am ftill here, whither I came for a week, and where I fhall probably make a ftay of two months. Economical arrangements had guided us in our firft refolution: our moral and phyfical welfare make us change our minds. Our mother, it is true, lives at as great an expence during our abfence, as if we were with her, and ftrangers occupy our places at table; but what then? We are here in the afylum of peace and liberty; we no longer hear a fcolding tongue going from morning to night; nor do we any longer behold a forbidding countenance, in which a want of feeling and jealoufy lousy are depicted by turns, and in which spite and anger are perceptible through the disguise of irony, whenever we meet with any success, or receive any marks of attention. We breathe a pure air, and can obey the dictates of friendship and confidence, without fearing to irritate by the manifestation of those sentiments, a hard heart, which was never acquainted with them, and which hates to see them in others. In a word, we can be busy, we can employ ourselves, or pass our time in soft dalliance, without the disagreeable assurance, that whatever we do will be blamed, criticised, misconstrued, &c.

These advantages are certainly worth a pecuniary sacrifice. It is impossible, however, to make such a bargain all the year round, without an absolute rupture; and for that purpose it was not worth while to meet. Well! have I told you enough this time? Do you believe I am still your friend? You may also believe, though I have the same affection for you as ever, I should never have spoken to you, nor to any one else, of my husband's mother, if he had not done so before. To confess the truth, however, these sorrows, which affected me so powerfully during the first two or three months, now appear infinitely more supportable: I know how to estimate them in a more rational manner. As long as it was possible to retain any hope of finding a heart among the whimsicalities of the most extraordinary disposition, I tormented myself in endeavouring to gain her favour, and was distressed beyond measure at my

want

want of fuccefs. Now that I fee in a proper point of view, a felfifh and fantaftical being, who is governed folely by the fpirit of contradiction, who never enjoyed any thing but the pleafure of tormenting others by her caprices, who triumphs at the death of two children, whofe fouls fhe fteeped in bitternefs, who would fmile at that of all of us, and who fcarcely takes any pains to conceal her fentiments, I feel my affliction converted into indifference, and almoft into pity; and my fits of indignation and hatred are become fhort and unfrequent. Every thing confidered, it was, neverthelefs, wife to come and to ftay here: the health of our child requires it more urgently than we imagined before our arrival. You will alfo believe, my good friend, we cannot poffefs great bleffings, without purchafing them at the expence of a few troubles. This nether world would be a perfect paradife, if, with a hufband fuch and fo dear to me, as mine, I had nothing elfe but fubjects of fatisfaction.

December 1.

I HAVE received your epiftles, and make a jeft of your morality: you might go far before you would find any one who ftands fo little in need of it as I do. I fhall take your letters to Lyons, whither I am going to-morrow with Eudora, and a man fervant, without a maid, becaufe I am to make but a fhort ftay, and becaufe my little apartment will be fufficiently filled by the doctor and my hufband, who

who have already inhabited it a fortnight. You may tell the excellent M. Parault, with my beſt compliments, this ſame doctor will call here again before he makes his entry into the capital: he muſt conſequently wait with patience till next year.

You aſk me, why I have not written you long letters for ſome time. I will anſwer you with a franknefs equal to your own : in the firſt place, I have not had time; but perhaps I ſhould have found it, if I had not thought I perceived my letters were a little leſs intereſting to you than formerly. I will not tell you what this idea is founded upon, for I do not know: it is not a judgment, but a ſentiment. It is indeed ſo internal, that I preſume, in reflecting on it, you are not ſenſible yourſelf of any change. The alteration in you, however, is not great, ſince you notice my ſilence ; and I rejoice at it. If you had been a woman, I ſhould already have made you ſome friendly reproaches; but without knowing why or wherefore, I do not feel myſelf at all indulgently inclined towards you male creatures; and when I cannot believe in a warmth of affection, and in a kindneſs, at leaſt equal to my own, my ſentiments concentrate themſelves, and I hold my tongue as a thing of courſe. Perhaps this will appear to you to be rather haughty than generous, and not conſiſtent with the frankneſs of friendſhip. I cannot account for it ; but ſo it is.

December

December 22.

WHY, how now, my good friend! you are in a terrible paffion! will you be pleafed to tell me why? You men are whimfical creatures: you clamour dreadfully whenever you are told the truth, and at laft confefs that it is fully proved.

Have I fcolded you? Have I made any complaint? I ventured an obfervation, which you confefs to be well founded; and it is for that you are difpofed to quarrel with me.—*It is no more poffible for the moral man to remain always the fame, than for the phyfical man not to alter.*—This is your anfwer, and the refult of your examination: why, who contefts either the fact or the principle? *I* had laid down the firft, as my own notion: *you* make a maxim of it. All this comes to the fame thing; nor can I any longer underftand your inclination to reproach me, or your idea that I have deferved it.

Am I then fo much to be blamed for the acutenefs and juftnefs of my feelings, and for having told you frankly what they enabled me to perceive? You would, perhaps, have wifhed me to enter into angry and doleful lamentations: it is the moft that could happen in a certain kind of connexion; but in a friendfhip like ours, the tone and colour may be more or lefs lively, and the nature of the thing remain for ever the fame. We fhall always find in our difpofition and way of thinking the fame

reafons

reafons for reciprocal efteem ; and in our inclinations and ideas we fhall ever have the fame points of contact, and the fame bonds of union: there is then a degree of confidence and kindnefs which will neceffarily fubfift without alteration. There remains, for variety, the greater or fmaller degree of attraction, eagernefs, and pleafure, in cultivating that friendfhip: in this refpect the field is wide and open. You were flame colour laft year; you are now of a fmoky grey; while I, who never run into extremes, preferve a pretty regular hue, and am witnefs to your ofcillations without confidering them as ftrange.

Tranquil and facred friendfhip has a point of fupport on which the balance ever refts. The paffions, at once delightful and cruel, tranfport us out of ourfelves, and at laft defert us; but fincerity of foul, and propriety of conduct, the confidence of a true and feeling heart, the moderation of a well-regulated temper, with good and fixed principles; thefe are the things that infure the continuance of a connexion, whatever alteration it may feem to fuffer. Thefe, my worthy friend, affure you that you will find me ever the fame. No doubt, as wife and mother, fixed to a point, and fatisfied with thofe happy titles, it is more eafy for me to preferve an equability in my intercourfe with my friends, than it can be for you, whofe unfettled fituation muft occafion a fluctuation in your affections: accordingly I make a due allowance for effects

effects and caufes, and, at the fame time that I am fenfible of your variations, continue to be your friend.

By the way, I cannot help laughing at my fimplicity in making fo particular an anfwer to a man, who, fince he wrote his letter, has been thinking of fo many other things, that he does not, perhaps, even know what I mean.

However that may be, I muft requeft you to do me a piece of fervice with all convenient fpeed: the matter in queftion is as follows:

A man of excellent fenfe, whom I particularly efteem, has undertaken to deliver a funeral oration on the Duke of Orleans; but does not know very well what to fay, any more than myfelf. It therefore becomes neceffary to collect facts and anecdotes, to come at the public opinion, to know fomething, in fhort, of the habits of that prince, that may ferve to give an idea of his way of life, both in the world, and in his own family—fomething that may be brought forward, that will furnifh the means of drawing inferences, and admit of embellifhment. Your acquaintance is fufficiently extenfive to enable you to pick up fome materials. Try what you can do, and fend me the refult: you can eafily perceive what I want. I know your activity is great, and I depend on your friendly exertions.

My good man is returned to Lyons; whence he is to fend me your letter which he took for himfelf,

felf, and to which he requefts me to fay in anfwer, *that he does not dread any one's reading what he writes to his friends; that he well knows people of great fenfibility are fufpicious, uncompliant, and fometimes even cruel; that at bottom, however, they are well worth other folks; that you are very much of that ftamp, as well as himfelf; and it is, no doubt, on that account he loves you.* If by chance he be in the right, and if your letter, which I take to be an anfwer to mine, prove entirely for him, you will not fail to hear of it in pretty plain terms.

Villefranche, Jan. 24, 1786.

WHAT are we to think, my good friend, of your fate, and of our own? I mean of the changes that ere this have taken place in your department, and of the little hafte you are in to inform us of them, as far as you are perfonally concerned. Do you fuppofe we no longer feel fufficiently interefted in that refpect, to look upon you as bound to fend us fuch information? On what can an error fo injurious to our friendfhip be founded? I cannot, indeed, believe it exifts. But how are we to account for your filence? Affuredly, after what you have already intimated to us, you muft have known for fome time, what you have to expect from changes, in which your intereft could not but be at ftake.

If any thing unpleafant have refulted from them, why have you not unbofomed yourfelf to your friends?

friends? If not, as I am more inclined to perfuade myfelf, how have you had the heart to leave us fo long in fufpenfe?

In a word, whatever may have happened, and however you may be, write to us, and do not reduce us to the painful neceffity of inquiring into the caufe of a filence which friendfhip cannot brook.

When you have made us eafy on your own account, fend us news of what is paffing in the capital, and of the Cardinal, of whom in the country we no longer know what to think. I muft once more remind you of the notes concerning the Duke of Orleans, whofe funeral oration is expected with impatience, while the author, in his turn, impatiently expects the information you are to fend.

Eudora grows tolerably faft, and begins to read: her father is at this moment very much engaged. We all embrace you, and earneftly beg you will fend us accounts of your fituation, of yourfelf, of yourfelf again, and of yourfelf above every thing. Adieu!—Do not forget friends whofe temper of mind, and fituation, make them very unlikely to change the fentiments they have felt for you fo long.

February 20.

THIS Paris is an abyfs, in which it feems to me friendfhip itfelf and remembrance are fwallowed up. We hear no more of you, than if you were dead. Even to the very doctor, who is

obftinately

March 17.

WE never feel more ſtrongly that we are your friends, than at the moments when you are afflicted. The little you have told me, makes me uneaſy. You ſpeak of bad news, but without unboſoming your-ſelf: you are in bad health and in bad ſpirits, and you content yourſelf with ſaying ſo, without giving way, I will not ſay to confidence only, but to the effuſions of friendſhip. Do you no longer then think of ours? Is it no longer dear to you? The tone of indifference in which you write, is cal-culated to give us pain, at the ſame time that we are tormented by your affliction.

Write, and explain yourſelf: we ſhall be uneaſy till we have further accounts from you, and are waiting for them with impatience. I only write to requeſt that we may hear from you. Our friend is juſt come in, after getting tolerably wet—Believe me, you occupy the thoughts of us all. Adieu, my good friend! recline yourſelf ſometimes on the boſom of that friendſhip which has united the whole of us for ever. We embrace you with more tenderneſs than I can find words to expreſs.

May 3.

THE reſemblance between us is but ſmall; for I am going to love you a little more than ever; my good man is ſet off, and every thing about him is become more intereſting in my eyes. He will ſoon be be in your prefence; you will fee him; you will renew the compact of facred friendfhip; imagination will bring me into the midft of you, and I fhall participate in your affections.

To-day, or to-morrow week, the well-beloved of my heart will arrive in your capital. On his way he is to pafs a few days at l'Epine and Longpont. Let me hear of his welfare, and your own: you will often hear from me; and I truft that you will take as much pleafure as formerly in promoting, and in partaking of our correfpondence.

I am to go next week into the country with my Eudora, who is ftill thin and weak, though advancing faft towards convalefcence. I intend to pafs the whole of my widowhood at the *Clofe*.—It is in the midft of fields, and by means of the charming fpectacle of nature, I fhall fupport the abfence of him who renders them more dear to me. You, who inhabit a great town, and many others befides, will perhaps confider thefe ideas, and thefe fentiments, as only fit for ruftics, or for books; nor are they lefs ftrange in our little country towns, than in your capital. I believe, indeed, that corruption is ftill greater in the former, where every little paffion is inceffantly fermenting, and produces its baneful effects without any compenfation. The only advantage a fmall town has over a great one is, that we can get fooner out of it, and may be every day in the fields. Adieu!—While I am moralizing, the clock is ftriking twelve; my mother is

fcolding,

scolding, and ordering the cloth to be laid, the servants are hurrying about, and the child cries: whether inclined to eat or not, I muſt ſit down to table.

Adieu!—I long to hear that you and my good man have met: mind, beforehand, that I join in your embraces.

Clos la Platière, May 12.

IN good truth, you are no better than a cameleon, or ſomething worſe. You begin your letter in the ſtyle of a *mountebank*; you proceed like a man of *ſenſibility*, and conclude like a *rake*. Tell me, in which part it is that Nature ſhows herſelf?

I ſhould like much to prove to you that my doubts are well founded; but I am not diſpoſed to enter into an argument. I would only wiſh you to know that I ſhall not hold myſelf obliged to you for my huſband's conſtancy; and that if he were only to diſcover *half a ſcruple* of fickleneſs, I ſhould lay the blame upon you. Learn then, in future, to employ more cunning and duplicity in your nefarious projects. You have the air of a mere ſchoolboy, or a merry-andrew; and though I am no more than a plain country-woman, I could buy and ſell a hundred ſuch as you, if I choſe to give myſelf the trouble. It becomes you admirably to ſay that he ought no longer to love me: believe me, it would become you better to confeſs that you have forgot me; for he will do nothing

but

but what is written *above*, as pious people fay. As to us women, the cafe is different—but the rain is over, a gleam of funfhine attracts me, and you muft not be angry with the fun, if his attractive force is more powerful than your own. I lay down my pen, wifh you a good night, and am going to breathe a little frefh air upon the terrace. Adieu.

May 30.

IN good faith, let it be to either one or the other, you may go alone : I am content with *the man* you know, hold the devil in great contempt, and hardly believe in God; but a woman cannot write the remainder of my thoughts.

It is very fine, indeed, to afk me whether I love you : pray, is that any bufinefs of yours ? It would be almoft neceffary for me to fee you, in order to make you a pertinent anfwer; for all truths are not fit to be told ; and if I had continued to beftow my affection upon you, in fpite of your being grown a little of a profligate, female dignity would not have allowed me to acknowledge it. Confefs your peccadilloes to me, if you can find courage enough, and then I will tell you my fecret. In the mean time, I feel myfelf much obliged to him, whoever he may be, who promotes my correfpondence with my hufband, and I wifh that he may find fomebody to do him the fame good office with an object worthy of his beft affection.

As to me, I do not fend you to any body, for I believe that you laugh as much at our *God*, either alone, or preceded by an *A* *, as at the *God-damn* of our neighbours.

I hope that my letter will not find you in Spain, and that you have no reafon to be afraid of broiling.

June 2.

UPON my word, I am quite at a lofs what to think. You have not then received the fermon I preached to my hufband concerning his mode of travelling? You have not then received what I wrote in anfwer to the pretty billet, which you concluded by fending me to God, or to the devil?

Well! I muft return to the latter to tell you, that as often as I am walking in peaceful meditation, in the midft of fome rural fcene, of which I relifh the beauties, it feems delightful to me to owe the bleffings I enjoy to a fupreme intelligence: at fuch times I believe and adore. It is only in the duft of the clofet, in poring over books, or in the buftle of the world, while breathing the corruption of mankind, that thefe fentiments die away, and that a *fombre* fort of reafon arifes enveloped with the clouds of doubt, and the deftructive vapours of incredulity. How fond we grow of Rouffeau! how much wifdom and truth do we difcover in his works,

* This appears to be an allufion to the valediction, *Adieu.*

when

when we have nature and him for our fole companions!

I bid you *adieu* then, in expectation of the obfervations, which you promife in the firft line, and which in the fecond you fay, you have not time enough to make.

Villefranche, Sunday, July 9.

I HAVE feen our good friend: we are met again; and I am determined he fhall go no more journies without me. He was with me in the country, when I received your laft letter, the particulars of which I cannot anfwer, becaufe I left it behind me at the Clofe. I will only tell you, that it gave me great pleafure, notwithstanding the greater pleafure which feemed to eclipfe every other—the pleafure of feeing my turtle-dove reftored to me.

Your ftory of the beehives is a very fine gafconade. I inquired after your lofs, and your forrows; and at firft you did not underftand what I meant, and then you laughed in my face. Whenever you come again with your pitiful tales, I fhall take it for granted, that you are laughing at ruftics.

Adieu!—Let us hear from you, and believe us ever and unalterably your friends.

Auguft 18.

OH! a great deal worfe than giddy—why, you are inconfiderate, impertinent—I know not what. How

How is it poffible that you can ever expect me to pardon you, for having made me lofe my time in copying the moft tirefome things in the world? Copy!—copy!—I copy! why, it is a degradation, a profanation; it is finning againft all the laws of tafte. It becomes you well, after this, to go fnuffing the wind, and ftrutting along; you, an interloper in the capital, whence I carried away a great part of what was good for any thing. Do not you know that I have upon my toilet both pens and journals, and, moreover, verfes to Iris; that I can talk of my country-houfe, of my domeftics, and of the ftupidity of the town at this time of the year; that I can pronounce fentence upon new books, fall in love with a work upon the report of the editor of the Journal of Paris, pay vifits, talk nonfenfe, liften to the fame, and fo on?' Is not that the utmoft effort of the wit and art of the elegant women in the great world?

Go your ways, young gentleman, you are not clever enough as yet for a *perfiflage*, nor impudent enough for fafhionable airs and graces. You have not even levity enough to encourage an experienced woman to undertake your education, without a rifk of expofing herfelf. Go your ways, pick up infects, difpute with the learned about a fnail's horns, or the colour of a beetle's wings; but as to the ladies, all you are good for is, to give them the vapours.

I am

I am much obliged to the amiable family of the Audrans for their remembrance; tell them fo when you fee them, and fay a thoufand kind things in my name.

Villefranche, Nov. 10.

ALSO by my fire-fide; but at eleven in the morning, after a quiet night, and the various cares of the morning, my hufband at his defk, my girl knitting, and I chatting with the former, overlooking the latter's work, enjoying my warm and comfortable fituation, in the midft of my dear little family, and writing to a friend, while the fnow is falling upon fo many wretched beings, overwhelmed with poverty and affliction, I compaffionate their miferable fate; I revert with pleafure to my own, and at this moment make no account of the unpleafant connexions and circumftances that fometimes feem to detract from my felicity. I rejoice at being reftored to my accuftomed way of life. We have had at our houfe thefe two months a charming woman, whofe beautiful profile, and pointed nofe, would make you fall in love at firft fight. She was the caufe of my going a good deal abroad, and receiving company at home; and was much careffed by every body here. We intermingled this diffipated life with peaceful days paffed in the country, and, what was ftill better, with agreeable evenings, employed in reading out to one another, and in converfing upon the fubjects

fuggefted

suggested by our books. At length it is necessary to return to our accustomed way of life. We are alone, and I am delighted at finding myself in the little circle nearest the centre: so much so, that, in spite of pressing solicitations, and almost an engagement to pass a part of the winter at Lyons, I have taken the resolution of not quitting the dovecot: my good man, however, cannot do otherwise than visit the principal town of his department, and make a considerable stay there; but I shall let him go alone, to cultivate our connexions, follow his administrative business, and amuse himself at the academy. I shall confine myself to my solitude for the whole of the winter, and shall only leave it when the fine weather sets in, in order to spread my wings in the beams of the vernal sun. I smiled at the conclusions you draw concerning what must necessarily have been thought of me, and what may be expected, as to gaming and visiting; and said to myself, This is the way in which our natural philosophers, chymists, and all the rest of our learned men, reason. They set off from *data*, of which they neither know the cause, nor the connexion; supply the deficiency by conjecture; varnish over the whole with a jargon of fine words, and gravely give the falsest results in the world, as if they were palpable truths.

Because upon a stranger's account I went into society, where any one might have seen that I made as good a figure as my neighbours, and have judged

that

that I muſt be very fond of home to remain there alone, while qualified upon occaſion to receive company, and to do the honours of my houſe, Mr. Philoſopher muſt needs take upon him to decide, that I have determined to live like other country ladies, always from home, and for ever at the card-table.

Becauſe I am aſtoniſhed that the child of a man of feeling, and of a good-natured woman, ſhould be of ſo obſtinate a temper as only to be overcome by harſh meaſures, and becauſe I regret the ſeverity I am obliged to aſſume in order to make her bend beneath the yoke of neceſſity, this wonderful reaſoner immediately concludes that I have caught the contagion, and that my daughter will ſoon have an iron collar round her neck, and a clog to her leg. Poor young man! if you ſucceed no better in your ſtudies, I pity you for loſing ſo much time. If you had been with me theſe three months, you would have come at a knowledge of more truths perhaps, than you will diſcover for a long while to come. In the firſt place, you would have become acquainted with all the people of note in a country town; I ſhould have aſſiſted you in judging of the diſpoſition, inclinations, talents, and pretenſions of every individual; of the relation of each to all the reſt, and of one to another; of their plans, duties, and paſſions; of the public and private operations of the latter; of their influence upon important meaſures, and upon actions the moſt inſignificant; of the reſult of all theſe things in regard to general manners,

manners, and thofe of private families, &c. It would have been a much more complete courfe of philofophy, ethics, and even of politics, than what you will be able to make up, in whole years, from your incoherent and fcattered obfervations. From thence I fhould have carried you to the country, in company with an Italian lady, full of fire, wit, graces, and talents, and joining to all thefe good qualities, a found judgment, a confiderable portion of knowledge, and an excellent heart; with a German lady, gentle by nature, rendered grave by a republican education; fimple in her manners, and combining great good nature with very uncommon information; and with a man of a referved difpofition, but good tempered, witty, and polite. The other perfonages you are acquainted with. Such is the compofition of our domeftic circle during the prefent vacation; to which may be added, a few perfons of the neighbourhood, with feveral originals, who fet themfelves above every body elfe. Befides this, you would have entire liberty, wholefome nourifhment, paffable wine, long walks, long converfations, entertaining readings, &c. I leave you to judge whether your courfe of philofophy would not have terminated pleafantly.

In the next place, you muft know that Eudora reads well; begins to leave off all playthings but the needle; amufes herfelf in making geometrical figures; is entirely unfettered by drefs; has no idea of the value fet upon fcraps of gauze

and

and ends of ribbons; thinks herself fine when she is told that she is good, and has a clean white frock on; and looks upon a cake, given with a kifs, as the greatest of all poffible rewards. You muft know too, that her fits of ill humour are more unfrequent, and of fhorter duration; that fhe walks in the dark as well as by daylight, is afraid of nothing, and does not think it worth while to tell a lie on any occafion whatever. Add to this, that fhe is five years and fix weeks old; that I do not perceive that fhe has falfe ideas on any fubject, of importance at leaft; and you will allow, that if her obftinacy has fatigued me, if her fancies have made me uneafy, and if her carelefs indifference has rendered it more difficult for us to keep her under, our pains, neverthelefs, have not been thrown away.

Upon fumming up every thing, I found by your letter that all the reafoning, of which you were yourfelf the direct object, was very juft; that you underftood very well what was conducive to your prefent and future happinefs; and that, confequently, you were a better philofopher than three-fourths of mankind. Continue at the fame time to be a good friend, and you will always bear a high value in our eyes, and in thofe of all good men. Adieu!—Noon approaches, and I fhall be called to dinner. I have only time to embrace you in the name of the whole family, Eudora included, who ftill remembers you, or your name.

Clos

Clos la Platière, October 3.

YOUR fervent prayers have recalled me from the abode of shadows, and I can once more converse with the living. I did not lose sight of you in the other world; but I saw you only in the distance, like those fleeting clouds which appear upon, and are hardly distinguishable from the horizon. Your orisons, and your efforts to attract attention, brought me back to you worldly folks with additional experience. When I had inhabited only one planet, I thought it was possible to cultivate the acquaintance of its inhabitants, without injury to our intercourse with the men of another. But I plainly perceive that it is not the case; and that Proserpine was in the right to divide the year alternately between Pluto and Ceres. As long as I remained in the study, nailed down to my desk, you heard from me often, and could judge of my way of life, and perhaps of my heart, by my correspondence; but as long as that correspondence was kept up with spirit, the people in our neighbourhood, and of our town, looked upon me as a hermit, who could only converse with the dead, and who disdained all commerce with her fellow-creatures. I laid down my pen; suspended my literary labours; walked forth from my museum, mixed in the world, and suffered it to approach me; talked, ate, danced, and laughed, like other people, with every body that came in my way; and then my neighbours perceived that I was neither an owl, nor a constellation, nor a female pedant; but a being both tolerable and tolerant; while you, on the other hand, thought me dead. I am about to refume my ftudies, to return to my folitude, and expect to hear you alter your note once more.

What have *you* been doing all the while? You have, no doubt, increafed the fum of your knowledge; but have you augmented your ftrength of mind, fo as to take mankind as you find them, the world as it goes, and fortune in whatever fhape fhe may prefent herfelf? As to me, I am in fuch a ftate as no longer to care about any thing that may contribute to that end. This you will fay is eafy for a perfon whofe neft is feathered; and who has a mate to help her philofophize, and the reft of it; but there are a number of circumftances and things which are independent of all this, and which have an influence over our happinefs: that influence it is that my reafon turns to good, or reduces to a cipher.

Only think how *nice** *(gentille)* I am!—*Nice!* this is not faying a little; for you muft know that at *Villefranche*, in the *Beaujolois*, the word *nice*, applied to either man or woman, means the practice of virtue, the love of ftudy, good fenfe, activity, &c. Accordingly you are a *nice* man, if you do your duty as a citizen, or a magiftrate, or any thing elfe. You

---

* As it was impoffible to tranflate the word *gentille* by any correfponding word in Englifh, fo as to retain the abfurdity which Madam Roland ridicules, the tranflator has fubftituted the word *nice*, which fometimes fuffers a fimilar perverfion of fenfe in this country, and almoft always in New England.

cannot

cannot laugh more than I do when I hear it gravely said of a father of a family, or of a good advocate, that he is a *nice* man. We are pretty spoken people in this country! And in that which you inhabit are the confequential, the fwaggerers, the Crœfufes, and the great talkers, as much refpected as ever? As to you, whom I think I fee at this moment, talking faft, walking like lightning, with a look which fometimes indicates fenfibility, and fometimes giddinefs, but which never has any thing commanding about it, when you affect to look grave, becaufe on fuch occafions you make *Lavaterical* grimaces, and becaufe activity alone becomes your countenance; you, whom we love with all our hearts, and who deferve our affection, tell us if the prefent *you* be fupportable, and the future promifing; for this it is that conftitutes the happinefs of that age, when the illufions of youth vanifh, and the cares of ambition begin.

January 19.

YOUR adulation, my dear friend, was thrown away: my lord and mafter is not yet returned, and I was not in a humour to be puffed up; but on his account I feel myfelf obliged to you for your intention. On my own, I thank you for your agreeable little letter, the receipt of which gave me much pleafure.

I did not imagine you were a Jew in any part of your character; but I find you not a little of a rogue in your way of excufing your want of memory.

We have had a variety of ſtories told us here about your Lyceum, in which the parliament interferes, by way of giving Monſieur de la Harpe a rap upon the knuckles: pray is there any truth in it?

I keep your third page for my well-beloved, who will be fenſible of its excellence. As to unworthy me, I like Arioſto's follies better than all the truths of your learned doctors, with their hard names, which there is no fuch thing as pronouncing.

To-morrow will be one of my happy days; I ſhall ſee my friend after two months abſence. My heart bounds at the thought, as much as it did ſeven years ago.

Eudora gives you as good as you bring, without ceremony, and without malice; but if you were a hundred leagues nearer, it is poſſible that there might be a little pouting.

May 2,

WHAT is come to you then, my good old friend? We hear no more about you: we only receive a few ſhort lines announcing ſome incloſure, or giving us an account of ſome commiſſion you have been good enough to undertake; but not a ſingle word of friendſhip; not one of thoſe little articles of chit-chat, which are ſo expreſſive of it, becauſe they proceed from the fulneſs of the heart, and are given with a confidence of their proving intereſting. Do you no longer love us? Have you met with better

friends,

friends, with perfons who value you more highly, who cherifh you more, or are more defirous of cultivating with you an agreeable and lafting connexion, founded upon reciprocal efteem, and fimilarity of tafte and inclinations?

I fhall not envy you the happinefs of having met with beings of more analogous minds, who enable you to enjoy the pleafure that refults from the communication of your thoughts and fentiments; but I fhall complain of your feeming to forget thofe with whom you formerly partook of that fatisfaction. I know that I have for fome time paft written lefs frequently than before; but I have told you the reafon. You ought to have pitied us on account of the multiplicity of bufinefs, and variety of cares, that prevented us from contributing as much as ufual to the commerce of friendfhip, and not to have written the lefs on that account yourfelf; but the contrary.

It is by mutually fupplying each other's deficiencies, according to circumftances, that we keep up the facred flame of friendfhip, of which candour, fimplicity, unbounded affection, and indulgence, are the neceffary attributes. To proceed therefore according to my principles, I forgive you whatever I may have reafon to complain of, and I dedicate to you the firft moments, not of leifure, but of liberty, which I can find in the midft of the more peaceful, though very bufy life to which I am returned.

We have juſt paſſed three weeks at Lyons, when the neceſſity of cultivating a variety of acquaintance and connexions, and of fulfilling the engagements they led us to contract, did not leave me a moment to myſelf.

Let us know then what your feelings are: take a ſolitary walk: you uſed to tell me, that it was in ſolitude that you became ſenſible that you had friends, and a heart; I hope that in ſuch moments we are not forgotten.—Is the revolution in public affairs likely to produce any in your department? Can you deviſe any project for your more rapid promotion? Or do you continue to conſole yourſelf for the contrary by the pleaſures of ſtudy? They are certainly great for a philoſophic mind. I lately met with a man reduced to the ſtate of preceptor, who is happy in that ſituation, and conſoles himſelf, by ſtudy, for a fortune of thirty thouſand livres a year, which he either loſt or ſquandered away. Much may be owing to his diſpoſition, it is true: and it muſt be confeſſed, that we often give credit to philoſophy for what is produced by a man's temper of mind.

October 20.

I RECOLLECT a certain certificate of confeſſion which you forwarded me: it contains an abſolution in proper form; and I feel myſelf diſpoſed to make a return for the favour: good day then; peace be with you. Perhaps I ſhould have anſwered it ſooner, if I had had more time: buſineſs on the one

one hand, cares on the other, and company into the bargain, are more than enough to fill up the day, and to take away the defire, or the power, of entering into chat with our diftant friends: befides —but we will fay no more on that fubject.

Whenever I have had a few moments to myfelf, I have employed them in digefting my little tour through Switzerland; to which I do a greater honour, as you may perceive, than to the one I made through England. I have not yet finifhed it; nor do I know when I fhall. Notwithftanding, however, the rain, the wind, the hail, and the cold, which befiege us during our vintage, and prevent its completion, I am confined here for a good part of the winter. You, good folks of the capital, ought to be much edified at feeing one of your country-women fet herfelf down in the midft of the woods, where the wolves are howling, while the neighbouring mountains are covered with fnow. But according to you, what fignifies the retreat we inhabit when once we are out of Paris? Lyons, or the woods of Alix, are all one in your eyes. What have you to tell me that is worth hearing? Pray let me know how you keep your head in order. As to your heart, it is a good fort of heart at bottom, and would go on very well, were it not for that fame head, which fometimes leads it aftray. And then the fciences, and your folitude? Have you found any means of rendering them compatible with one another, or do you court them by turns?

turns? Among so many revolutions, which threaten so many persons, does your situation promise you promotion? Now take up your pen in your turn; let us hear from you, and let us strengthen the bonds of a friendship of so many years standing.

October 24.

I AM glad you join me in my detestation of this everlasting guzzling, and these slovenly houses. If I could do as I like, or were alone with my turtle-dove, I would not give a dinner for these three years to come; but would have elegant apartments in town, and a delightful little box at the *Close:* but according to all appearance I shall not go to paradise in such a hurry.

The wind which is here called the *bise* (the north-east) is blowing; and I keep a Christmas fire. The lesser veronica and pimpernel are hardly to be seen in the fields; and in the hedges there is nothing but half-blown violets and primroses peeping out from among the leaves. I have met with a kind of insect resembling the little wood-lice, that are found running about in closets among books and papers, only a great deal larger, that takes up its abode in the shell of a snail, exactly as the *hermit** does in that which it adopts. It was my intention to go to Lyons next month; but I am prevented by household affairs, and regret it much; for I am

* A marine animal of the cancer kind.

very

very defirous of improving my acquaintance with Madam de Villiers: fhe is the only woman I can find to my liking in this quarter of the world: fhe is polite, kind-hearted, gentle, modeft, like her fortune, goes little into company, is very well informed, and exceedingly attached to her hufband, who is much older than herfelf, and whofe labours in the ftudy fhe partakes of. I do not know if you are acquainted with that grave philofopher; an excellent man at bottom, very ftiff in his opinions and manners, tolerably well verfed in chemiftry, and various other branches of the fciences, and particularly fkilled in entomology. He has a very interefting cabinet of infects, collected by himfelf and his wife. This is almoft the only connexion, either at Lyons or here, that has any charms for me. I fhould, however, have occafion to fee in the former place feveral very interefting perfons in various points of view. Bufinefs muft take place of every thing: I therefore leave you in hafte to make up for the half hour I have devoted to you.

April 6, 1788.

REALLY and truly, my good friend, I have been thinking of applying to a third perfon, in order to learn what is become of you: it is fo long fince we have had any accounts from you, expreffed in the tone of confidence, which keeps up that of one's friends, that I almoft doubt whether my correfpondence

refpondence upon the old footing will be well received.

Have we not a new acquaintance to make? Or do you, who formerly wrote me word that you changed every year, refemble the *you* of three years ago? It is highly neceffary that you fhould let me know; for however long we may fuppofe the telefcope to be, mine does not enable me to fee things a hundred leagues off. I can only judge by approximation. For inftance, I recollect to have known you in poffeffion of a true and affectionate heart; and as that is a thing which does not eafily change its nature, I fuppofe you in poffeffion of it ftill, and love you accordingly. But it feems to me alfo, that you are fometimes in your mode of expreffion, and in your ftyle, the reverfe of goodnature, or thereabouts; it feems to me alfo, that you do not like to be told of it; but then I recollect that I have paid you in your own coin, when your ill-temper has made me lofe mine, and I afk myfelf in what ftate things are at prefent? Is the tinge grown deeper, or is it gone off? I am for the latter fide of the queftion, when I figure to myfelf the effects of ftudy, of meditation, and of happy inclinations; but I am for the former when I confider the influence of the world, the fociety of fools, the fenfe of injuftice, and the hatred of prejudices, and of tyranny. I fhall therefore continue in this ftate of incertitude, until you remove my doubts. But that

that you may have none in regard to me, I will give you my barometer, as it ſtands in the different places I inhabit. In the country, I forgive every thing: whenever you know me to be there, you may venture to ſhew yourſelf, ſuch as you are, at the moment of writing: an original, a cenſor, or, if needs muſt, moroſe: my ſtock of indulgence is inexhauſtible, and my friendſhip tolerates all ·kinds of appearances, and every ſort of tone. At *Lyons* I make a jeſt of every thing; the company I ſee there puts me in good humour, my imagination grows more lively, and if you rouſe it, you muſt take the conſequences; it will not let a joke eſcape, without ſending it back with a ſharper point. At Villefranche I deliberate upon every thing, and ſometimes am a cenſor in my turn. Grave, and full of buſineſs, I receive the due impreſſion from every thing; I ſuffer that impreſſion to be ſeen without diſguiſe; and am more than uſually inclined to reaſon, though my feelings there are as ſtrong as elſewhere.

You muſt allow that I give you great advantage in the game: you know all my cards before I ſee yours. Amidſt all this I do not forget your diſſertations, which are not at all in my favour: they take up a great deal of your time, damp your imagination, and do not leave room for the leaſt word of friendſhip. I no longer know whether your ſyllogiſms are in *baroco* or in *feriſon*; and having forgotten Ariſtotle's Categories, being acquainted with no infect but the *lady-bird*, knowing nothing of Linnæus but a score of phrases for culinary and medicinal purposes, I am sadly afraid left our friendship should fail for want of some rallying-point. By way of reviving it, I will speak to you of my daughter, whom you are pleased with, because she puts me out of all patience. In the first place, she has still that claim to your kindness, although she gives me hopes that it will not always be the same; she begins to fear reproaches almost as much as doing penance upon dry bread; she is, perhaps, more sensible of the approbation bestowed upon her when she behaves well, than of the pleasure of eating a bit of sugar; and is fonder of being caressed, than of playing with her doll. What a sad degeneration, you will say; what a fine progress we have made!

She is very fond of writing and dancing, because they are employments that do not fatigue her head, and will make a great proficiency in both. Reading amuses her, when she has nothing to do that she likes better, which does not frequently happen; but she cannot bear stories that require more than half an hour to come to the end: she is still a long way off from Robinson Crusoe. The harpsichord sometimes makes her gape: it requires the head to work, and that is a thing she does not excel in: there are sounds, however, that she is fond of, and when she has strummed an air of *The Three Farmers*, with both hands, she does not fail to be mightily

proud

proud of her performance; and to repeat three or four notes that pleafe her five or fix times over. She is very fond of a clean white frock, becaufe fhe is the prettier for it, and becaufe fhe thinks it muft make her appear more agreeable. She does not fufpect that there are rich dreffes which entitle the wearers to greater confideration, and likes a leather fhoe bound with rofe-coloured ribands, better than one of filk of a *fombre* hue. But fhe would like ftill better to be running about in the country, than to be neatly dreffed, and to fit primming up in company. She has a ftrong inclination to fay and do the very contrary of what fhe is defired, becaufe fhe thinks it agreeable to act in her own way; and this fometimes carries her to great lengths. But as fhe is fure to be repaid with intereft, fhe begins to fufpect that fhe might do better, and gives herfelf as much credit for an act of obedience, as we fhould do for a fublime effort of the mind. Her fair hair takes every day a deeper hue. Her complexion is rather pale, unlefs when fhe takes fome violent exercife. She fometimes blufhes from embarraffment, and is always in great hafte to make me acquainted with any blunder that fhe has committed. She is very ftrong, and her temperament has fome refemblance to that of her father. She is now fix years, fix months, and two days old. Although fhe plays a great deal with her father, fhe reveres him fo highly, that fhe begs of me, as the greateft favour poffible, to conceal her little

mifdemisdemeanours from his knowledge. She fears me lefs, and fometimes fpeaks to me in a very flighting way; but I am her confidant upon all occafions; and fhe is very much at a lofs what to do when we quarrel, for fhe has then nobody to whom to apply for any indulgence, nor to whom to tell her little tales. We are in doubt whether we fhall have her inoculated or not; it is a queftion that gives great anxiety and occupation to my mind. If it were for a perfon lefs dear to me, I fhould eafily come to a decifion, for probabilities are much in favour of the operation; but I fhould never forgive myfelf for having expofed her to the unfavourable chance, if fhe fhould prove the victim of it, and fhould rather wifh that fhe might be cut off by the hand of Nature, than that it fhould happen by my means. Befides, I dread the taint of a ftranger's blood, which might be communicated by inoculation; an objection to which I have not yet heard a fatisfactory anfwer.

Find me then, if you can, good reafons to bring me to a decifion.

Adieu!—I am going to return to my ftudies: tell me if I have given much interruption to yours. I wifh you peace of mind, and every thing that can contribute to your entire fatisfaction; and if you be ftill our good friend, as I hope, I embrace you with all my heart.

Monday,

Monday, April 7.

YOU will readily underſtand, my worthy friend, that I had not received your little epiſtle of the fourth, when I wrote you the incloſed. You will therefore take no more than what is good at all times, and will paſs lightly over the raillery, by which I endeavoured to provoke you, in order to make you break ſilence.

I was highly ſenſible of this mark of your friendſhip, which made me perceive that I retained a greater attachment for you, than I either ſaid or thought I did. Tell me then what are your ſubjects of ſorrow: nobody will more readily ſhare them than ourſelves. I have perfectly made up my mind as to all uneaſineſs about the place; as ſoon as my huſband's health gives me any, I feel that in compariſon with that object, every other is nothing.

He is better ſince he went to Lyons; but his cheſt is affected as ſoon as ever he begins to write with any aſſiduity. I am therefore at great pains to make his labours for the Encyclopedia laſt as long as poſſible, by means of moderation and intervals, and to partake of them myſelf as much as I can.

Villefranche, April 21.

WE have received your agreeable epiſtle with the greateſt pleaſure, and with the warmeſt feelings of friendſhip. It is not neceſſary for me to be at the *Cloſe*, in order to find it to my taſte. You wrote

wrote it at a moment in which you did not ſtand in need of the indulgence of your friends, and in which they difcover you to be every thing that they can defire. You vifit the unfortunate, and you endeavour to confole them: it is one of the moſt effectual means of preferving and increafing the native goodnefs of the heart.

I have alfo that painful advantage: my neareſt neighbour has loſt an excellent hufband, whom fhe loved as I love mine. This woman, whofe mind is of the common caſt, is rendered fublime by her grief; fo much does a ſtrong and lively fentiment render us fuperior to ourfelves. She has a great number of acquaintances, all of whom endeavour to divert her attention from her lofs. I am, perhaps, the only one who never attempt to confole her; and who weep with her fincerely: my tears render her's lefs bitter, and her affliction lefs grievous.

Our eldeſt brother fet off this morning at five o'clock: pray examine him *lavaterically*. I believe that his pointed nofe will pleafe you, and that his mouth will give you fome pain: it feems, at leaſt to me, to be at variance with every thing like wit and taſte. As to his forehead, I am at no lofs what to think of it; but I will not foreſtal your obfervations. You know what I wrote to Lanthenas concerning the triumph which I offered him over elderfhip; pray be of the party; and let the praife of the younger brother, and the care of enhancing every thing that is in his favour, fhew

his

his elder, that a man may enjoy great confideration in fpite of primogeniture.

You are very fortunate to be able to apply yourfelf to a fcience fo agreeable as natural hiftory: I cannot figure to myfelf a ftudy which agrees better with our peace of mind, or which is better fitted to defend us from thofe paffions that difturb it.

Adieu!—I embrace you.

May 22.

MANY thanks for your news: it brings us a little acquainted with the world again, from which we were a hundred leagues off. I am very much of your opinion, both as to the principles, to the bufinefs itfelf, and to the refult that we ought to defire.

We get nothing but falfified intelligence. The journals are garbled, and fent a fecond time to the prefs: it is a great pity. My health is but indifferent, and I am threatened with another dofe of phyfic. An ounce of hardnefs of heart, and the fame quantity of indifference, might do a great deal of good to my conftitution; but thofe drugs, common as they are, are not to be bought, and I fhould abhor making ufe of them.

Send me then your journal, if it be not in Latin: as to the fowls, I cannot promife you them in exchange, but I can promife you fome pretty fpecimens of quartz, upon yellow ftones, with which our Clofe abounds. Is not that ftill better for a man of fcience, although not fo digeftible? Give us a good receipt to deftroy caterpillars, and then you may come, and eat your fhare of our apples. In good earneft, fhall you never be able to make a pilgrimage to this part of the world? We would take you a walk through our woods, and over our mountains; from our terrace you would fee Mont-Blanc, which our peafants, I know not why, call The Cat's Mountain, and we would go in a body to vifit Mount Pila. Throw off your fetters for a little while, and join us in our retreat: you will find there true friendfhip, and real fimplicity of heart. A woman of Lyons has betrayed me; her hufband has done ftill worfe; and between them they have printed one half of my tour through Switzerland. I have infifted upon the cancelling of my name, and of every thing that might ferve to point me out, and it has been done; but there are fo many blunders, and the cenfor (an abbé) has fo curtailed me, that I am quite ftupified at it, and hardly know my own work.

Clos la Platière, June 18.

I SEND you a treafure for a naturalift, but the deftruction of our kitchen gardens. You will find in the box that accompanies this, feveral individuals of a fpecies of infect which preys upon artichokes. Thefe villanous little animals, of a fhape fomewhat refembling that of caterpillars, have at the end of their tails a kind of fcaly mantle, which

they

they throw over their backs, and thus brave every danger. When once they fet to work upon the artichokes, they devour the pulpy fubftance of the leaves; the whole plant turns white, and withers; ceafes to be productive; and fometimes abfolutely dies. We are ignorant, in this country, both of the name of the infect, and of the way of deftroying it. They do not often make their appearance; and, if I may judge from the prefent year, the firft in which they have been feen fince I came to this part of the world, they never fhew themfelves but after a great drought.

If it be unknown to you, it is a prefent I am making you, and I afk in return a receipt to get rid of them: if you can procure us one, you will render a fervice to the whole province. You will find two individuals, which I furprifed, in a different fhape: they are larger, and in their prefent drefs refemble a wood-loufe.

You will be able to judge by fome bits of artichoke-leaves, inclofed in the box, of the ftate to which thefe little black animals reduce the beft of our vegetables.

I have juft opened the box again, and find nothing left already of my pretended wood-loufe, but a fkin of a greenifh white. The black animal has crept out of it, and is now running about like the reft, with the mantle, which gives them the appearance of little *prickly balls*.

July 4.

HONOUR to the fciences, and ftill more to men of fcience, for their admirable expedients! Are not my artichokes well protected? And have I not made a notable addition to the fum of my knowledge, by learning to give the name of *larva*, to what I defignated fo well, by that of the little black animal?

You do not fo much as tell me what the two perfect infects, *hatched on the road*, refemble, though I had informed you, that you would find in the box two individuals in a new drefs. But I have met with fome in my garden in a third fhape, with a handfome green cuirafs, running brifkly along, and no longer making me fick with their difgufting appearance, although they fall directly upon the artichoke itfelf, and pay no further attention to the leaves of the plant. You and your brother muft agree as you can about the two bottles of oil: in the mean time I muft inform your fcience, that it is for the ufe of the human fpecies alone, and that it is the laft and moft powerful remedy for worms. The dofe is a few drops, in a fpoonful of any fort of fyrup. By thefe means grown-up perfons have been fnatched from the grave, after all other remedies have proved ineffectual, and when they have been almoft expiring in convulfions. Eudora once took fome in a violent fit of ficknefs, and fhortly after voided a very large worm, the only one which fhe

ever

ever brought away in her life, and of which the expulsion was the signal of better health.

Perhaps this discovery may be new to some of your doctors, and will be more useful to them, than your preservatives against the *caffida viridis* will to me: this is the way in which I am resolved to revenge myself for your want of knowledge.

I expect your severe critique; but I beg you to suspend it as far as relates to the article Lavater, as I have new matter to furnish.

You no longer say any thing about your men of science, and the intriguers, and so on, that pretend to it: what is that little nation doing, while the great republic is in disorder, and money as scarce in the coffers of the state, as water was in our cistern in the months of April and May?

I have now, however, enough to baptize you, if you will come and see us; and I may venture to defy every thing reprehensible about you, with an element so pure, a site so excellent, and so deep a solitude. My good man is still at Lyons; nor do I very well know when he will come back. My health is tolerable, as long as I have nothing to affect me, or make me uneasy; but my stomach is not in a state to bear without injury the emotions of my heart, or the agitation of my mind: when they are too much employed, the former goes quietly to rest, and will no longer do its office. We must put up with these old servants, who take it in their head to govern.

Adieu!

Adieu!—I have a great deal to do, and I amufe myfelf with chit-chat. It appears to me that you have dropped your correfpondence, fince I have been living in retirement. I have only heard once from you at this place, where I have been ever fince the fifteenth of laft month. Health and friendfhip!

October 1.

HANG yourfelf, dainty Crillon*; we are making jellies and jams, and fweet wine, and fweet-meats, and you are not here to tafte them! Thefe, elegant Sir, are my prefent occupations. The vintage in the mean time is going on amain, and very fhortly it will be only in the cellar of the mafter, and in the cupboard of the miftrefs of the houfe, that the grape, and its delicious juice, will be found. That of this year will be excellent; but we fhall have little of it, on account of the vifit paid us by the hail: an honour which always leaves a dear and lafting remembrance behind it.

Why then do you not write to us? you who have no vintage to attend to; can there be any other occupation in the world befide?

But you are quite loft in the labyrinth of politics, and exhauft yourfelf in differtations upon the good

---

* An allufion to a letter of Henry IV. beginning in thefe words Hang yourfelf, brave Crillon; we have been fighting at Arques, and you were not there,—*Tranf.*

to be done, that will never take place. What is M. Necker about? They fay that there is a terrible party againſt him. And the tall devil of an archbiſhop. He was ſaid to be ſet off for Rome; but it is now reported that he is in cloſe cuſtody.

May God grant peace to the good, and annihilate the wicked! Devote a few moments to the recollection of your friends at the world's end, who do not forget you, and who embrace you without ceremony, except Eudora, who might already have her objections

How do the ſciences go on in the midſt of our political convulſions, and our financial diſtreſs? and the men of learning, and the great talkers, and the collections, and the courſes of lectures, and La Blancherie, and the muſeums, and the *muſards* (loungers?)

We are told here that Necker's anſwer is ready; but that he muſt leave the kingdom in order to publiſh it. What is ſaid of it in your part of the world? We, who think him pretty much of the *charlatan*, in ſpite of his *character*, have great doubts of the exiſtence of that anſwer, or of its being good for any thing, in caſe its exiſtence be real.

Carra's manner beſpeaks him exactly what you repreſent him to be. I ſhould be very glad to be more particularly acquainted with him.

Tell my brother-in-law what I have not been able to let him know, that the Intendant came here to infiſt upon the regiſtering of the edicts, after which

which our bailiwic, though very happy at this little piece of violence, affected to be in no hafte to take its meafures in confequence. Next comes a letter from the Intendant to his fub-delegate, defiring to know if the court had begun to fit, and pointing out the neceffity, in cafe any difficulty fhould arife, of informing government, &c. The bell of the town-hall is ringing, and our magiftrates are affembling, probably to form a *prefidial** court.

The grand bailiwic of Lyons held its firft fitting on Friday, upon a threat of its being transferred to Macon, in cafe of any refiftance.

But Macon refufes to fubmit to the jurifdiction of Lyons.

Neverthelefs, the little tribunals are upon the whole well fatisfied with the revolution.

We poor plebeians, whofe pockets will be emptied, without any one faying *by your leave*, were the only perfons difpleafed with this fame bufinefs of regiftering, and this formation of a *plenary court*, compofed of creatures of the crown.

It appears to us befides, that the right of jurifdiction given to the inferior courts is too confiderable. In fmall places, where goffiping and prejudices have fo much influence, the fortune of almoft every individual is left at the difcretion of judges, very eafy to be impofed upon and deceived.

---

* In France an inferior court of judicature, from which an appeal lay to the provincial parliaments.—*Tranf.*

Let

Let us wait and fee—let us blefs America, and weep over the banks of the river of Babylon. Adieu!—We love you as much as ever.

December 4.

COME, now, Mr. Doctor, have the goodnefs, I befeech you, to let me know *fubito*, for that is the way to pleafe the ladies, if the famous turnips, at prefent fo much extolled at Paris, and fo much cultivated in its vicinity, be of the genus *raphanus* or *braffica*. Then you will tell me, *en paffant*, in what genus you include the *turnip-radifh*, which you Parifians eat at breakfaft; and then, whether you are acquainted with the *long* and *round* radifh which grows in Flanders, and in fome of our provinces, and what you call it. Let your decifion on all thefe points be exact and precife: it will terminate very learned difcuffions, in which you may confider it as a great honour to be chofen for umpire. But let that decifion be accompanied by the Linnæan terms; for we have a great many things to attend to, and very few books. Should I be fatisfied with your fcience, and fhould you notwithftanding be unacquainted with our *radifhes*, the moft falubrious, the mildeft, and the lighteft of all poffible kinds of food for man and beaft, I will fend one of them at your head of five or fix pounds weight, *long* or *round*, as you beft like.

Adieu!

Adieu!—Do not altogether forget your friends of the laſt century, who embrace you with ſincere affection.

Clos la Platière, October 8.

WE hear nothing from you, my dear friend, and yet the parliaments are coming forward, and acting in a moſt extraordinary manner. Are the friends of order and liberty, who defired their re-eſtabliſhment, then doomed to regret it? What effect have their refolutions produced upon the public mind? Their mention of the ſtates-general of 1614, their pretenſions, their tone, and their language, are very ſingular.

The queſtion then is only to know, whether we are to vegetate miferably under the rod of a ſingle tyrant, or to groan beneath the iron yoke of ſeveral united defpots? The alternative is dreadful, and leaves us no choice, for there is no making one between evils of the fame magnitude. Though the national degradation may be leſs general in an ariſtocracy, than under the defpotifm of an unbridled monarch, the fituation of the people is ſometimes harder, and would be ſo among us, where the privileged claſſes are every thing, and where the moſt numerous clafs is counted for little more than a cipher.

We are told that the principal financiers have entered into a league againſt Necker: what is that
miniſter

minister about? Has he not yet fixed himself firmly in the saddle?

July 26.

NO, you are not free: nobody as yet is so. Public confidence is betrayed: our letters are intercepted. You complain of my silence, and I write to you by every post. It is true, I entertain you very little with my personal affairs:—who is the traitor, that at this moment minds any business but that of the nation? It is true also, that I have written still more vigorously than you have acted; and yet if you do not take care, all you have done will be only a vain parade. Neither have I received the letter from you which our friend Lanthenas speaks of. You send me no news, and yet there must be a great abundance. You busy yourselves about a municipality, and you suffer heads to escape, which are about to conjure up new horrors.

You are nothing but children; your enthusiasm is a momentary blaze; and if the national assembly do not bring two illustrious heads to a formal trial, or if some generous Decius do not strike them off, you will all go to the devil together.

If this letter do not reach you, let the base wretches who read it blush, on learning that it is from a woman, and tremble on reflecting that she is able to make a hundred enthusiasts, who will make millions more.

August

August 15.

IT is not to the citizen only that I addrefs myfelf to-day, but to the naturalift alfo. We do not give up politics: they are at this moment too interefting; nor fhould we deferve to live in a free country, if we grew indifferent to the public weal. But the days are long; people of a lively imagination, and ardent minds, foon draw their conclufions; letters and converfation can only fill up a part of our time, when we are not actors in the bufy fcene ourfelves; nor can we for ever feaft upon the fame difh. Furs are then coming once more upon the carpet: they are interefting on account of their immediate relation to a part of natural hiftory. There is no work indeed in which we cannot, in fome fhape or other, introduce and fet forth the rights of juftice, and the true principles of adminiftration.

We are ftudying with much pleafure the *Mammalia* of *Erxleben*, and I think we may quote him with confidence: we have, however, remarked, that his own quotations of the different works of Linnæus, Buffon, Bomare himfelf, and a thoufand other authors, are from editions more than twenty years old.

For thefe twenty years paft natural hiftory has been very generally cultivated: it has made a great progrefs, and we fhould perhaps run a rifk of finding ourfelves behindhand in feveral articles, if we

were

were to place our principal dependance upon an authority of such ancient date.

We should be glad to know then whether any able naturalist exist in Europe, who has published since that period; and whether you chance to be acquainted with any work of later date, which is worth consulting, and deserving of faith. Communicate to us what you know in that respect, and try to procure us all the information you can. Did Erxleben publish nothing but his *Mammalia*, particularly since he gave that work to the world? And have not some of the learned men of Germany, or England, gone over the same ground since with equal success?

As soon as you have it in your power, we shall expect a satisfactory answer on that head, and in the mean time will beg you to explain to us one of his passages: we comprehend the words, but as we do not understand the signification of the figures, the whole is lost upon us.

It is in page 42, *Naturales* hic subesse, *ordines* generum, 1—7; 9—11; 12—20; 21—24; 25—31; 32—40; 41—46; 47—51; apparet; neque male conjungi crediderim, 7 and 8; 11 and 12; 20 and 21; 24 and 25; 31 and 32; 40 and 41; 46 and 47.

Fiat lux.—That is your business.

We embrace you heartily.

August 25.

YOU deserve a few friendly lines for your last letter, which gave us great pleasure. I can easily conceive how much you must be occupied; and accordingly I do not complain of your momentary silence, as of a fault which you commit, but as of a privation which I suffer. Courage then; continue to assemble: by dint of uniting for the common weal, the sphere of good-will is extended, ideas are propagated, and the public spirit is fixed upon a firmer footing.

Our silly country towns are a hundred leagues behind you in all possible respects: vanity there is so great, that each individual thinks he is grown one half smaller. Every one looks only to himself; and the consequence is, that the whole see nothing but fools. I believe that the honest Englishman is in the right, and that we must have a small touch of civil war before we are good for any thing. All these little quarrels, and insurrections of the people, seem to me inevitable; nor do I think it possible to rise to liberty, from the midst of corruption, without strong convulsions. They are the salutary crises of a serious disease. We are in want of a terrible political fever to carry off our foul humours. Go on and prosper then: let our rights be declared; let them be submitted to our consideration; and let the constitution come afterwards.

We

We shall come to blows: I fully expect it: what is to be done? We must arm ourselves with courage. I will lay aside the sciences, and all the rest of it, to talk and think of nothing but politics. At this moment can any other interest come in competition with our political concerns? But it becomes us to keep in our proper places, and not to rebel against the influence of those about us.

Adieu!—Health and friendship, in unity of heart, as fellow-citizens.

September 4.

YOUR kind letter brought us very bad news. We blushed on hearing it, and on reading the public papers. They are going to patch us up a bad constitution, in like manner as they garbled our faulty and incomplete declaration of rights. Shall I never then see an address of reclamation for the revision of the whole? Every day we see addresses of adhesion, and other things of that sort, which bespeak our infancy, and confirm our shame. It behoves you Parisians, to set the example in every thing; let a temperate but vigorous address shew to the assembly that you know your rights, that you are determined to preserve them, that you are ready to defend them, and that you insist upon their being acknowledged! Without this bold measure, every thing will be worse than ever it was. It is not at the Palais Royal it should be done: the united districts ought to act; but if they do not shew themselves felves fo inclined, it fhould be done by any fet of men, provided they be in fufficient number to command refpect, and to lead on others by their example.

I preach all I can. A furgeon, and a village curate, have fubfcribed for Briffot's journal, which we have taught them to relifh; but our little country towns are too corrupt, and our peafantry too ignorant. Villefranche overflows with *ariflocrats*, people rifen from the duft, which they think they fhake off by affecting the prejudices of another order.

You will be able to judge of the happy days I pafs, by figuring to yourfelf my brother-in-law more prieftly, more defpotic, more fanatic, and more obftinate, than any prieft you ever met with. The confequence is, that, though we have little intercourfe with one another, he contrives to teafe us a good deal; and I am well perfuaded, that, out of hatred to our principles, he will do us, perhaps, all the mifchief he is able.

I do not know whether you be amoroufly inclined; but I well know that in the circumftances in which we are placed, if an honeft man be free to follow the torch of love, it is not till he has lighted it at the facred fire of that of his country. Your rencounter was interefting enough to deferve mention; and I feel myfelf much obliged to you for making us acquainted with it; but I can hardly pardon you for being ignorant of the name of fo worthy a creature.

I have

I have this inftant heard of the proceedings of the king, his brothers, and the queen, with the affembly. They were devilifhly frightened! That is all that the ftep they have taken proves; but to believe in the fincerity of their promife of leaving every thing to that body, it would be neceffary to forget all that has paffed. It would have been neceffary for the king to begin by difmiffing all the foreign troops.

We fhall be nearer the moft dreadful flavery than ever, if we fuffer ourfelves to be blinded by delufive confidence.

The French are eafily feduced, by fair appearances on the part of their mafters, and I make no doubt but one half of the affembly was moved at the fight of Antoinette recommending her fon. *Morbleu!*—A child is of great confequence, to be fure! It is the falvation of twenty millions of men that is at ftake. All will be loft if we do no not take care.

Have we not reafon to be afraid of freezing, even in the remembrance of our friends, in fuch fevere weather? Receive this *billet* then as a little faggot to feed the facred fire, and watch over it faithfully, that it may not go out.

As to us, good country folks, who have nothing but cheering friendfhip to divert our attention from the bitter blafts that afflict thefe regions, there is no fear of our neglecting its worfhip. Join us then, as far as intention goes, in our fincere prayers, and let us pay homage together to that amiable divinity, at the renewal of a year which adds to the date of our friendſhip. Are we to have no more of the chit-chat from you, that we uſed formerly to receive? And does the Latin of Linnæus leave no room for the communications of ingenuous friendſhip? Adieu!—If to this *oremus* you anſwer *amen*, we may begin again; in the mean time receive the embraces of all our little family.

Eudora is tall, with fine *fair* hair, which falls down her ſhoulders in natural curls; very dark eyelaſhes encircle her grey eyes; and her little noſe, ſomewhat turned up at the end, gives her already a roguiſh look.

Clos la Platière, 17 May 1790.

A TRUCE for a moment with your politics: let us return to natural hiſtory, to the ſtudy of which the country invites. But our ideas concerning it have been ſo diſturbed, that we are puzzled to find our way even with the help of Erxleben.

For inſtance, I think I have formed a juſt conception of Linnæus's diviſions, of which the *claſſes* are the firſt; the *orders*, ſubdiviſions of claſſes; the *genera*, ſubdiviſions of orders; the *ſpecies*, ſubdiviſions of genera; and the *varieties*, ſubdiviſions of ſpecies. It appears to me that Erxleben ranges his diviſions in the ſame way: however, when I look for examples, I think I perceive contradictions. His Mammalia confiſt of only one claſs, in which he has included

cluded 51 orders. The first of those orders, *homo*, has only varieties; but in the fourth order, *cercopithecus*, I consider as genera the *hamadryas*, the *veter*, the *senex*, the *vetulus*, the *silenus*, the *faunus*, &c. How happens it then that he says, after the synonimy of *faunus*, *barbatus*, *cauda apice floccosa* SPECIES *obscura adeoque dubia* ?

This word *species* deranges all my ideas, and I can no longer understand the author's arrangement.

I should like to find in his *Mammalia* an example to justify his statement of the subdivisions: I should wish to find in one of the 51 orders a genus having both *species* and varieties belonging to it, or to know why the denomination *species* is applied to a division which I had reason to consider as a genus.

Give me the clue of this labyrinth, in which I am lost, and out of which I can no longer find my way.

The weather is delightful; and in six days the country has undergone a total change: the vines and the walnut-trees were as black as in the dead of winter.—The touch of a necromancer's wand does not change the appearance of things more suddenly, than the genial heat of a few fine days has done: every thing is verdant, and in leaf; and we can now find a pleasant shade, where before nothing existed but the gloomy aspect of torpor and inaction.

I could eafily in this place forget public affairs, and the difputes of mankind: contented with the range of the manor, with feeing my hens hatch their young, and with tending my rabbits, I no longer think of the revolutions of empires. But, as foon as I am in town, the mifery of the people, and the infolence of the rich, excite my hatred of injuftice and oppreffion; and I no longer afk any thing of heaven, but the triumph of truth, and the fuccefs of our regeneration.

Our peafantry are very much difcontented with the decree concerning feudal rights: they look upon the rate of redemption for fines and quit-rents as exceedingly burdenfome; and will neither redeem nor pay. We muft have a reform, or we fhall have more châteaux burnt. The mifchief perhaps would not be fo great, were it not to be feared that the enemies of the revolution would take advantage of this difcontent, to diminifh the confidence of the people in the national affembly, and to excite fome diforder, which they long for as a triumph, and as a mean of recovering their loft ground.

Preparations are making at Lyons for a camp: fend us then brave fellows to make ariftocracy tremble in its den. It had been made a queftion, whether women fhould be allowed to approach the camp; apparently thofe who raifed the doubt had fome treachery in contemplation; but the idea was too offenfive, and did not take.

Adieu!

Adieu!--Send us a little chit-chat for once and away.

Clos la Platière, Monday, Sept. 27.

IT was only by Saturday's poſt that we received your letter of the twentieth, becauſe it did not reach Lyons till after our departure from that place. We had been longing for accounts from you for ſome time, and we welcomed them joyfully; but your obſervations concerning public affairs afflict us the more, becauſe they are perfectly conſonant with what we hear from other quarters. It is not, however, from the public papers that you think you ought to procure us information: not one of them is calculated to give an idea of the bad ſtate of public affairs; and that very thing ſerves to render it more complete. This is the moment in which patriotic writers ought to denounce by name thoſe corrupt members who, by their hypocriſy, and their manœuvres, deceive the hope, and betray the intereſt of their conſtituents. They ought to publiſh without reſerve what you ſay of the General. What purpoſe does the liberty of the preſs anſwer, if the remedies which it affords againſt the evils that threaten us be not made uſe of? Briſſot ſeems to be aſleep; Louſtallot is dead; and we have lamented the loſs of him with many tears: Deſmoulins will have occaſion to reſume his employment of procurator-general of the lantern. But what is become of the energy of the people? Necker is ſet off without

without throwing any light upon the abyfs of the finances, and nobody thinks of exploring the labyrinth he has abandoned: why do you not remonftrate againft the bafenefs of that committee which dares to defend d'Artois' debts?—The ftorm is howling; the knaves throw afide the mafk; the bad fide triumphs, and the people forget that infurrection is the moft facred duty when our country is in danger! O Parifians! how much do you ftill refemble that fickle people whofe *effervefcence* was falfely ftyled enthufiafm! Lyons is fubjugated. The Germans and Swifs domineer in that place by means of their bayonets employed in the fervice of a treacherous municipality, which is in league with the minifters, and other bad citizens. Soon we fhall have nothing left to do but to weep over liberty, if we do not die for her. We dare no longer fpeak, fay you: be it fo: we muft *thunder* then. Join yourfelf to fuch honeft men as you can find; complain; reafon; fet up an outcry; wake the people from their lethargy; fhew them the dangers by which they are threatened, and try to give new courage to the fmall number of members who poffefs any underftanding, and who would foon recover their afcendency, if the voice of the people were raifed in their fupport.

I have not the heart to entertain you with an account of the life we lead, and of our rural excurfions. The republic is neither happy nor affured; and our felicity is difturbed by it. Our friends are

endea-

endeavouring to make profelytes with a zeal which would be attended with fuccefs, if they could preach for any length of time in the fame place.

December 20.

GET a decree paffed declaratory of the way in which minifters are to be made refponfible; get a bridle put in the mouth of the executive power; and haften the organization of the national guards. A hundred thoufand Auftrians are affembling on your frontiers; the Brabanters are conquered; the kingdom is drained of its fpecie, without any one's inquiring how; we pay the princes and fugitives, who with our own money manufacture arms to fubdue us.—Death and deftruction! What fignifies your being Parifians? Why, you cannot fee to the end of your nofes, or elfe you want vigour to make your affembly get on! It was not our reprefentatives who brought about the revolution: take away a dozen or fo, and the reft are beneath it.—It was the *public opinion*; it was the *people*, who are always in the right, when that opinion is properly directed. It is Paris that is the feat of that opinion. Finifh then your work, or expect to fee it watered with your blood.

Adieu!—Your fellow-citizen and friend, in life, and in death.

29 January 1791.

I WEEP for the blood that has been fpilt: it is impoffible to be too fparing of that of our fellow-creatures! But I am very glad that there are dangers. I do not fee any thing elfe capable of goading you on. The fermentation prevails throughout France, it fluctuates along with external meafures; the public force is not organized; and Paris has not yet fufficiently influenced the affembly to oblige it to do every thing it ought!

I expect vigorous refolutions from your fections: if they deceive my expectation, I fhall think myfelf doomed to weep over the ruins of Carthage, and though continuing to preach liberty, I fhall defpair of feeing it eftablifhed in my unfortunate country. Lay afide your natural hiftory, and every other fcience, except that of becoming a man, and diffufing public fpirit.

I have heard Lanthenas fay, that members of the affembly went to ftudy botany in the Garden of Plants: good God! and you did not make them afhamed of themfelves! And thofe worthy citizens, who fee with pain corruption furrounding them, do not rife up with energy to oppofe its progrefs! do not follow it through all its ramifications! do not call upon public opinion to ftop the torrent! Is this the way in which they fhew their courage? Is this the way in which they do their duty?

Why

Why do you not put them in mind of it? If I perceived the smallest intrigue directed against the welfare of my country, I would hasten to denounce it to all the world.

The wise shut their eyes against the faults or the foibles of a private individual; but the citizen ought not to forgive his own father, when the public weal is at stake.

It is easy to see that these good quiet men did not admire Brutus, till the revolution had brought him into fashion.

Bestir yourselves, and may we hear at one and the same time of your efforts, and of your success.

Lyons, February 7.

I AM told that you are playing the *Rodomont*, and that you write fine things to puff off the Parisians and yourself, but that no effects follow. It is certain that the armaments which you get decreed are highly ridiculous, while our national guards remain every where unorganized, unexercised, and without arms. It is very fine, to be sure, to reckon twenty-five millions of men, among whom there are not three hundred thousand in a state of defence! and in the mean time the enemy's frontiers are covered with armed men; and the great despots, the petty princes, the fugitives, and the discontented of the interior, are preparing for us, in concert, the most bloody scenes. Read the printed address that you will find inclosed, and you will see that this is not a

time

time for boasting, but for shewing ourselves by our good works.

You may say what you please; but as long as I see your tyrannical, ignorant, or corrupt committees proposing trifling decrees, amusing themselves with matters foreign to the constitution, or setting up nothing but scarecrows, I shall assert, that the Parisians are not so brave as they appeared to be, or that they have lost all their cleverness. Shew yourselves men, or I will tell you the same thing to your face.

Adieu!—I shall write to you to-morrow concerning our lodgings. In the mean time we embrace you in return for your kind expressions, and I take my leave of you in order to pack up. In less than a week we shall be with you.

Madam Roland wrote me by almost every post from the beginning of the revolution, letters as replete with patriotism as the above; but I only kept those which it was not worth while to circulate. Whether they were intended for me or Lanthenas, I sent them to the latter, who used to communicate them to Brissot, and other persons; and they never came into my possession again. Many of them served to make articles in the different journals, particularly the Patriote François, and were remarkable for their energy, and for the just reflections they contained.

END OF THE FOURTH AND LAST PART.

www.ingramcontent.com/pod-product-compliance
Lightning Source LLC
Chambersburg PA
CBHW032140010526
44111CB00035B/626